MAKING A GAMESALAD® FOR TEENS

MICHAEL DUGGAN

Cengage Learning PTR

CENGAGE
Learning·

Professional • Technical • Reference

Australia • Brazil • Japan • Korea • Mexico • Singapore • Spain • United Kingdom • United States

Making a GameSalad® for Teens
Michael Duggan

Publisher and General Manager, Cengage Learning PTR:
Stacy L. Hiquet

Associate Director of Marketing:
Sarah Panella

Manager of Editorial Services:
Heather Talbot

Senior Marketing Manager:
Mark Hughes

Senior Acquisitions Editor: Emi Smith

Technical Reviewer: Clayton Crooks

Senior Production Director:
Wendy Troeger

Production Manager:
Sherondra Thedford

Senior Content Project Manager:
Stacey Lamodi

Project Manager:
Prashant Kumar Das

Interior Layout Tech: MPS Limited

Proofreader and Indexer:
MPS Limited

Cover Designer: Mike Tanamachi

Cover image(s):
© Hiro-Hideki/www.Shutterstock.com

For product information and technology assistance, contact us at
Cengage Learning Customer & Sales Support, 1-800-354-9706

For permission to use material from this text or product, submit all requests online at **cengage.com/permissions**

Further permissions questions can be emailed to
permissionrequest@cengage.com

GameSalad is a registered trademark of GameSalad, Inc. in the U.S. and/or other countries. All other trademarks are the property of their respective owners.

All images © Cengage Learning unless otherwise noted.

Library of Congress Control Number: 2013933087

ISBN-13: 978-1-285-44011-8

ISBN-10: 1-285-44011-0

Cengage Learning PTR

20 Channel Center Street

Boston, MA 02210

USA

Cengage Learning is a leading provider of customized learning solutions with office locations around the globe, including Singapore, the United Kingdom, Australia, Mexico, Brazil, and Japan. Locate your local office at: **international.cengage.com/region**

Cengage Learning products are represented in Canada by Nelson Education, Ltd.

For your lifelong learning solutions, visit **cengageptr.com**

Visit our corporate website at **cengage.com**

Printed by RR Donnelley. Crawfordsville, IN. 1st Ptg. 06/2013

Printed in the United States of America
1 2 3 4 5 6 7 15 14 13

For the game designer in all of us. Where there is a will and an aptitude, we will wow the world.

ACKNOWLEDGMENTS

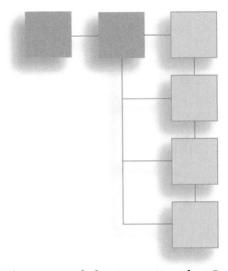

Thanks to the editing team and layout artists who took my rough brain matter that I spewed onto paper and turned it into the glossy cool tome you now hold in your hands. If they had not helped me, this book would not be what it is today.

ABOUT THE AUTHOR

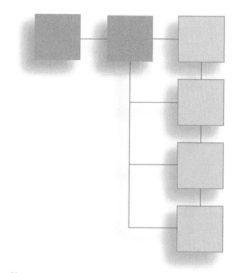

Michael Duggan is a Southern-based author and illustrator of game development books. He works full-time as an applications developer at North Arkansas College. He spends his spare time as a game designer, tattoo artist, cartoonist, and amateur ventriloquist.

CONTENTS

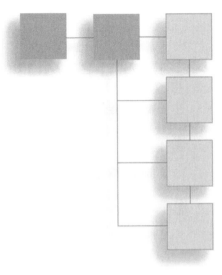

INTRODUCTION

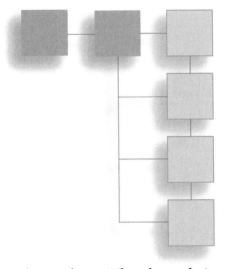

Face it. Video game designers are the rock stars of this day and age. They have their photos appear on the cover of magazines. They are interviewed by television networks. They foster a collection of adoring fans. What is truly remarkable is that they do all this without having to step on stage or scream into a microphone. All they have to do is spend long hours putting together a video game and getting it played by the public.

Are you a hardcore or casual gamer? Have you ever considered creating a video game yourself but had no idea how or where to start? Perhaps you were playing one of your favorite games, and an idea wormed its way from the hindbrain to the fore with startling clarity, telling you, "This is the kind of game you should make!" Or maybe you overheard your friends chatting about what kind of game they would like to play, but which does not exist yet, and you knew you ought to build it.

Once you get inspiration, you will want to make a video game. Yet no matter where you look, the task seems to be a difficult one, full of math, physics, and late nights staying up staring at a computer screen, not knowing how to implement the features you dream about.

What if I told you that you, too, could become a game developer, and you do not even have to graduate high school or have a fancy career at Blizzard Entertainment to do so? The instructions within this book reveal one route to making your own video games and getting people to play them. Yes, you could become a modern-day rock star by embracing the role of a maker of video games.

To build video games, you need first to understand them. Whether you have played every game on the shelves at your local video rental store or only fiddled with a Facebook game app once or twice, you probably do not know everything there is to know about video games and how they became so popular. So take a moment to reflect on the history of the video game industry.

In their early days, playing video games was often seen as a sub-cultural hobby activity and substitute for physical sports or outdoor activities. Video games have changed a lot since then. *Spacewar!*, a multiplayer game programmed by MIT students in 1962, is widely considered to be the first influential video game, even though it was predated by a missile simulator game created by Goldsmith and Mann in 1947. The 1970s was dominated by *Oregon Trail* and *Pong*. *Oregon Trail*, developed by three student teachers at Carleton College in Minnesota, is still used as a teaching tool today. *Pong* is an astonishingly simple but addictive game based on the tabletop game Ping-Pong. It involves two paddles, a dotted line for a net, and a dot for a ball.

In the 1980s, video games swelled in popularity, mostly thanks to *Pac-Man*, a game developed by Namco and designed by Toru Iwatani. *Pac-Man* fever swept America during the 1980s, primarily because it appealed to boys and girls as well as adults.

Today, video gaming is viewed as a serious industry, comparable to the movie and music industries. News outlets cover video game console releases in the same matter as they would the release of a highly anticipated motion picture.

A video game is any electronic game with human interaction and a user interface that generates visual feedback on a video device. The *video* part of the term *video game* originally referred to cathode ray tube (CRT) display devices, but now refers to any display device that produces a two- or three-dimensional image. The type of electronic system you use to play a video game is known as its *platform*. Examples of different platforms include personal computers, laptop computers, and video game consoles like the Xbox 360 and Nintendo Wii. These platforms can range from large desktop computers to small handheld devices.

One platform is the video game arcade, which is not as strongly significant as it was during the 1980s but still exists in some parts of North America. In a video game arcade, games can be played on fixed machines in a public place. The machines are typically coin operated, meaning that they require change or tokens to be put into their slots to play them.

The input device used to play a video game is called a game controller, and varies depending on the platform. For instance, a controller might be a button, joystick, keyboard, or mouse.

Video games typically use various sensory means for providing interactivity and information to the player besides just video. Audio is almost universally used; indeed, sound can impart a lot of telltale information throughout a video game. There are even whole games made for the visually impaired. These games focus primarily on the use of sound to guide the player through seemingly three-dimensional environments. Other feedback may come via haptic peripherals, such as vibration or force feedback, with vibration sometimes used to simulate force feedback in a game.

The video games industry is a rapidly developing phenomenon. Technological innovation results in continual improvement in the devices people use to play video games. As the market develops, players become more sophisticated, and the types of games they play change. In addition to what goes on in the mainstream media, thanks to the Internet, there is plenty of activity on the fringe of game development, such as Web browser–based games, user-developed modifications (mods), and independent game design.

With so many possibilities, this is an exciting time to become involved in making video games. It can also seem like a frightening time because where do you start and what skills do you need to become a video game developer?

Video game development and authorship, much like any form of entertainment, is frequently a cross-disciplinary field. Video game developers, as employees within this industry are commonly referred to, primarily include programmers and graphic designers. Over the years, this has expanded to include almost every skill set you might see prevalent in the creation of a film or television show, including sound engineers, musicians, and other technicians, as well as skills specific to video games, such as the game designer and character modeler. All of these roles are managed by directors and producers.

The three essential skills necessary to make video games are as follows:

- **Graphic design:** Making pretty pictures on the computer
- **Rudimentary animation:** Making those pictures move
- **Programming logic:** Making those pictures interrelate with each other and interact with the player's input

While the first two skills contribute to the appearance of the game, the game is nothing without the gameplay. That leads you to the programming logic, which is truly the bread and butter of any video game. From designing a heads-up display that ticks off the player avatar's health, to dialog boxes that pop up in-game, to the character movement controls, none of this would be possible without the logic. As you will see, the game-authoring software you will use following the steps in this book makes the logic part a cinch with drag-and-drop behavior blocks.

In the early days of the industry, it was more common for a single person to manage all of the roles needed to create a video game. Such people were called *game sages*. As platforms became more complex and powerful in the type of material they could present, larger development teams were needed to generate all the art, programming, and other substance required of a video game.

However, this is not to say the age of the one-man shop is over. You still see this in the casual and handheld gaming markets, where smaller games remain prevalent. Independent game developers still have some clout, and game-authoring technology that makes the process simpler for users keeps the independent market alive.

With the growth in the size of development teams in the game industry, the problem of cost has increased. Development studios need to be able to pay their staff a competitive wage to maintain the best talent, while publishers are constantly seeking to keep costs down to turn a profit. Typically, a video game console development team can range in sizes upward of 50 people, with some teams exceeding 100. One game project reportedly had a development staff of 450 people!

The growth of team size combined with the pressure to get completed projects into the market to begin recouping production costs has led to an increasing occurrence of missed deadlines, rushed games, and the release of unfinished projects. Therefore, there is more practical simplicity in keeping a project smaller. For one thing, you can build a game yourself in a reasonable amount of time with a limited amount of resources, especially if you select a game-creation tool that will afford you the greatest flexibility for the least cost.

This book will show you one such game-creation tool, GameSalad Creator, and how you can use this 100% free tool to make your very own video games—without having to recruit a large team of other developers or spend a fat bank roll on asset acquisition.

WHAT YOU'LL FIND IN THIS BOOK

No single book could ever hope to give utterly comprehensive coverage of such a vast and dynamic subject as game development. Rather like a guidebook, this book provides you, a novice designer, a good grounding in gaming principles and indications of how to achieve your aspirations.

You will use a free game-development tool, GameSalad Creator, to mix your own video games through practical exercises that require some of the skills and techniques necessary to become a video-game designer. With GameSalad Creator, any game you build you can convert to and publish for all kinds of different gaming platforms, including Mac, PC, mobile devices, and online.

There are roughly three games you will make during the course of this book:

- A shooter, in which the player pilots a spaceship to duck enemy missiles while tackling alien motherships
- A platformer, in which the player runs and jumps around a level, collecting stars while avoiding hungry ghosts
- An adventure game, in which the player is a repair Android awakened from deep-space hibernation to fix the spaceship's computer guidance system before the ship veers too far off course

The content of this book is intended to start you off on the long but exciting journey to become a professional in the games industry. May you find your time with it, and your experiences with GameSalad Creator, rewarding.

WHO THIS BOOK IS FOR

Want to try your hand at making your own video game? It might seem impossible at first, but it can actually be done more easily than you might think. If you want to make a video game, this book will teach you how from start to finish.

You do not have to be a math whiz, a computer genius, or a talented artist to make a video game with GameSalad. It helps, but by all means, you could be an amateur when it comes to those fields and you will still be capable of following along with the instructions within these pages. You will still make three games with the Game-Salad Creator toolkit, regardless of your previous experience or skill level.

However, any computer design requires patience, as making creative works in a digital environment involves managing a lot of tedious little details. If you are easily frustrated, you might not finish a project you start. Pay careful attention to detail, and if you find yourself getting upset, pause and take a few deep breaths or even a brief break before marshaling on. Even in large game development companies, where dozens of professionals work in tandem in the same office area, they have water coolers to visit and take short breathers while busy so they can remain focused on the project at hand.

If you already have prior experience making video games, or just dealing with art editors or programming languages, you will find this text's instructions familiar and perhaps more relaxed than if you did not have previous knowledge. Nevertheless,

I guarantee you will learn something, and the games you make with GameSalad will be no less satisfying. In fact, you may take what you know from before and push the parameters of GameSalad even further, developing your own unique creations to show off your abilities to the world.

So, beginner or intermediate computer user you may be, you will find something deeply rewarding by *Making a GameSalad for Teens.*

How This Book Is Organized

This book is broken into neat and easy-to-follow chapters that contain the instructions you need to become familiar with GameSalad and build three different types of games.

- **Chapter 1, "Start with the Proper Ingredients":** This chapter tells you how to download and install the necessary software to begin making games with GameSalad Creator. Most of the instructions, including the following chapters, focus primarily on using a Windows PC operating system, although you are just as capable of using an Apple Macintosh operating system to accomplish the tasks. Please read the system requirements for the software thoroughly and make sure you have the necessary technology recommended to perform the lessons.

- **Chapter 2, "Understanding Your Recipe":** Before delving into the step-by-step instructions for making video games, it is good to know a little about the game industry—how game studios push a project from green light to gold master, and what actually goes into making a top-shelf video game title. This chapter will also introduce you to some of the basic game industry terminology and popular game genres.

- **Chapter 3, "Creating a Basic Shooter":** The first game you will design will be a shooter game. The player will pilot a spacecraft and have to shoot alien space fighters and emergency beacons while avoiding missiles and kamikaze aliens. This may sound daunting for a first game project, but really it is not. It will be easy as 1-2-3 with GameSalad Creator.

- **Chapter 4, "A More Advanced Shooter":** After accomplishing the first steps in making a shooter, you will be shown how to make your shooter better by raising the difficulty, adding new levels, and spawning more enemies.

- **Chapter 5, "Creating a Basic Platformer":** The next game you will design will be a platformer. This is perhaps one of the most historically noted genres next to shooters. A platformer has a playable character that moves from left to right across the viewing screen, and the character can run and jump across multiple platforms while avoiding hurtful obstacles such as deathly spikes and roaming enemies.

- **Chapter 6, "A More Advanced Platformer":** Once you have the basics down for making a platformer, I will show you how to make the platformer even better. You will learn how to add dangers and ramp up the tension, pushing the player to edge of his or her seat.

- **Chapter 7, "Tossing an Adventure GameSalad":** Now for something totally different. After you have finished building a shooter and platformer, you will make an adventure game. An adventure game focuses more on exploration and puzzle-solving than hand-eye coordination. Players work at their own pace to figure out how to find their way out of complex scenarios. In this case, they will need to find the right tools to fix a computer before the spacecraft they are on floats too far off course.

- **Chapter 8, "Taking Your Game to Market":** With decent starts to three different game projects, you will need to know how to publish your game. GameSalad makes this part a snap with its Arcade, where you can publish your game online for others to find and play. You will also learn a few trade secrets about Web advertisement, including how to promote yourself in social networks and via Web design.

- **Chapter 9, "Cross-Platform Publishing":** You will learn some of the basics of publishing for different platforms besides the personal computer. Instructions will show you how you can publish a game for mobile devices such as the Android. With multiple platforms to target, you can hit a broader market for your games and garner even more players.

- **Appendix, "Resources":** For easy reference, this appendix has bulleted lists of all the Web-based resources used within this book.

- **Glossary of Terms:** Forgot what a specific term means? You can refer to the glossary to look up the definition of a specific behavior, function, or other important vocabulary word.

COMPANION WEBSITE DOWNLOADS

You may download the companion website files from www.cengageptr.com/downloads.

CHAPTER 1

START WITH THE PROPER INGREDIENTS

Perhaps you are a casual player of App Store games like *Angry Birds*, or an avid gamer with countless hours building your character in *Runescape*, or a digital artist who would like to branch into more dynamic interactive content for your website. Regardless of the reason you have picked up this book, if you have ever wanted to make a video game but have been nervous because of all the programming jargon, then this book is for you.

Merriam-Webster defines a video game as any game "played by electronically manipulating images produced by a computer program on a television screen or display." Most Americans under the age of 40 have played video games since childhood and are more than passingly familiar with them. Some are even what you might call "core" gamers, who play video games between 12 and 30 hours per week. Video games have found a strong niche within the media market, right beside music and movies, and will become even more entrenched over time.

Similarly, the past two generations of kids have desired nothing more than to make video games themselves. It is as difficult to learn and become proficient at making video games as it is to develop the skills needed to become a filmmaker. These fields share cross-disciplinary skill sets like graphic design, sound engineering, animation, writing, and programming. Colleges and summer workshops have sprung up across the country in an effort to get this knowledge into the hands of willing learners.

If you have ever thought, "I want to make a video game," before, but did not know where to start, then this book is the perfect place to begin. Imagine it as a recipe for success.

You, too, can make great video games for use on multiple platforms such as the iPhone, Android, Mac, PC, and World Wide Web. Just by learning rudimentary features of a popular package called the GameSalad Creator, you can build video games that you can then share with your friends and family or add to your portfolio to snag a job in the ever-growing field of game development!

THE GAMESALAD CREATOR

The GameSalad Creator, simply called the Creator by most, is a game-authoring system developed by GameSalad, Inc., formerly known as Gendai Games (see Figure 1.1). Michael Agustin, Dan Treiman, Tan Tran, and Joshua Seaver founded GameSalad, Inc. in August 2007 on the belief that all people should have the tools to make popular games, limited only by the boundaries of their imaginations. GameSalad provides a game-authoring system by which people can do just that. GameSalad empowers everyone to express and share his or her ideas through games. GameSalad has studios in Austin, Texas; Los Angeles, California; and San Francisco, California.

Figure 1.1
The GameSalad Creator.
Source: The GameSalad Creator, © 2013 GameSalad®, Inc. All Rights Reserved.

A game-authoring system is computer-based system that enables users, usually non-programmers, to create or author content for video games. GameSalad, Inc. expressly aimed the Creator at non-programmers by providing visual editors and basic behavioral logic to compose games in a loose, drag-and-drop fashion. This makes the Creator very easy for beginners to pick it up and run with it.

Currently, hundreds of consumers and creative professionals such as graphic designers, animators, and game developers use the GameSalad Creator for rapid prototyping, building, and self-publishing cross-platform games and interactive media.

The Creator began as an application that ran only on Mac OS. On November 20, 2010, GameSalad unveiled a new "Free to Make" model, making basic membership free to all users of the Creator, including users who wished to publish their games for iOS devices.

Although the Creator still runs on Mac OS X for producing games for the iPhone, on June 11, 2012, GameSalad unveiled a Windows PC port of the Mac program, allowing Windows PC users to create games with the Creator, including iPhone publishing. The concept is the same. However, GameSalad made some changes to the layout in the Windows PC port, as it could not support some features of the original. They optimized their Windows PC port for producing games on Android devices. To publish games to the Apple App Store, you must convert games developed on Windows to Mac OS files.

Major Features

The GameSalad Creator enables you to build completely original games and applications without typing a single line of code with logic and assets. *Logic* refers to the combination of rules, behaviors, and attributes that jointly define how a project operates. Assets include the images and sounds you import into your project.

The Interface

The Creator provides a graphical user interface, or GUI (pronounced "gooey"), for describing the rules and behaviors of game objects, which it calls *actors*. Users do not have to possess prior knowledge of programming or scripting languages to use the Creator. *Behaviors* are components of an actor that instantly or persistently affect the actor depending on rules. The Creator comes with a vast library of behaviors—some for movement, changing attribute states, affecting collision, saving the game, and so on—that you can insert into rules and other behavior groups to create new behaviors.

Actors and Scenes

You can place and manipulate actors anywhere within a scene. You add actors to the scene by dragging and dropping them. You organize actors in a scene into different layers to change how you visualize actors, such as rendering order (who goes in front of who), parallax scrolling, and so forth. Parallax scrolling is where, in two-dimension side-scrolling games, the background scrolls right-to-left at a slower speed than the foreground does.

Real-Time Editing and Previewing

You can edit a scene while the game is still running. The initial state of actors can be toggled to display translucently to show their original orientation when the scene started playing.

For Mac and iOS developers, the GameSalad Creator offers a specific preview mode for debugging and testing performance and memory usage of games on the desktop and the iPhone. You can install a viewer application separately to an iPhone so you can click a toolbar button in the Creator to upload games to your iPhone over a wireless (Wi-Fi) network.

Integrated Physics and Expressions

The GameSalad Creator utilizes a rigid-body physics simulator for handling realistic motion and collision within the games made with it. Rigid-body physics refers to virtual objects given artificial substance, so they collide with one another for interesting effect. You can manage and optimize how objects collide by organizing actors with tags. You can choose to have an actor collide with a group of many other types of actors.

For more advanced users, the GameSalad Creator has an Expression Editor to define complex behavior and state changes with mathematical expressions and a library of functions.

Cross-Platform Publishing

The GameSalad Creator has one common dialogue-based interface for publishing to multiple platforms, including the iPhone and Mac. The Creator can also publish to Android devices such as the Nook, and to the Web as an HTML5 widget. This is an unprecedented number of devices you can publish to, all from a single source!

The GameSalad Website

The GameSalad website (www.gamesalad.com) has three major areas to help users:

- The Marketplace is for users to sell and/or buy electronic files such as GameSalad project files, graphics, audio files, and more.
- The Forums are a place you go to ask for help, answer other people's questions, announce your game once you have designed it, and much more.
- The Cookbook is a site to look up a question if someone has already asked it or ask a question if they have not.

The GameSalad Distribution Network

In January 2013, GameSalad, Inc. announced the launch of a new and powerful feature for the GameSalad community: the GameSalad Distribution Network (GSDN).

One of the biggest obstacles indie game communities have faced over the years is the issue of discoverability, or being found. With mammoth publishers moving into mobile gaming and spending large media budgets to attract gamers, indie developers have had to struggle to break into the top charts and attract new players at a reasonable cost to them.

Simultaneously, new acquisition techniques have emerged, and many savvy developers have benefited from utilizing cross-promotion tactics to attract gamers without spending an exorbitant marketing budget. With this in mind, GameSalad, Inc. built the GameSalad Distribution Network, a network that would leverage cross-promotion techniques to take full advantage of the thousands of games and millions of players throughout the GameSalad universe.

GameSalad promotes a variety of high-quality games made with the GameSalad Creator, including select Game of the Month winners. Pro developers (any user with the money to pay for a Pro account) can use cross-promotion technology in their games and receive traffic in exchange for referring traffic to other GameSalad games. Basically, this means displaying ads for other GameSalad games with your game so that those other games will advertise your game, too.

A TRIAL RUN

To download the GameSalad Creator, head over to www.gamesalad.com/creator (shown in Figure 1.2) and click the Download button to get the most recent version of the Creator. You must be 13 or older to agree to the terms of use, so have an adult help you if you must. Choose the appropriate version for your machine.

Figure 1.2
The Download page for the GameSalad Creator.

I will be using the Windows PC version for this book, although you can find correlative material if you choose to use the Mac version. If you do use the Mac version, keep this in mind when comparing your work to the screenshots contained within the following pages.

After the Creator has finished downloading to your machine, install it and you are good to go. Do not be concerned if GameSalad has to install prerequisite software like the Haali Media Splitter during installation, as this is normal.

Although you can download and use the Creator without registering for a GameSalad account, you will not be able to publish without logging in, so I highly recommend you take the time to register for an account if you have not already done so.

The Dashboard

After starting Creator, the Dashboard will be the first screen that you will see if you are using the Mac version. If you are using the Windows PC version, the first screen will be the Editor, but you can open the Dashboard by choosing File > Open Dashboard in the top menu bar. I show the Windows PC version of the Dashboard in Figure 1.3.

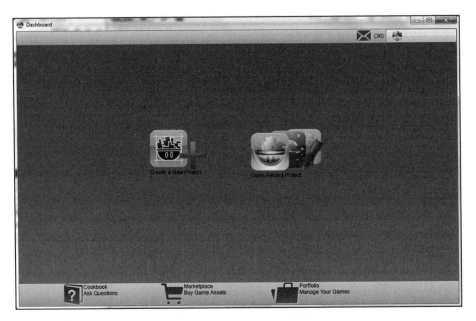

Figure 1.3
The Dashboard.

From here, you can log into your GameSalad account, access your portfolio of previously published projects, examine sample project templates, and start your very own project. With the Dashboard, you can also browse uploaded games, run tutorials, message other GameSalad members, and download shared templates uploaded by other GameSalad members.

When you are a little more familiar with the Creator's options and functionality, I recommend you peer at some of the project templates found in the Dashboard. For now, though, return to the Editor (Windows PC users) or start a new project by double-clicking My Great Project (Mac users).

If you are a Mac user, you will have to select your project info after starting a new project. Leave all the text fields as is for now. The only decision you need to make on the project-creation screen is what platform you want to use to develop your game. Of course, you can change this later, but the decision will affect the starting screen resolution of your project, so it is something to bear in mind. For now, set Platform to iPhone Landscape.

The Scene Editor

Click the Scenes tab at the top of the screen (Mac users) or click the Scenes tab in the Library panel on the left of your screen (Windows PC users). A black-and-white movie clapboard icon is used to denote scenes. See Figure 1.4.

Figure 1.4
Scenes.
Source: The GameSalad Creator, © 2013 GameSalad®, Inc. All Rights Reserved.

Scenes, like levels in a game, are the primary way you will divvy up your project. You can give different scenes unique scene attributes, such as size, gravity, and X/Y wrap, and actor placement. X and Y refer to the dimensions of two-dimensional space. In the Creator, X governs the horizontal axis (left and right), while Y governs the vertical axis (up and down). If you have taken geometry in grade school, you will be very good at understanding how the axes work in tandem and the principle of coordinates, or finding where a point exists in space given an X and Y designation.

You start with a single empty scene that contains default scene attributes. You add more scenes by clicking the plus (+) icon in the bottom-left corner of your screen (Mac) or at the top-right corner of the Library panel (Windows PC). Clicking the minus (−) icon will remove the selected scene.

Before adding a new scene, you always want to ask yourself, "Is it alright if the player waits briefly for the next scene to load?" You could continue to add to your current scene instead, but bear in mind that continuing to add actors and behaviors may decrease performance quality. So weight the option. Should you continue expanding your current scene, or add a new one and transfer the player to it instead?

You rename existing scenes by clicking the name and typing the new name (by default, the starting scene's name is Initial Scene). I changed the name of the starting scene to My First Level, as shown in Figure 1.5.

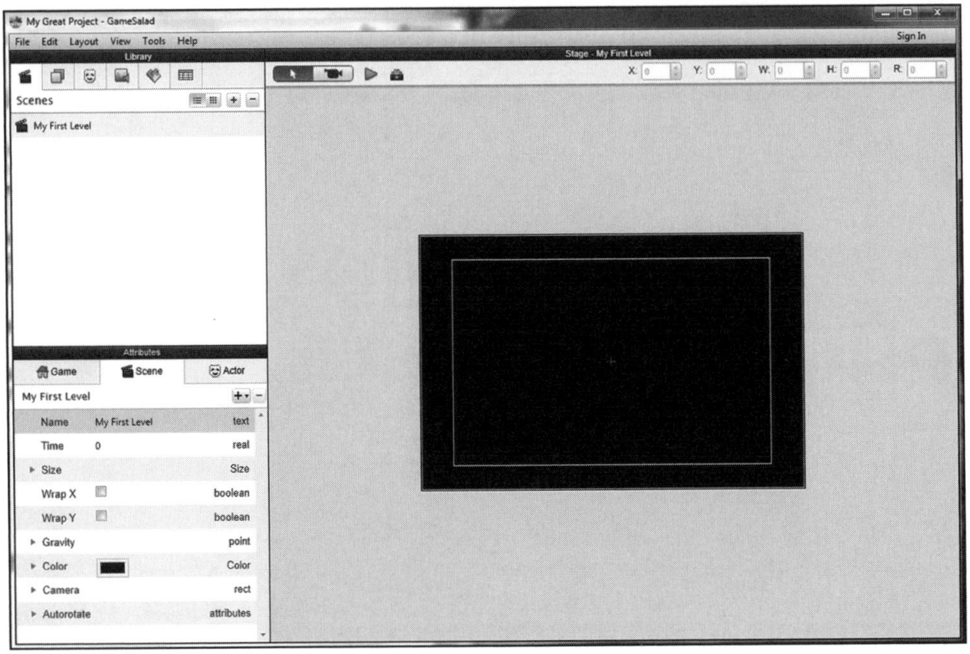

Figure 1.5
I changed the starting scene's name to My First Level.
Source: The GameSalad Creator, © 2013 GameSalad®, Inc. All Rights Reserved.

Switching between scenes is not something that happens at random or automatically within a GameSalad project. Instead, you must trigger scene change with a behavior aptly named Change Scene.

If you are using the Mac version of the GameSalad Creator, double-click your starting scene, named Initial Scene (unless you renamed it), to view the Scene Editor, which opens by default on the Windows PC version. The layout of the Scene Editor is different in the Windows PC and Mac versions, but shares much the same components, just in different locations. The Preview button (a green "play" button) is in roughly the same place, but the Library panel is at the bottom left in the Mac version and the top left in the PC version, and the Inspector panel is at the top left in the Mac version but replaced by the Attributes panel in the bottom left in the PC version. Most of the lessons herein I have based on the PC version, with slight suggestions how Mac users could do the same.

Do not panic just because there are several options and pieces of information visible in the Scene Editor all at once. The basics are straightforward, and that is all you will focus on right now.

Behaviors Tab

Mac users will find the Behaviors tab in the bottom left, and Windows PC users will find it in the top left, denoted by a colorful jigsaw puzzle piece icon, as shown in Figure 1.6. The Behaviors panel contains lists of all standard, custom, and in some cases, Pro or version-specific behaviors. Behaviors add computer logic to your game, including collision and interaction between actors.

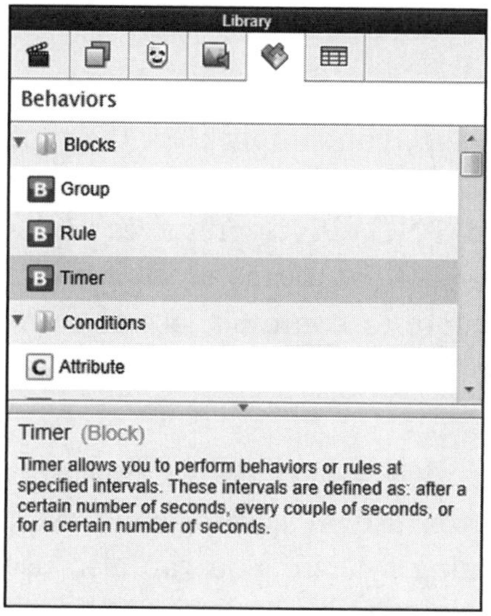

Figure 1.6
The Behaviors tab.
Source: The GameSalad Creator, © 2013 GameSalad®, Inc. All Rights Reserved.

Media Tab

Beside the Behaviors tab in the Mac version, you will find two other tabs, named Images and Sounds, which GameSalad groups together in the Media tab in the Windows PC version (located beside the Behaviors tab and denoted by a graphic image and speaker symbol, as shown in Figure 1.7). These enable you to access your art and sound assets.

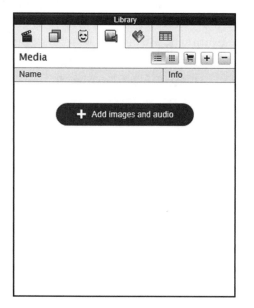

Figure 1.7
The Media tab.
Source: The GameSalad Creator, © 2013 GameSalad®, Inc. All Rights Reserved.

While media libraries start empty, you can easily import your own files into the Creator as long as they are the appropriate file type. To do so, you simply click the plus (+) icon. Image files should be in the PNG (pronounced "ping") format, although many other file types will convert automatically into PNG. PNG preserves alpha transparency, which is why it is preferred. Alpha transparency means an image can have a see-through background. All the images are square (a common fact of computer graphics), but alpha allows the square edges to be hidden either partially or wholly.

Acceptable sound file formats include WAV, OGG, and M4A. Windows PC users will find it easier to get their hands on WAV files for use in games, while Mac users will recognize OGG files as native to that operating system. You can also use MP3 files, as GameSalad automatically converts them to OGG on import.

Actors Tab

Mac users will find the Actors tab in the upper left in the Inspector panel, while Windows PC users can find it the middle tab in the Library panel in the upper-left corner. Greek drama masks denote actors, as you see in Figure 1.8.

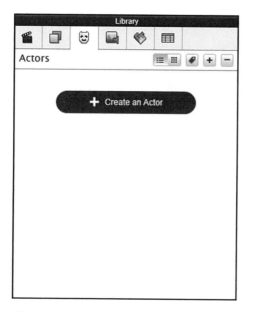

Figure 1.8
The Actors tab.
Source: The GameSalad Creator, © 2013 GameSalad®, Inc. All Rights Reserved.

Actors are the primary agents in all projects. You will find every actor that exists in your current project in the Actors tab, not just those used within the current scene. In addition, you use the Actors tab to create new actors, by clicking the plus (+) button.

When you drag a prototype actor into the current scene, you create an instance of that actor. *Instances* are essentially duplicate copies of the prototype. New instances include all the prototype's logic and attributes, and start out locked to the original prototype. While the instance is locked in this way, almost any change to the prototype will affect every instance. In this way, you could create a dozen instances all tied to the same prototype. Instead of going through each one to edit them identically, which would be a time-consuming and daunting task, you simply edit the prototype and GameSalad automatically updates all the instances for you.

You will know you are editing a prototype when you see the word "prototype" in parentheses next to its name in the title bar. Similarly, you will know you are editing an instance when you see the Revert to Prototype button. This button grays out as long as you have a locked instance; selecting it on a non-locked instance will relock it, reverting any attributes or logic that may have changed back to the default settings inherent in the prototype. When an actor is selected, you will see the prototype rules and behaviors displayed in its own tab in the Backstage panel. Selecting that tab will allow you to edit the prototype's rules and behaviors.

Attributes

The last area of the Scene Editor with which you must be familiar is the Attributes panel (Windows PC) or Attributes tab (Mac).

Attributes are one of the powerful aspects of the Creator, and are essentially value placeholders. GameSalad designed attributes to store numerical or text values so you can use them in different situations. They are how actors in your project know when to spawn new enemies, how much life or ammo the player character has left, when to show the Game Over screen, and much, much more. Understanding how to use attributes properly is crucial to unlocking the full potential of the GameSalad Creator.

GameSalad divides attributes into three main categories: scene, game, and actor. All three are grouped in the bottom left of the Scene Editor for Windows PC users, as shown in Figure 1.9.

Figure 1.9
The Attributes panel.

Existing attributes record data about your game, scene, and actors, such as their size, location, color, and more. Custom attributes contain data unique to your game—for instance, how many blocks remain to be moved in a puzzle game. You click the plus (+) icon to add attributes. The Creator will prompt you to pick a type for your new attribute:

- **Boolean:** These are true or false values. One example of a Boolean attribute could be the status of a door, where true equals opened and false equals closed. All actors start with at least one Boolean attribute by default under Physics in their attribute list to toggle whether the actor is moveable. You change Boolean attributes to true/false in games with the Change Attribute behavior.

- **Text:** These are alphanumeric (letters and numbers) values. You primarily use text in conjunction with the Display Text behaviors to display scene titles, actor names, and so on.

- **Integers:** These are whole number values, such as 0, 9, 22, and 3,250. A few of the many possible uses for integers are storing the game's score, specifying a set number of enemies to spawn, or keeping track of how many reward objects are left in the current scene.

- **Real:** You use these in place of integers whenever you are dealing with fractions or decimals, as real numbers allow for decimal points, such as 0.142 and 24.5.

- **Angle:** Angles range from 0 to 359, representing the degrees of a circle. You can use decimal values within this range if you like. You primarily use angles with objects that rotate or have some form of angular movement, such as tossed grenades, cannon balls aimed at a target, and so on.

- **Index:** These are only positive whole numbers. Essentially, index values are the same as integers, except an index value can never drop below 0. Therefore, for instance, if an actor's health was told to drop −6 points after an attack, and that actor only had a health of 3, the reduction would have to stop at 0.

Be sure to give any new attribute you add to your game, scene, or actor a descriptive name so it makes sense to you and you will be able to remember it later, such as "puzzle blocks remaining."

The Relationship between Actors and Behaviors

This would be a good time to create your first actor, so you can learn about rules and behaviors.

1. Click the Actors tab in the Library panel.

2. Click the plus (+) icon to create a new prototype actor. Note that at this point, the newly created actor does not exist in any scene. (Actually, prototype actors never enter scenes; only instances of them do.)

3. Double-click the newly created actor's name (Actor 1 by default) and type a new name to rename it.

4. Click the Actor tab of the Attributes panel (Windows PC) or within the Actor Editor (Mac). As you can see, the actor already has some default attributes aligned to it (see Figure 1.10). However, it will not have any rules or behaviors yet.

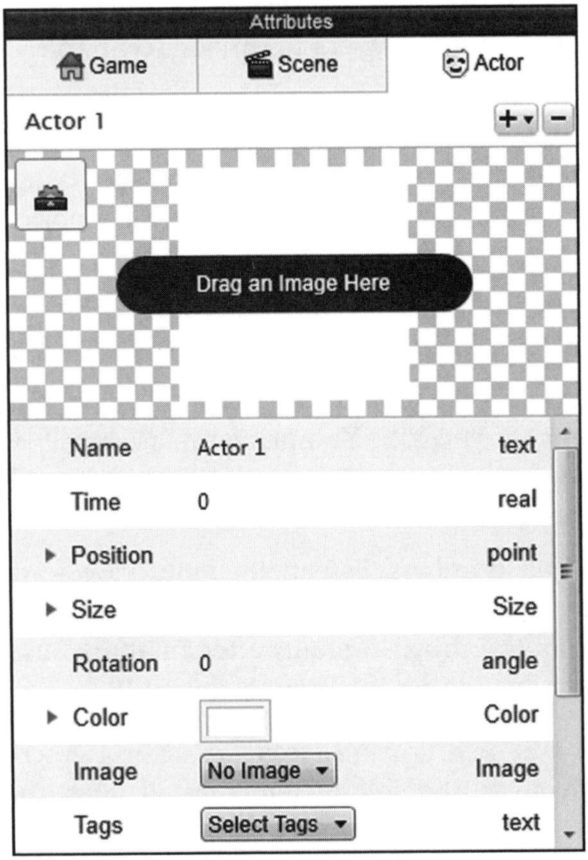

Figure 1.10
The Actor attributes.
Source: The GameSalad Creator, © 2013 GameSalad®, Inc. All Rights Reserved.

5. To add a new rule, click the Create Rule button in the upper-right corner just below the blue Help icon in the Actor Editor (Mac) or click the Edit Rules button (as shown in Figure 1.11, it looks like a shelf with a gear in it) just under the Actor title in the upper-left corner of the Attributes panel (Windows PC). The Actor 1 (Prototype) rules appear to the right in the Backstage panel.

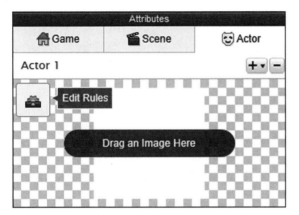

Figure 1.11
The Edit Rules button.
Source: The GameSalad Creator, © 2013 GameSalad®, Inc. All Rights Reserved.

6. Click the + Rule button to add a new rule. A new rule will appear in front of you (see Figure 1.12), ready to be turned into a feature of your game. Before you add behaviors, you should examine the individual components that make up a rule.

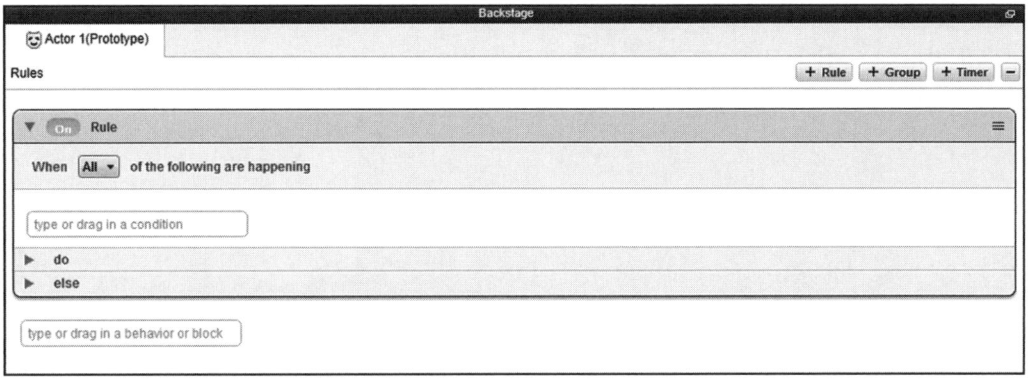

Figure 1.12
A new rule appears.
Source: The GameSalad Creator, © 2013 GameSalad®, Inc. All Rights Reserved.

The conditions section at the top lets the rule know when it should trigger. A rule can be triggered based on user input, such as the following:

- A key pressed on the keyboard
- A mouse click
- A touchscreen press (iPhone or Android)
- An accelerometer tilt (tilting the iPhone or Android left/right or up/down)
- An event such as one actor colliding with another
- The game or device clock hitting a specific time
- When a game or actor attribute is or is no longer a specific value

Once triggered, a rule will look to the Behaviors section to determine what it should do next. It will then execute all behaviors included in the order they are listed.

It is crucial you understand that rules and behaviors fire off in a top-down or cascading order. That means if you put two Change Scene behaviors in the same rule, the second Change Scene behavior will never get a chance to execute because it is superseded by the first one, even if the rule itself is valid and triggering properly.

The final portion of a rule is the else or otherwise section, which is collapsed by default. This section lets the rule know what it should do if it is *not* triggered. This can be tricky to use properly, so for now I recommend focusing on the first two sections.

Right now, the sky is the limit. Rules can make any number of adjustments to your game. Animations can be initiated. Actors can be moved around the scene. Music or sounds can play. Additional actors can be spawned. The player's perspective can be shifted. Scenes can be changed. The value of actor attributes can be altered. Alterations of those attributes may even cause other rules to trigger, and so on, until (before you know it) you have made a game!

CHAPTER 2

UNDERSTANDING YOUR RECIPE

Many fans of video games, even those people who want to make them, are not clued into the amount of work a video game takes to put together. Perhaps this is because some of the most noted games each year are so incredibly polished, they make video-game development look simple. This is not the case. In fact, every video game takes long months, dozens or even hundreds of collaborators, and enormous toppling budgets to build. That being said, game development is not impossible, even for the "one man band." This chapter will show you how it is done.

THE MAKING OF VIDEO GAMES: BEHIND THE SCENES

So you want to make video games with GameSalad. What has prompted this? Do you think this could be a "sure thing," with lots of money potential and very little work? If that is what you think, you have never seen how a game goes from inspiration to store shelves, and how much work and sweat is actually involved.

The Developers

Team leaders hire game developers based on personality, because everyone on the team must get along and work well together, and on demonstrable skills. Developers fall into several classes based on their skill sets.

The broadest classes of individuals making up a game development team are as follows:

- **Designers:** Game designers are responsible for the look and feel of a game. They generate the concept, story, game world, and mechanics behind the game.

They are concerned mostly with the aspects of a game that grab the public attention and make it a potential success. Under the general designation "designer," there will be sub-roles such as director, scriptwriter, and level designer. Posts range in seniority from junior positions to leads, who manage the staff.

■ **Artists:** A game's graphics include the commercial (box) art and in-game graphics. Visual appeal is one of the first things a gamer assesses, so graphics can make or break a game's success. Therefore, the art has to look spectacular. Game art includes two-dimensional (2D) and three-dimensional (3D) art, both of which are important in video-game design. The art and animation staff gives eye-catching form to the game designers' ideas, from 2D drawings up to fully realized 3D models and animations. These visualizations are necessary to develop the game's unique style. These roles can overlap with those of the digital modelers and animators who create the assets to be included in the game. The GameSalad Creator appeals to artists because it does not require a whole lot of setup or programming to make their game graphics truly shine.

■ **Programmers:** These people are the ones who talk straight to the computer via programming or scripting languages (including C++, C#, Lua, Perl, Java, and more). They create the code for the engines that deliver games. Despite coming from highly technical backgrounds, many programmers have a creative streak. They make the most money out of everyone on a development team because a game could not work without them. Their job is the trickiest and most stressful of all because if they cannot work out an algorithm to make a feature successful, the game just will not fly, no matter how impressive the graphics might be. One of the great things about using the GameSalad Creator is that you do not have to be a programmer to build a game. If you plan to customize the inherent behaviors, however, you do need some programming skills.

■ **Audio specialists:** Sound is just as important in video games as the graphics are; you just cannot see sound, so it is not readily apparent until you start to play the game. Designers listen for the right kind of sound because it helps set the mood and put the player into the game. The roles of musician, composer, and sound engineer are critical. These roles may cover the design aspects of the game as well as the more technical side, when incorporating the soundtrack into the game programming.

■ **Writers:** Not all games have storylines, but the majority do—and where there is story, there must be a storyteller. The writers not only construct the plot a game must follow, but they also describe the game in blurbs and commercial advertisements, write the game manuals, and produce copious documents for producers and capital investors to peer over.

- **Testers:** There is this persistent myth that testers get paid big money to play games all day, but that is not true. Game developers outsource or find volunteer testers to get fresh eyes on their games. Testers sit in offices, plowing repeatedly through a single level or one section of the overall game and jotting down loads of notes to the development team to let them know what works and what does not.

- **Managers:** These people keep the whole development cycle on track, making sure the team meets each deadline (also called *milestones*) on time and accurately. Managers must communicate with everyone, from artists to programmers, so understanding the culture and vocabulary of each department can add to their effectiveness.

Of course, many teams have noted cross-pollination between these disciplines. A writer may become an artist, while a programmer may become a director, often switching between game projects. As an independent beginner, you will serve all the roles simultaneously (unless you can find some friends to help you out). As you practice making games yourself, you may learn you like one discipline more than another and gravitate toward that specialization.

You might wonder how many developers it takes to make a game. That is a difficult question to answer because it depends on several elements, including what kind of game it is being made and how large a budget the team has to work with.

Electronic Arts (EA) and other large game publishers expect video games they choose to publish to be AAA (triple-A) game titles. The AAA title description refers to an individual title's success or anticipated success. In other words, AAA titles are defined by the cost and the return on investment. Most AAA title games cost between $10 and $12 million to make and become a smash hit, selling well over a million copies.

In contrast, an average video game requires a team of 20 to 300 or more individual developers and may cost upwards of $500,000 to make. However, it is not unheard of for a small independent team of developers of one to 20 people to make a video game in their spare time, or even in their parents' basement or garage, for a petty budget of less than $1,000.

Indie Developers

Although much of the game industry's big-budget efforts come from large team efforts, toiling on the production line is not the only game-development model out there. Lovingly crafted creations from independent (indie) game developers have proven that creativity flourishes when you put the development process back into the hands of a solo designer.

As an indie developer, you can make any game you want. Because you are not taking anyone else's money to make your game, you can try radical things no one else has tried before. Working alone to build a game with art, music, and compelling play may seem daunting to a first-timer, but it has never been easier for developers to create original titles without committing themselves to programming from scratch or shelling out an exhaustive budget.

Best of all, there is no reason to wait for permission to start working on a game. You can start right now and do it all by yourself. Working alone on a game not only gives you complete control, but it also infuses your work with a personality that big-team development rarely has.

When a corporate giant such as Electronic Arts pours millions of dollars into creating a big-market game, they expect huge payoffs to compensate for their costs. They are understandably unwilling to take risks, even if the payoff might come in better innovation or storytelling. This undeniable fact is why you see so many game sequels and imitation knockoffs instead of original or groundbreaking games on store shelves. If you want to see real innovation in the game industry, you have to peer at the margins, at the indie developers.

Producers of game-authoring systems like GameSalad target the indie development community because they know that indie developers do not have an exorbitant budget but still want to make great games.

Game Genres

Game media, just because it is recent on the scene, did not originate in a vacuum. It sprung from other media, so it borrows heavily on their categorization by genre typing.

Just as the fiction book and film category has its genres, like Westerns, science fiction, and horror, video games have their genres, too. Video-game genres sometimes parallel fiction genres, as many games you see on store shelves today fit the aforementioned categories. Subject matter is vital to games because fiction genres appeal to different players. If someone likes horror games, for instance, they will probably play all the horror games they can get their hands on.

That being said, game genres are also divisible by their gameplay, or the underlying way you play the games.

You must understand that game genre boundaries are still fuzzy. Many games take part in more than one style of gameplay. While this adds broader interest to the experience, it is risky, because you run the risk of alienating fans of either genre who are not interested in the new mix of elements.

For example, take the game *Darkwatch*. Here you have a horror Western game with a mixture of first- and third-person shooting action. The design team was directly inspired by the tabletop game *Deadlands*, but it was still a risky move on their part. They took the chance that fans of Westerns would hate it and that fans of horror would think it too campy for its Western trappings. Ideally, the game targets a niche market of folks who like Stephen King's *Gunslinger* trilogy. It paid off in the end for the makers of *Darkwatch*, but their sales never reached astronomical success.

In addition, because game genres are still new and emerging, confusion can settle in. What one website might call an "adventure game" may be no more than a platformer, and while there is certainly some adventure in playing it, it does not fit the actual definition of a true adventure game.

What follows are some traditional video-game genres.

Action Games

This is the oldest of all video-game genres and still represents a large portion of the game market today (almost 30% of games sold in the United States). Action games include all the different games in which a player's reflexes and hand-eye coordination make a difference in whether he or she wins or loses. The most popular action games consist of the following:

- **First-person shooters (FPS):** Seen through the eyes of the main character, these games focus on fast-paced movement through detailed game levels, shooting at enemy targets, and blowing up everything in sight. Because of the intimacy of "being the character," these games have the deepest player immersion. However, because of the frantic pacing of these games, the player rarely has time to stand still and take in all the scenery, no matter how much gorgeous detail the level designers have imparted in the game environments. Examples of first-person shooters include *Quake, Hexen, Doom, Wolfenstein, Duke Nukem, Call of Duty, Halo, Half-Life,* and *F.E.A.R.,* to name a few.

- **Third-person shooters:** In these games, the player sees the action through a camera, which hovers above the ground in the air and aims down at the main character or over the character's shoulder. These games still focus on shooting and blowing stuff up, but the character is always visible onscreen and may have additional controls for actions like jumping, climbing, and performing martial arts.

■ **Platformers:** In these games, the player's character is visible onscreen, sometimes from a side angle. The action no longer focuses on shooting and blowing up enemies; instead, the main action focuses on the character running and jumping from one platform to the next in a fast-paced animated world. The first platform games were called *side-scrollers* because the background scrolled from one side to the other. In them, two-dimensional characters started on the left of the screen and jumped and ran their way to the right of the screen (think *Super Mario Bros.*, *Sonic the Hedgehog*, and *Earthworm Jim*). Figure 2.1 shows an example of a side-scroller being built in the GameSalad Creator. Games like *Mario 64*, *Super Mario Sunshine*, *Spyro the Dragon*, *Ratchet and Clank*, *Jak and Daxter*, and *Crash Bandicoot* revolutionized platformers by bringing them into fully realized 360-degree 3D game worlds.

Figure 2.1
A side-scrolling platformer built in GameSalad Creator.

- **Racing games:** Racing games feature fast vehicles along twisting tracks and difficult terrain in an all-out race to the finish line. The goal is usually to come in first and as far ahead of the rest as possible.

- **Sports games:** Sports games are simulations of a real-world athletic competition, where the player wins or loses on a virtual playing field. They feature rules and scenarios just like their real-world counterparts. Sports games focus on popular sports such as golf, soccer, basketball, football, volleyball, and baseball, although any pastime can be a prospective electronic game. The best include realistic motion-captured animation, moves that follow accurate physics, referees, cheering crowds, announcers, and other little touches to make them more vibrant.

- **Fighting games:** A fighting game is any duke-'em-out arcade classic where the player competes against other contenders in an enclosed arena. Using combination attacks and devastating blows, the player tries to take his or her opponent down before losing too much of his or her own health. Games such as *Street Fighter, Mortal Kombat, Tekken, Soul Caliber, Double Dragon, Dead or Alive,* and (to a certain extent) *Devil May Cry* and *Onimusha* have set the standards for this genre.

- **Stealth games:** For those players who do not like rushing headlong into battle, there are games that reward players for sneaking into and out of places invisibly and striking their enemies silently. Sometimes the player is taking on the role of a master thief (*Thief: Deadly Shadows*), while at other times the player is a slick assassin (*Hitman: Absolution*) or special-ops master (*Splinter Cell*). This is one subgenre that is slower than most because the player must rely on patience, hiding in the dark and taking advantage of enemy blind spots.

Adventure Games

One of the first interactive fiction games played on a computer (and one of the best games ever released for the Commodore 64), *Zork* was the forerunner of modern adventure games. The word "zork" is hacker jargon for an unfinished program, but by the time Infocom was set to release its game with the name *Dungeon* in 1979, the nickname *Zork* had already stuck. For many, the name *Zork* conjures up dim images of a computer game prehistory, before graphics became the norm. *Zork* set several precedents for the genre.

Adventure games evolved from the two-word combination text-parser games of the 1970s, the most popular of which was *Zork*. They are about exploring a world and experiencing a story, usually by solving a variety of puzzles. Adventure games do not rely on action, strategy, or management skills to be successful. They move at a slower pace, have better stories, and often can include awe-inspiring graphic settings.

What pulls the game together is an extended, often twisting narrative, calling for the player to visit different locations and encounter many different characters. Often, the player's path is blocked, and he or she must gather and manipulate certain items to solve some puzzle and unblock the path. Adventure games primarily center on story, exploration, and mental challenges. Most, if not all, adventure games do not even have violence in them.

Another type of adventure game you might have seen and even played before is the hunt-the-pixel or "hidden image" game. This manner of adventure games, a trendy genre for amateur game developers to undertake, consists of a series of graphic puzzles that has the player going on a virtual scavenger hunt.

Examples of adventure games include *Colossal Cave*, *Secret of Monkey Island*, *Myst*, *Siberia*, *Still Life*, *Legend of the Broken Sword*, *Gabriel Knight*, *Grim Fandango*, and *Maniac Mansion*.

Role-Playing Games

By definition, a role-playing game (RPG) is any game in which the player takes on the role of another person and in doing so goes on various quests. This could practically describe all video games today, as the player adopts the role of an onscreen avatar and pursues goals within the game world.

Computer RPGs are an offshoot of pencil-and-paper ("tabletop") RPGs started in the 1970s with Gary Gygax's *Dungeons and Dragons*, a variation of the British war gaming, which was a popular hobby of British veterans that used miniature soldiers and world maps laid out on tables to reenact battles. Players of *Dungeons and Dragons* would sit around a table and, using paper character sheets and rolling many-sided dice, imagine they were wizards, warriors, and rogues exploring vast treacherous dungeons in a fantasy world.

Today's more complex computer RPGs, like *Neverwinter Nights*, *Asheron's Call*, *World of WarCraft*, and *Elder Scrolls V: Skyrim*, help players create their own characters from scratch. The goal of each game is often making their characters stronger and finding better weapons while facing a rising level of adversity. The adversity comes in many startling guises, from trolls to giant spiders to fire-breathing dragons.

One of the major resources you see in almost every RPG is experience. Players get experience for completing missions and beating monsters, and they spend experience to raise their character's skills or gain new powers.

Another popular part of RPGs is communicating with non-player characters, or non-player characters (NPCs), through multiple-choice conversations called *dialogue trees*. Depending on what players decide to say to NPCs, they might make friends, or they might find the NPCs rushing them with swords drawn!

The downside to this genre is that the industry itself has typified RPGs as classic, quest-driven fantasy games where players beat monsters and gain treasure, all in order to beat tougher monsters and gain better treasure. Players complain they feel more like itinerate gofers or second-hand arms dealers. They are always looting corpses, breaking into treasure chests, and trading with shopkeepers. This has caused hecklers to call such games "monty-haul" or "hack-and-slash" games, which even fans of *Torchlight* and *Diablo* cannot deny. RPGs like *Vampire: Bloodlines*, *City of Heroes*, and *Fable* have set out to challenge this dichotomy, with limited success.

Tip

There is a great application you can use to make fantasy RPGs called RPG Maker. If you want to learn more about it, look for my book *RPG Maker for Teens,* from Cengage Learning PTR. In that book, I show you how to make a fantasy game RPG using Enterbrain's RPG Maker software.

Strategy Games

Strategy games envelop a great deal of mental challenge–based games, including real-time strategy (RTS) games, turn-based strategy (TBS) games, and construction-management simulations (CMS). In each, the core play has the player building an empire, fortress, realm, world, or other construct, managing the resources therein, and preparing against inevitable problems like decay, hardship, economic depravity, revolution, or foreign invaders. Strategy games emphasize skillful thinking and planning in order to achieve victory.

In most strategy games, the designer gives the player a godlike view of the game world and allows him or her to manipulate battle units. Thus, strategy games are a closer comparison to classic British war games than RPGs, even though RPGs were the first electronic games to originate from war games.

Keynote strategy games that have helped define the genre include *Age of Empires*, *Civilization*, *StarCraft*, *Command & Conquer*, and *Shattered Galaxy*. CMS game examples include *The Sims*, *Spore*, *Ghost Master*, and *Roller-Coaster Tycoon*.

Casual Gaming

When video games entered homes during the console movement, the rules for video games became more complex, and only the most hardcore gamers dominated the consumer market. However, this is not the only type of video game audience out there, and developers, especially mobile game developers, have recognized that.

A casual game is a video game targeted at or used by an audience of casual gamers. What are casual gamers? Casual gamers are those who do not have the time, patience, or obsessive passion to learn difficult, complex video games but still want to be entertained.

Casual gamers include the young and old but are more often female, with more than 74 percent of casual gamers having a pair of ovaries. Casual gamers tend to seek out games with comfortable gameplay and a pick-up-and-play entertainment that people from almost any age group or skill level can enjoy.

Casual games can be any type of genre. You can distinguish them by a simple set of rules and particular lack of time commitment required. Casual games often have one or more of the following features:

- Extremely modest gameplay played entirely with a single-button mouse click or cell phone keypad
- Gameplay accomplished in short episodes, such as during work breaks or, especially in the case of mobile games, on public transportation
- A game that either is quick to complete or has continuous play with frequent or no need to save your spot in the game
- A game that is usually free or a try-before-you-buy download

Microsoft's *Solitaire*, which comes free with Microsoft Windows, is widely considered the very first casual game, with more than 400 million people having played it since its inception.

When Nintendo released its Gameboy, the company included a free, built-in *Tetris* game, a casual game if there ever was one, which critics partially credited with the success of the Gameboy.

With the invention of Flash animation software came a boom of Web-based casual games. One of the most prominent titles was *Bejeweled*, which even former president Bill Clinton admitted to being addicted to playing. Flash game sites have cropped up all over the Internet, and Facebook third-party application developers got into action with casual games like *Farmville* and *Mobsters*. Another popular casual game is the diner type, where the player is a server at a dining or drinking establishment and must make sure the customers leave happy, as shown in Figure 2.2.

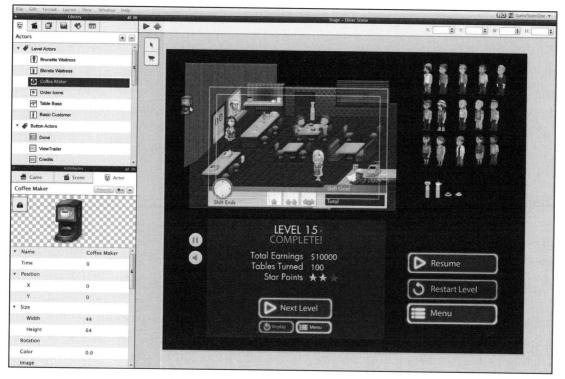

Figure 2.2
A diner game built in GameSalad Creator.
Source: The GameSalad Creator, © 2013 GameSalad®, Inc. All Rights Reserved.

Today, casual games on the Web and on mobile devices have exploded, with a wider and much more approachable audience than any other known game type. Casual games are also remarkably well placed for indie game developers to get their feet in the door.

CAMERA MODALITY

There is another component to consider when designing a video game besides genre. It is the playing perspective, also known as the point-of-view (POV), just as in the development of fiction stories.

In film, cinematographers have to arrange the composition of all their camera shots to tell the story. In contrast, games use fixed or active cameras, which you can think of as floating eyes, to witness the action in video games. The position of these cameras, whether fixed or not, defines the POV of the game. The following are the most popular playing perspectives seen in video games today.

First-Person View

Just as fiction has a first-person perspective—the "I," "me," and "our" voice, told from the perspective of the narrator—so too do games have a first-person perspective. The approved choice of 3D shooters because of the ease of aiming, first-person perspective, or view, enhances sensory immersion by putting the player directly into the shoes of the character played. In other words, the player sees through the eyes of his or her character, and usually the only part of the character the player can see is the hand holding the gun out in front of him or her.

Caution

It is important to remember when designing a first-person game that the player will start to think of himself or herself as the avatar character, so cut scenes that suddenly show the character or asides where a particularly incongruous voiceover supposed to belong to the character will take away the player's suspension of disbelief and (worst-case scenario) cause frustration.

Suspension of disbelief, a concept first postulated by poet Samuel Taylor Coleridge, is that magical realm where the audience goes along with fantastical fiction elements as long as they are not brought back down to reality by some flaw in the writing. This concept is best demonstrated by watching a stage magician performing. You want to believe in his act, that he is really doing magic, but your suspension of disbelief is worn down if he constantly goofs or shows you how he does his tricks.

Third-Person View

In fiction writing, you typify the third-person (omniscient) style with the "he," "she," "they," and "it" voice. Similarly, video games have a third-person perspective. The video-game third-person perspective is much more cinematic and immediate, however, in that the gamer can see his or her character on the screen and therefore can watch every move the character makes. This leads to a greater identification with the player character but less player immersion overall.

The worst restriction to this viewpoint is that the character is *always* onscreen, and often from behind. As a result, the character must look exceptional or gamers are going to complain about always looking at an ugly butt. Both Mario from *Mario 64* and Lara Croft from the *Tomb Raider* series were used in this perspective and rose to "movie star" fame because they literally became game icons and representatives of their gameplay.

Film cinematography features an over-the-shoulder (OTS) camera view, which has recently made its way to video games as a variation of the third-person perspective. Surprisingly well-done examples of this are Capcom's *Resident Evil 4* and *Resident Evil 5* (see Figure 2.3).

Figure 2.3
Resident Evil 4 for the iPad demonstrates the over-the-shoulder (OTS) perspective.
Source: Capcom Corporation.

Top-Down (Aerial) View

The top-down or aerial view is a view looking straight down at the playing field. You see this perspective in games like *Solitaire*, the early *Ultima*, or *Zelda: Link to the Past*. It limits the horizon for the player, so he or she has a harder time seeing what obstacles might be coming up, but it adds finer detail to what is on the surrounding map. *Grand Theft Auto*, before its 3D days, began as a vintage 8-bit top-down game.

Isometric View

Isometric is the favored tilted three-quarter view hovering off to one side of certain RPGs such as *Diablo*, *Baldur's Gate*, *Bard's Tale*, and *Planescape: Torment*. Developers use this perspective to give a fair impersonation of 3D, even when the characters and environments are 2D. Isometric games for this reason are popular in RTS and RPG but rarely seen in action shooters because of the limitations to aim and visibility. Isometric games offer player movement in eight directions: north, northwest, west, southwest, south, southeast, east, and northeast.

Side View

The side view perspective reflects the traditional view of Sega and Nintendo's side-scrolling platformers, as popularized in *Sonic the Hedgehog*, *Super Mario Bros.*, and *Earthworm Jim*. Although largely unused in newer games, being thought of as too retro, some games do still simulate the side view on occasion.

Adventure Scenes

Adventure games are well known for having their characters explore static backdrops, each scene acting like a diorama. Sometimes, there is no player character at all, just a diorama to explore. This type of perspective is fixed and unmovable. Whenever the player moves to an exact location onscreen (say, a door leading to a hallway), another scene is drawn (say, the interior of that hallway).

The player navigates and clicks through each adventure scene, sometimes having to backtrack many times or click throughout a scene to find elements to interact with. If the designer is not careful, this can quickly degenerate into "hunt-the-pixel" frustrations.

Because of the scene structure in GameSalad Creator, as you can imagine, adventure scenes are perhaps one of the easiest ways to set up and manage in that game authoring system.

Closed-Circuit Cameras

First pioneered by the game *Alone in the Dark*, the closed-circuit camera (CCTV) or "fixed cameras" perspective became the basis for the *Resident Evil* cameras. In fact, many developers simply call this playing perspective "RE cameras" for that reason. Developers copied the style for *Silent Hill* and countless other survival horror games in succession because they believed it heightened suspense.

In closed-circuit camera view, fixed cameras pan to follow the player characters as they wander through their virtual environments. When a player character gets too far away from one camera, another camera switches on and picks up the action so that the player character is always on display.

Unfortunately, this perspective style has gotten a lot of opposition. Players have griped that this style, while maintaining a suspenseful mood, can be downright frustrating when trying to aim and shoot at enemies coming around corners or being able to tell if you are approaching a potential hazard. This complaint is one of the reasons that *Resident Evil*, starting with *Resident Evil 4*, switched to using over-the-shoulder third-person perspective.

THE FOUR FS OF ALL GREAT VIDEO GAMES

There are four Fs of all great video games. Whenever making any design decision, it helps to list them in order of priority and to reflect on them. They help ensure every game you build is fantastic. The four Fs are as follows:

- Fun
- Fairness
- Feedback
- Feasibility

Fun

By their very definition, games are supposed to be fun. Indeed, fun is a word often synonymous with play. Even the smallest child will begin inventing his or her own personal game when bored, an innate instinct meant to stave off ennui.

You know what fun is intrinsically, but fun is actually very abstract and subjective. You cannot dissect fun and have it laid out before you in its constituent parts. It loses its nature when you do so. Yet there are some tricks you can do to make sure your game will be fun.

A game is any fun activity conducted in a pretend reality that has a core component of play. Because it is play (not work), that is a huge distinction to keep in mind when making a game. However, even play has rules.

How to Play

Play is any grouping of recreational human activities, centered on having fun. The pretend reality of most games is based on the players' mental capacity to create a conceptual state self-contained within its own set of rules, where the pretender can create, discard, or transform the components at will. The complexity and character of people's games evolve with their age and mental acuity. A game that is beyond a participant's age or understanding will swiftly tire the participant and leave him or her feeling bored. A boring game is no fun at all, as boredom is the antithesis of fun.

Note

Remember: Boredom is the antithesis of fun!

Video games are different from traditional board or card games. In video games, developers hide most of the rules. The game has rules, but those rules are not always written down for the player to consult before jumping into play. Instead, video games allow players to learn the rules of the game as they play. Harder games, or ones with entirely new or unheard-of rules, will sometimes offer players training levels to learn the rules early in the game. These are levels in which players learn the rules through moderated experimentation. Given this route for learning rules, gamers with practice playing a specific game are better informed and therefore can optimize their choices.

Hiding the rules offers video games one huge advantage over traditional games: Because the computer sets the boundary of the pretend reality involved in play, the player no longer has to think of the game as a game! This level of immersion is lacking in most traditional games.

Motivation

All games—not just video games—are driven by motivation and objectives. In sport games, the players are motivated to be the best, to become legendary for their talent on field or court, while their objective is to win the match. These principles translate directly to the world of video-game design.

- **Personal motivation:** Motivation in a game can have emphasis on the main character and those he or she loves. For instance, perhaps the evil villain has kidnapped the hero's girlfriend and taken her to his hard-to-reach lair.

- **Global motivation:** What about world peace? Instead of making a personal gambit, this type of motivation makes the hero care about saving the world as a whole. Perhaps the evil villain is threatening to blow up Canada with his death ray.

- *Die Hard* **motivation:** Making the motivation both personal and global (as in the movie *Die Hard*) creates a great impetus for your character to act. Nearly all the successful action films follow the *Die Hard* motivation pattern. The evil villain has not only kidnapped the hero's girlfriend (or estranged wife, as the case may be), but he is also threatening Canada with his death ray, and only the hero can stop him!

Objectives are the obstacles between the player and his or her ultimate goal. A structure for game objectives developed early on was to reach the end of one level and kill the boss monster. This basic structure prevails in modern games, though masked by complex storytelling and graphical finery. Players need to feel a sense of progression.

The boss battle is a sign to the player that he or she has successfully completed one chapter of the game.

Within game levels, a useful device you can use is a mini-objective. Mini-objectives help maintain player's interest by offering intermediate challenges before the eventual face-off with the boss. These mini-objectives could be as simple as "break into the vault," "steal the diamond," and "get out of the museum unseen." These examples are fine, but as with the primary motivation, the more incentive you can throw at the player, the better.

Player Interaction

When a player picks up the controller or takes over the keyboard and mouse or presses the touchscreen on his or her iPhone, that player wants to be able to explore make-believe worlds and interact with the game environment. Games are not passive entertainment forms, such as watching movies. Games are active; they expect you to react!

Games are not like traditional stories. Stories are typically a series of "facts" that occur in a sequential order. In a game, however, the audience cannot understand the story from a typical sequential order. Rather, the audience is free to make choices and come at the options from every angle. This freedom of interactivity leads to immersion, which sells games. Indeed, a game with a lot of immersion in it is a game that players will want to play repeatedly to explore new opportunities and avenues for expression.

Players do not want you to tell them a story. They want to discover the story themselves. Listening to long-winded expositions, watching time-consuming animated sequences, and even talking with NPCs should always be secondary to exploration, combat, manipulation, and puzzle solving. In other words, story is supplementary to interactivity.

Putting the controls in the player's hands can sound scary for any designer at first. You are abdicating some control to allow the player to interact with—and possibly lose—the game you have provided. However, without elevating your player to the status of coauthor of your game, you will never make a fun game because fun games are all about interactivity.

Note

If you fail to empower your player with interactive control, your game will fail.

Part of interactive control is giving the player fun choices to make. This involves having two main things present in your game:

- Difficult decisions that have to be made by the gamer
- Tangible consequences for making these decisions

There is a partnership between you, as the game designer, and your future gamer. You essentially pass off partial control of your game and its contingent story to the person who plays your game. Collaboration can be exciting!

When creating decisions for the player to make, keep these simple rules in mind:

- **Make each choice reasonable:** Do not ask your player to go in a door marked "Great Stuff Inside" and then have a brick wall on the other side of it. Likewise, do not ask your player to choose between getting a magnificent sword and a pile of junk; the player will pick the sword every time. The choices a player is given should be reasonable ones.

- **Make each choice real:** Do not invent arbitrary decisions, such as asking your player if he or she would rather go through Door A or Door B when both doors lead to the same room. To the player, this is as bad as cheating. The best choices to present your gamer with are difficult ones, especially when there is a perceptible tension surrounding the outcome of the decision.

- **Keep your player informed:** You must give the player enough knowledge to make a proper decision when faced with one. If you leave out the fact that if the player keeps the Sword of Eons, she will have to use it to slaughter her only surviving sibling, you are sure to see a player throw a tantrum.

Balancing Gameplay

Developer Dino Dini defines gameplay as "interaction that entertains." Developer Sid Meier calls it "a series of interesting choices." Gameplay comes first because it is the primary source of entertainment in all video games. Art and story are almost window dressing. When designing the core mechanics, gameplay must be the foremost element you consider.

Gameplay differs from game to game, based on the player actions, options, and challenges. The challenges are central to the game, often varying by genre, and the options are the choices open to the player to overcome challenges. The gamer's actions are steps that gamer takes to achieve his or her goals throughout the game. One of the thorniest facets of successful game creation is making sure the game has balanced gameplay. If just one component in play gives the player (or for that matter, the enemy) too much power, the whole game is a wreck.

Players try to find the laziest and most efficient way to beat any game because they understand games have an underlying competitive challenge. So be on the lookout for minor imbalances in the core mechanics and repair those imbalances so your player cannot cheat.

Always Remember to Make Your Game Fun

Give your players a fun, fresh, and original experience—one that encourages gamers to play it again and again, and to advertise it via word of mouth—and you have done your first duty as game designer. If your game is the slightest bit offbeat, offers cathartic release, or is irreverent and funny, it will get played.

Games can seem like hard work and can sometimes be frustrating to play, but players are willing to put in as much work as required if they get back enough high-quality fun. Fun is what games are all about. If your game does not provide the player with enough fun moments, you have to stop, rewind, and erase what you are doing right now and start building your game on the premise that every part of it must be fun. As noted by game aficionado Duane Alan Hahn:

> *Play is supposed to be the opposite of work, but most video games are just jobs with a little bit of fun thrown in. These games can leave players feeling abused, frustrated, and overly aggressive. Your game can either irritate or alleviate. Which would you rather do?*
>
> —*Duane Alan Hahn, www.randomterrain.com*

Fairness

You must respect your player's time. A great game should offer the quickest, easiest ways to have fun and conquer all the challenges unless there is some entertaining reason to prevent it. Frustration can be a healthy motivator in games, challenging gamers to achieve greater heights for themselves, but frustration can also lead to players giving up before beating your game. So tamp down frustration by playing fair with your player, and you will receive greater rewards in the end.

Players should always be able to understand the reasons for things happening to their on-screen personas. As a player, there is nothing worse than feeling cheated. Whether this is by bad luck or by the devious actions of an opponent, it usually means that players become so unhappy with the game that they never play it again. This can be disastrous for a video game if players feel cheated by poor design or inconsistent controls.

Do not force gamers to repeat complicated moves in the game or learn their lessons by seeing their character die repeatedly. Endless repetition can be maddening, so never let your player fall into a rut. Never set players up so that they have to perform a knotty set of maneuvers to get their character avatars to the top of a 100-foot platform, only at the last minute having them fall all the way back down to the bottom to have to start all over again. Likewise, do not kill the player's character off suddenly or inexplicably without giving the player a heads up as to why. Shun meaningless repetition or wrist slapping such as this.

Avoid frustration by making the game easier for the player. Do not remove challenges from the game completely, but relieve the buildup of tension that could potentially cause the player's attention to wane. For instance, it is common practice now to have extremely brief death or game-over sequences and allow the player to jump right back into play without missing a beat.

Players will delight in challenges of all types depending on the game, from the hidden sniper to the complex pattern puzzle. It is your job as a designer to make sure you entertain players by your challenge and not dissuade them from play.

The most common game challenges include the following:

- **Gates:** Gates, also called lock mechanisms, fence the player in, preventing access to some area or reward in the game world until that moment when the player beats the challenge and unlocks the next area or recovers the reward. The simplest and most prosaic gate is a locked door. Players are so familiar with this kind of gate, they know they should immediately start looking for a key to unlock it. Blood locks are another kind of gate. In a blood lock, you lock the gamer within a single area with hordes of foes to defeat; the exit does not appear until the gamer destroys the entire onslaught of enemies.

- **Mazes:** Below-average gamers can get lost in standard game levels, so making the level more difficult by adding lots of twists, turns, and dead ends might quickly cause a gamer headache. On the other hand, used wisely, a maze can become a wonderfully entertaining way to break the monotony of locked doors.

- **Monsters:** Battles with monsters typify the combat mechanic in many games, including fighting games, shooters, and role-playing games. As classic as the gateway guardians of mythic lore, monsters are another form of obstacle to overcome, and always with some reward. See the example of the pterodactyl in the GameSalad Creator scene in Figure 2.4. The toughest of all are the "boss monsters" that pose the largest threat in a level.

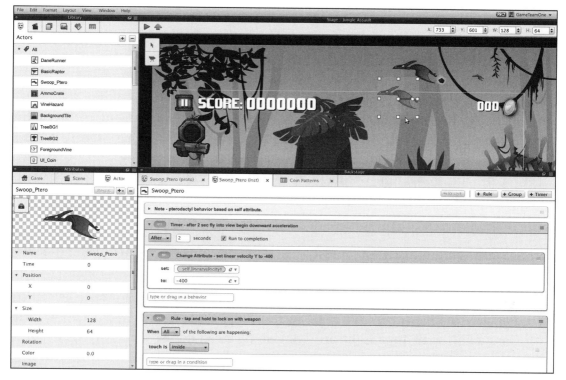

Figure 2.4
A pterodactyl makes a terrific flying monster in this GameSalad game.
Source: The GameSalad Creator, © 2013 GameSalad®, Inc. All Rights Reserved.

- **Traps:** Traps are a hodgepodge of suspense, scenery, and intrigue. Good traps can have whole stories behind them. Give some thought to each trap you place.

- **Quests:** Quests are special sets of challenges that take place in both stories and games, thus linking narrative and gameplay. Quest games, like the *King's Quest* game series, have quests in which the player must overcome specific challenges to reach his or her goal. When the player successfully surmounts the challenges of the quest and achieves the goal, he or she unlocks another part of the game story.

- **Puzzles:** Aside from actual puzzle games like *Bejeweled* and *Tetris*, developers can use puzzles to further the story or as mini-games within a game. Some puzzles are cryptographic or clue driven in nature, where the player must supply a crucial bit of info, such as a password, key code, or similar, to pass by a guard, open a locked door, or open a wall safe. Clues can be left lying around in convenient journals, computer e-mails, or tape recordings, or discovered by talking to people.

Feedback

Video games are all about pushing a player's buttons. A game world is little better than a Skinner box, a special lab apparatus developed by psychoanalyst B.F. Skinner to show you can train a rodent to press a lever to get food. Feedback is just one of the primary components of the human-computer interface. Providing the player with adequate feedback will help the player know what to expect out of the game and frames the choices that player will make from then on. In other words, if the player does something downright stupid, show the player it was wrong to try that particular action by punishing him or her. On the other hand, if the player does something right, give him or her a reward.

There are two critical rules to remember with regard to punishments and rewards:

■ You should make your punishments and rewards fit the actions and environment, and you should always be consistent with your use of them.

■ You should make your punishments and rewards happen immediately so the gamer sees the cause-and-effect relationship. Gamers are eager to know that they are doing something right or wrong so they can adjust their play style and master the game. They listen for the bells and whistles to instruct them in how to play better. You can use this knowledge to your advantage by creating a better game.

Also, the game world must react reasonably to the game's player. That is, the environment must be reactive. Having reactive environments means that the game world responds to the player in logical and meaningful ways that help immerse the player in that game world. For example, if the player sees a weak spot in a wall, a strong enough force should be able to knock a hole through it. This empowers the player to explore the game's environment and to treat it as if it were its own self-contained world. When in doubt about whether to make the game background more interactive, always opt for the affirmative answer, even though it usually means more work for you.

Feasibility

Encourage player immersion whenever and wherever you can in your game. To this end, avoid inconsistencies and a little terror called *feature creep*. Feature creep happens when a game designer gets too close to his or her project and begins adding "neat features" that add nothing to the game or do not fit with the original game concept. Keep your games simple. Anything goes as long as it is fun, fair, provides adequate feedback, and makes sense.

As president of Cerny Games and video game consultant Mark Cerny notes, "Keep the rules of the game simple. Ideally, first-time players should understand and enjoy the game without instructions." Keep your game rules simple and feasible. CCP founder Thorolfur Beck puts it this way:

I would say simplicity is a key factor in any good game design—simplicity in interface, game systems, and so on. Simplicity does not have to mean few possibilities (just look at chess), but creating a really good, well-balanced, simple game system is a much harder task than creating a very complex one.

—Thorolfur Beck, www.randomterrain.com

THE GAME-DESIGN PROCESS

When you play a game, you do not see the years of sweat and hard work it took to polish that game into the final piece of electronic make-believe you play. Game developers do not jump in feet first and start to work without a thought or a plan. That would be foolish and waste a lot more time than would prove justifiable. Instead, before a team creates a game, they write up a blueprint called a *game-design document* and put forth a task schedule of when certain milestones need reached.

The process outlined here is the ideal way in which a video game should come together, from the initial concept to the finished piece. This process can be remarkably complex when working on a large game title. There is no set order to follow to achieve the end result, and every company has its preferred method for organizing resources. Game companies are constantly changing and refining their development process to suit specific games and situations.

The Inspiration

The start of the design process comes when there is an idea for a new game. The idea can come from several sources. These include the following:

- **Intellectual property:** Occasionally, a video game will be developed based on an existing intellectual property (IP), meaning the game is intended to embody an existing idea in another form of media. Possible media include films, TV, comic books, or even existing computer games. Development of spinoffs from existing stories, characters, worlds, or concepts is quite common in the modern game industry, partly because it can be extremely lucrative. Competition for the rights to certain intellectual properties can be cutthroat and cover all sorts of fields from sports to comics, to movies, to other games.

- **"Me too" games:** Suppose game company A has a successful title concerned with fantasy chess. As the director of game company B, you might direct your designers to come up with a similarly themed game with enough differences to avoid copyright infringement. Although some folks say this copycat method demonstrates a lack of originality or imagination on behalf of the second company, occasionally the second company's game is better than the first. Publishers also like giving the green light to proven concepts.

- **Frankenstein games:** Seemingly new game ideas can come from mixing ideas from old genres. Often, these inspirations stem from a "what if?" discussion. The "what if?" scenario might be an alternate history or the transposition of one story into a different age or setting. You can see this in the musical *West Side Story*, by Leonard Bernstein, Arthur Laurents, and Stephen Sondheim. They loosely based their story on William Shakespeare's play *Romeo and Juliet*, but set it in the 1950s New York.

- **Jumping off a cliff:** Brand-new ideas are perhaps the rarest and riskiest propositions in game development. Few game designers have achieved both critical acclaim *and* commercial success off new ideas. As a result, directors tend to be nervous about such propositions and wary of players not accepting the game's concept, story, characters, or setting. Even though the danger is understandable, you should not entirely shun new ideas. Although few will see the green light of production, raw creativity can help move the industry forward.

Writing a Game-Design Document

As soon as one or more of the game's initial creators conceives of a great video game, the team begins fleshing out the game, just to see if it would be doable. Artists come up with concept artwork, like sketches of characters, vehicles, environments, and weapons they might use in the game. Writers write the game-design document, a hefty document that will become a blueprint for how the team will make the game. This document includes every single detail of every character, environment, and event that will appear in the game, including each twist and turn in the narrative and what outcomes the players might witness.

There is no greater test for a killer game idea than putting it into words on paper. Usually, ideas in and of themselves are sublingual—full of images, emotions, and vague details. But putting your idea on paper and then reading it aloud to hear how it sounds helps you focus and reveals weak spots that might have made it past your original mental process. You might find there are words you used that do not work as efficiently as some others.

As you develop your game-design document, you should write a game outline that encapsulates your killer game idea. A game outline is a short description of a game that is detailed enough to start discussing it as a potential project. The outline forms a general idea of how you intend to entertain someone through gameplay and, more importantly, why you believe it will be a rich, compelling experience.

First, take stock of whom your target audience will be. In a play-centric design, you put the players first and design the game around their expectations. Although you could design a game for yourself and hope there is another person out there exactly like you who will find your game as appealing as you do, it has been proven time and again that you will do better if you make a game for a specific group of gamers instead. So look around at types of gamers you see and who you think would like your game.

Next, write your outline on paper. At a minimum, your outline should include the following:

- A two-to-three sentence description of your game, similar to those blurbs of upcoming shows seen in the *TV Guide*. Can you describe the game concisely in just one paragraph? If not, then your idea may still need refining until you can. This is particularly important as you will need to sell your idea to others, either as part of a team promoting ideas with the public or as an indie developer looking for a publisher. When you are selling your idea, you need to grab and hold other people's attention from the outset.

- Who the player will be in the game, if they have a character they can see onscreen, and what role they fulfill.

- What the game world is like, if there is one.

- The game genre (if applicable). Game genre, like film genre, is an easily understood and quick way of categorizing your game. You are trying to establish the game's provenance at this stage. Relating it to a known genre will help you establish exactly what your game is all about.

- Who your target audience is, including their demographic (their age, gender, income level, and so on). The types of people likely to make up your audience and their age range are extremely important factors in game design. Establishing the target audience will relate the development of the game to the players' perceived expectations. If you are going to meet, challenge, and even exceed these expectations, you must have a clear vision of whom you target with your game. Age considerations are also relevant for classification. The Entertainment Software Rating Board (ESRB) is a non-profit organization that provides international ratings for the video-game industry. Audience age dictates what is admissible in a certain game.

- A short summary of how the game will progress from level to level, including a synopsis of the storyline.

Production

At the outset of the design process, there might be only one or two individuals or small teams working on fleshing out the ideas and planning. These could be senior designers within the company or specialist idea-generation teams tasked with brainstorming new concepts. After an idea is approved for further development, it might be assigned to a larger team.

Depending on whether there is enough money for the game company to make the game, the team sometimes creates a game proposal or short playable demo, often referred to as a *prototype*. They can then shop this around to potential financial backers or game publishers.

The team takes inventory of what software and hardware they have to start with, whether they have the office space needed for production, and how many members they need to add to the team by either hiring or outsourcing. This inventory helps shape their budget.

The team grows as production starts rolling. The asset artists design 3D models, 2D artwork, textures, and environments on their computers. The programmers code the player controls and character behaviors, as well as the physics engine. The writers set out dialogue and scripted events. The cinematic artists take storyboards and create short, animated cut scenes that appear throughout the game. User interface (UI) artists develop the menu screens you see in-game, like the ones being laid out in GameSalad Creator in Figure 2.5.

Figure 2.5
Shell menus and user interface.
Source: The GameSalad Creator, © 2013 GameSalad®, Inc. All Rights Reserved.

The production process often starts dreamily and becomes more stressful the closer to deadlines. Team members may work obscene hours during crunch time. Finally, the team creates a gold master, which they send to the manufacturer for publication. The gold master is the final unalterable version of the game, as it will appear when published.

When you feel your game is finished and ready to publish is when you lock it down as a gold master yourself and publish to your platform of choice. GameSalad makes the publishing process a snap.

Post-Production

After the game is finished, it is still not finished. Even before the game hits store shelves, it must start selling well; to foster this, the public relations (PR) department makes sure people know about the game before its release and that the target audience wants to buy it. Most companies release their games to coincide with the Christmas rush, although games may come out year-round and new ones hit retail stores every week.

Game magazines will feature previews of early prototypes of the game or interviews with its developers. Web forums are also a great place to hit the target audience. Any way the PR people can whet the appetite of the public and make folks curious about an upcoming game is a good way to advertise it before its release.

Whether or not the development team's game was shipped with any flaws or glitches in it, the team sets up technical support for their players to contact. They fix major bugs by releasing patches. Mistakes can make for glaring errors in a game's release, causing word-of-mouth advertisement to work against the game developers as players spread around how awful some of their game's flaws were.

The game may prove wildly successful, and the developer may have to begin work on expansion packs, downloadable content, or sequels. If not, the game-development team may get a moment to take a few breaths before starting their next game project.

You, too, might be so thrilled with your endeavors that you start on new projects right away. As a beginning game designer, a caveat veterans often give is that your first several game projects will suck. Get over it. They are for practice anyway. It takes time and repeated practice to get good making video games. So as soon as you finish your first one, start on another. Eventually, you will be making games you will be proud of and want to share with everyone.

CHAPTER 3

CREATING A BASIC SHOOTER

Shoot-Em-Ups are also known as "shmups" and, as the name suggests, involve shooting things up. A typical shmup has the player controlling a spaceship with a quick-firing weapon. Enemies attack the player's ship; the objective is generally to destroy them as quickly as possible.

The first shmup was *Spacewar!*, which was created in 1962. It ran on a DEC PDP-1, an early computer system the size of an automobile. *Spacewar!* was created by Stephen "Slug" Russell while a member of a club at M.I.T. This was not only the first shmup, it was also arguably the first ever video game.

Space Invaders, released in 1978, was the game that captured the public's attention. It was the first mass-market video game. It was also a shmup. Created by Toshihiro Nishikado, it had easy-to-learn controls (move left, move right, and shoot) and a simple objective. *Space Invaders* incorporated many unprecedented features, such as waves of enemies, bonus points for shooting harder-to-reach enemies, ramping difficulty, and so on. It not only pushed the design of video games forward, it also made hundreds of millions of dollars in arcades. At that time, arcades were the only places video games could be played, costing players a small amount of money for each game. The incredible commercial success of *Space Invaders* marked the video game industry as a viable business opportunity. New companies sprang up in short order, attempting to copy the money-making formula.

For this chapter, you will open an existing template so you have some resources already available. You will be developing a shmup of your very own.

INSTALLING THE BASIC SHOOT-EM-UP TEMPLATE

First, you will need to download the template. It is called "Basic Shoot-Em-Up" and is a side-scrolling shooter game that should feel very familiar to gamers who like *Metroid* and other classic platform shooters. The template comes from GameSalad, but is available for download on the companion site for this text. Download the template from www.cengageptr.com/downloads. Type this book's title or ISBN into the search box to quickly find the resource materials provided. You will download a compressed ZIP file. The ZIP file format is a common form of data compression and archiving. ZIP file contains one or more files that have been compressed to reduce file size. What that means in layman terms is "squishing a file or bunch of files so that they take up less space on your computer." You can usually tell a ZIP file by the zipper on its icon. After you have downloaded it, unzip the ZIP file using WinZip, WinRAR, B1, or whatever decompressing software you have on your machine. If you cannot find a service on your machine that will "unzip" the ZIP file, download one from the Internet. Most Windows PCs come with built-in Win-Zip. To unzip, simply double-click on the file. Your unzip program will automatically open, and you can then choose where you want the unzipped (expanded) version of that file to be saved on your computer.

Once the file is unzipped, you can move the GAMEPROJ file folder to your desktop or to a special directory where you are storing your other game projects. Make sure the place where you put your GAMEPROJ file is easy to access. I try to keep all my game project files at one place, so I do not become confused when looking for files I might need to edit or import. Next, open the GameSalad Creator and load the template. Click File > Open and navigate to the location where you put your GAME-PROJ file. There you will select the Basic SHMUP.gsproj file and open it.

Once the template is loaded on to Creator, you can begin to edit it. (See Figure 3.1.) If you click the Media tab in the Library panel (Windows) or the Scenes and Actors tabs (Mac), you will notice you already have some art and sound assets available to you through this template.

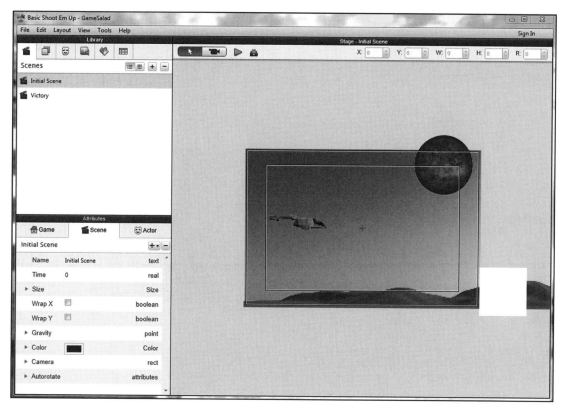

Figure 3.1
The Basic Shoot-Em-Up template.
Source: The GameSalad Creator, © 2013 GameSalad®, Inc. All Rights Reserved.

CREATING A NEW SCENE

Leave the assets, including the actors, alone; you can use those later. For now, follow these steps:

1. Click the Scenes tab in the Library panel.

2. Click the plus (+) icon to create a new scene.

3. Rename the scene. To do so, click on the scene's default name until it appears highlighted, type Battle Scene, and press Enter (Windows) or Return (Mac).

4. Delete the Initial Scene and Victory scenes in the Library panel. To do so, first click the Initial Scene entry in the Library panel; then click the minus (-) icon to delete it. Repeat to delete the Victory entry. As shown in Figure 3.2, this sets you up with a blank slate from which to work.

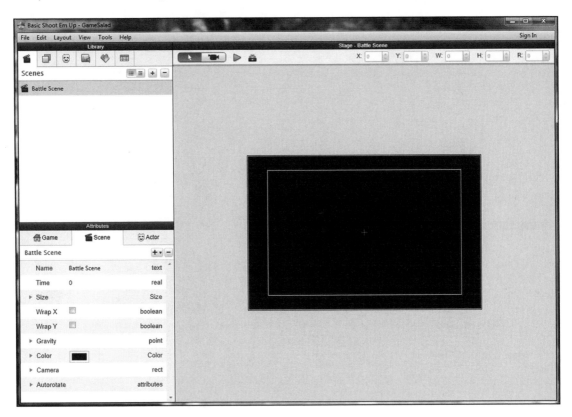

Figure 3.2
Start with a single empty scene, called Battle Scene.
Source: The GameSalad Creator, © 2013 GameSalad®, Inc. All Rights Reserved.

Scene Attributes

The following attributes define each scene and are modifiable:

- **Name:** A descriptive way for you to refer to different scenes within your game.
- **Time:** The number of seconds a scene has been active. This attribute can be read and incorporated into your rules/behaviors, but not set.
- **Size:** The pixel dimensions (width and height) of the current scene.
- **Wrap X:** When enabled, actors that exit the left side of the scene will re-enter from the right side of the scene (and vice versa). When disabled, actors continue moving indefinitely off-screen unless they are explicitly destroyed (via behaviors you've set).
- **Wrap Y:** Similar to Wrap X but in the up/down direction. When enabled, actors that exit the top of the scene will re-enter from the bottom of the scene (and vice versa). When disabled, actors continue moving indefinitely off-screen unless explicitly destroyed (via behaviors you've set).

- **Gravity:** The strength of gravity in the scene. The default value is 0. Using a value between 100 and 1000 will provide approximately "normal" gravity. I caution against using any values significantly above 10,000. Please note that gravity can be directed in both X and Y directions; negative values will cause items to go in the opposite direction. Gravity affects all the movable objects in the scene.

- **Color:** The background color of the scene, represented via red, green, blue, and alpha integer values between 0 and 1. You can edit any of these individual values, or you can select a color from a color picker.

- **Camera:** A compound attribute with the following sub-categories:

  - **Origin:** The starting X and Y position of the lower-left corner of the camera relative to the scene.

  - **Size:** This sets the width and height describing how much of the scene will be shown when the game is played. These values are set depending on the resolution selected at the opening of a new project and cannot be modified manually. To adjust a scene size, Mac users can click the Home button, select the Project Info tab, and use the drop-down Platform menu; selecting any of these options will automatically resize all scenes in the game to match that platform's screen size. Windows users can use the Game tab in the Attributes panel and expand Display Size to edit the resolution of scenes.

  - **Tracking area:** You can give actors within your scene a control camera behavior, which ensures that the camera will follow the actor as it moves through a scene. This tracking area sets the boundaries (width and height) for when to begin scrolling a scene (if possible) based on the position of an actor with the control camera behavior. The camera will snap to the actor with that behavior unless it would force the camera to move beyond the edge of a scene.

  - **Rotation:** The rotation of the camera, which changes based on auto-rotation. This cannot be modified manually.

- **Autorotate:** Rotates the scene to adapt to a player turning his or her device. For example, if a player turns his or her device upside down, you may want the game to auto-rotate to portrait (or landscape) upside down to adjust to this new view. In contrast, if you are creating a maze or tilt game, you would not want the scene to rotate as the player tilts the device to navigate the ball (or whatever object) around the maze.

CREATING A NEW ACTOR

To create a new actor, follow these steps:

1. Click to the Actors tab in the Library panel.

2. Click the plus (+) icon to create a new actor. Actor 1 appears at the bottom of the Actors tab list.

3. Double-click Actor 1, rename it Spaceship, and drag the white square from the list on the left side of the screen and drop it on the stage. (See Figure 3.3.) This adds an instance of the Spaceship actor to the Battle Scene template. This instance is locked to the prototype of the same name.

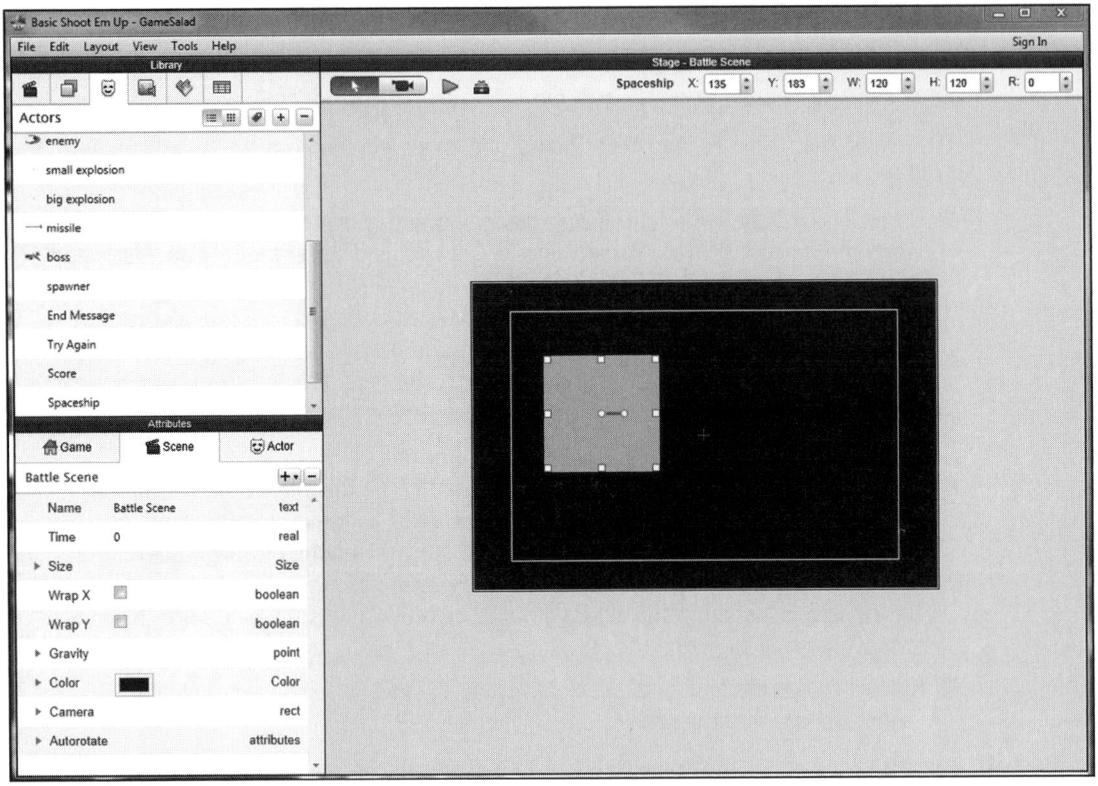

Figure 3.3
Drag an instance of your new actor into the Battle Scene template.
Source: The GameSalad Creator, © 2013 GameSalad®, Inc. All Rights Reserved.

Note

If you dropped more than one instance of Spaceship onto your stage, they would share the same name and game attributes, being nearly identical to one another. However, they would each have their own separate self attributes, such as X and Y position. Self attributes are unique from game attributes in that each instance autonomously keeps track of its own self attributes. For instance, if you set up a self attribute such as Health Points for enemy ships, each new enemy ship spawned would keep track of its own version of that self attribute. If you attempted to do that with a lone game attribute, hurting one enemy ship would affect all of them.

As you can see in Figure 3.3, this actor is not much to look at right now. You will need to edit it. Click the instance within the scene to display the screen you see in Figure 3.4 (or one similar to it). This in-your-face message lets you know that you are thwarted from attempting to edit an instance, as it is still locked to the prototype by the same name. If you were to click the lock icon, you would unlock the instance and break it apart from its prototype, which means you could edit the instance without changing the prototype. However, if you ever edited the prototype, those changes would not affect the instance because it has been unlocked.

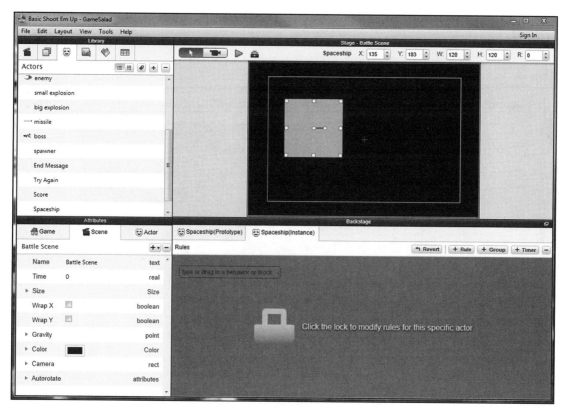

Figure 3.4
This instance is still locked to the prototype.
Source: The GameSalad Creator, © 2013 GameSalad®, Inc. All Rights Reserved.

Say, for example, you have created an enemy spaceship prototype actor with three engines. You have added a few instances to your scene and unlocked each to add separate decals on each of the spaceships. Later, you decide you only want two engines, not three, on the enemy spaceships. You would have to revert each instance back to the prototype to make the changes because simply editing the prototype would not have any effect on its constituent unlocked instances.

To edit the Spaceship actor, follow these steps:

1. Keep your current Spaceship instance locked to the prototype. If you unlocked it, simply lock it again by clicking the Revert button (Windows) or selecting Revert to Prototype under Preview (Mac). Edit the prototype instead.

2. To change the appearance of the prototype from a white box to something with more contextual appeal, drag the ship (128 × 64) file from the Images or Media tab to the white box representing your prototype. When your cursor is over the white box, it should change colors to indicate you the image file can be added to this actor. When you drop it, the actor automatically updates to show the ship, as you can see in Figure 3.5.

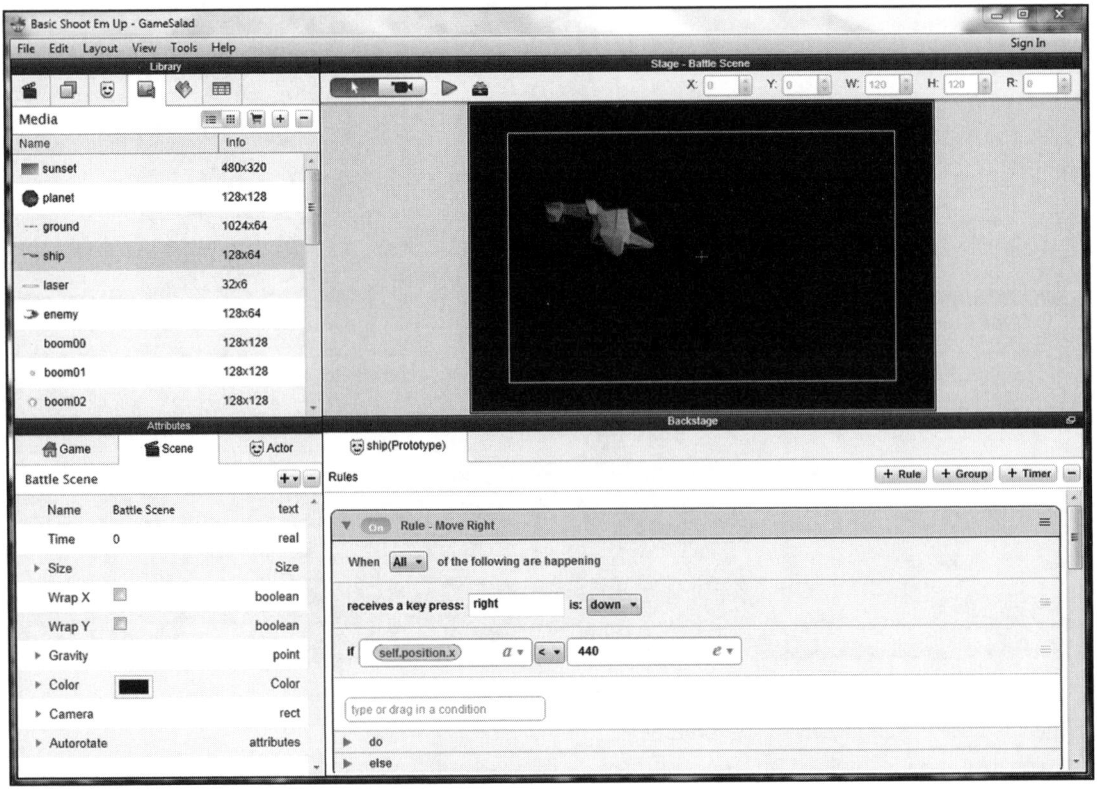

Figure 3.5
Replace the Spaceship instance's empty white box with the ship graphic.
Source: The GameSalad Creator, © 2013 GameSalad®, Inc. All Rights Reserved.

3. The default dimensions of the actor make the ship look stretched out. Change these attributes in the Actor tab of the Attributes panel to 128 (Width) and 64 (Height), as shown in Figure 3.6.

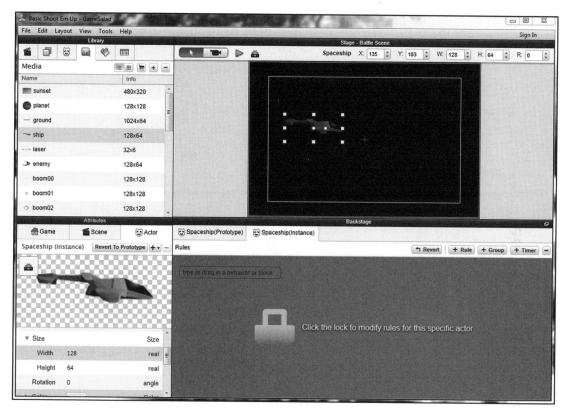

Figure 3.6
Resize the Spaceship actor so the graphic is not squashed.
Source: The GameSalad Creator, © 2013 GameSalad®, Inc. All Rights Reserved.

CREATING RULES AND BEHAVIORS

With regard to your Spaceship actor, you will want to focus on two main behavior types:

■ **Movement:** You want this ship to be the player avatar, so the player will want to control its movement in the scene.

■ **Weapons:** The player may want a defense against enemies, so he or she will want to be able to fire weapons on them. To add an element of danger, and therefore conflict, to the mix, you must make sure the ship can be damaged by enemies. If the damage gets too low, however, the game will be over and the player will lose. For this reason, you'll want to incorporate armor into the ship.

Movement

Start with movement. Follow these steps:

1. Create a new rule. To do so, click the Create Rule button (Mac) or the +/Add Rule button (Windows) in the Rules panel for the Spaceship (Prototype).

2. In the When [All] of the Following Are Happening section, type key in the Type or Drag in a Behavior or Block field. Start typing the word "key" and a Key option should pop up as a suggestion. Use your cursor to select the Key option by clicking it or, if you are still typing the word "key", press Enter (Windows) or Return (Mac) to automatically add that option.

3. Click the Receives a Key Press field. Whatever key you type on your keyboard will become the operable key for this rule. In this case, press the right-arrow key on your keyboard. You will see the word "right" appear where your cursor used to be, as shown in Figure 3.7.

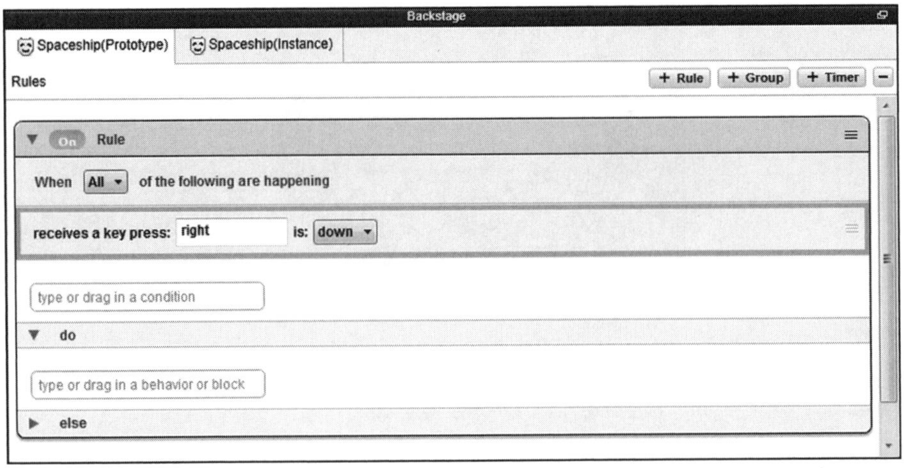

Figure 3.7
Press the right-arrow key to add "right" as the key command for your new rule.
Source: The GameSalad Creator, © 2013 GameSalad®, Inc. All Rights Reserved.

4. Examine the "do" section below the Receives a Key Press field. What do you want the system to do if the right-arrow key is pressed? In the Type or Drag in a Behavior or Block field, type move. As you type, the Move option should appear; select it.

5. Parameters such as what direction you want the avatar moved and how fast will be displayed. In the At a Speed Of field, type 150. (See Figure 3.8.)

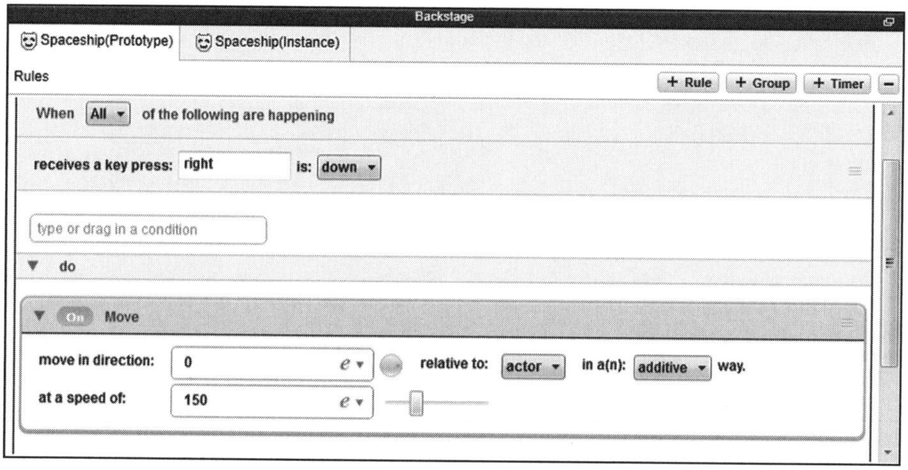

Figure 3.8
Add directional speed of 150 or half the default speed.
Source: The GameSalad Creator, © 2013 GameSalad®, Inc. All Rights Reserved.

This rule is complete. Whenever the player presses the right-arrow key on his or her keyboard, the Spaceship actor will move to the right of its current position.

Movement in Different Directions

Rather than create three more individual rules similar to this for the other directions, you can duplicate this rule, changing it slightly each time. Follow these steps:

1. Select the rule as a whole. Then hold down the Alt (Windows) or Option (Mac) key, and drag the rule to the blank space below. This will create an exact duplicate of the logic you selected. Your next step is to simply edit the key command and movement direction for this new logic.

2. For the first duplicate, set the key command to the up-arrow key, the speed to 150, and the Move in Direction setting to 90, so it will take the Spaceship actor up.

3. Create a second duplicate, setting the key command to the down-arrow key, the speed to 150, and the Move in Direction setting to 270 (see Figure 3.9).

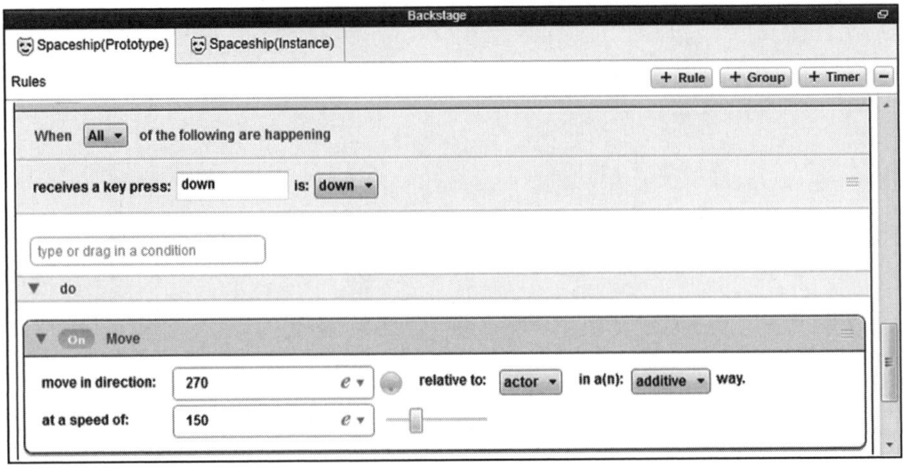

Figure 3.9
For each new rule, set the key command, direction, and speed appropriately.
Source: The GameSalad Creator, © 2013 GameSalad®, Inc. All Rights Reserved.

Tip

Beside the Move in Direction setting is an orbital direction button that looks like a circle within another circle. The small interior circle is a direction indicator. Simply click on the orbital button where you want the direction indicator to point, and the input value will jump to that degree angle.

4. Create a third duplicate, setting the key command to the left-arrow key, the speed to 150, and the Move in Direction setting to 180 to move the Spaceship in the opposite direction.

To test your game so far, click the Play/Preview button (it looks like a green play button). In the Preview window, shown in Figure 3.10, you can test your game logic and how it plays. Notice that unfortunately, as you move the ship around using your keyboard, it is possible to fly completely out of the visible area. The player could get lost and frustrated if you left it this way. Your next priority is to fence the player in.

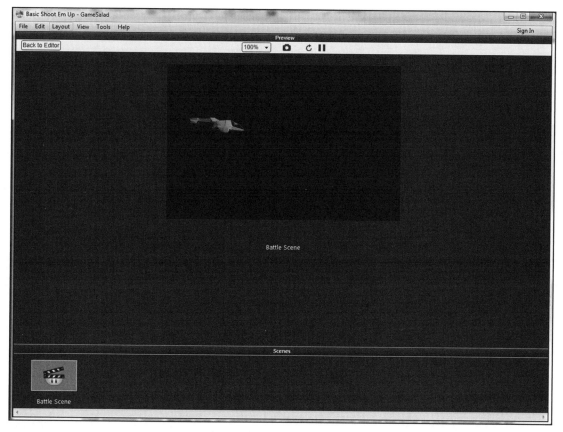

Figure 3.10
Preview your game.
Source: The GameSalad Creator, © 2013 GameSalad®, Inc. All Rights Reserved.

Restraining Movement

Fencing the player in means adding another condition to your rules. Follow these steps:

1. Click the Back to Editor button to return to the Editor.

2. Scroll up the list of rules you added until you find the first one for the player moving the ship right.

3. In the empty If field, just below the one where you put the key-press condition, type `attribute`. An option by the same name will appear; choose it.

4. Click the drop-down arrow in the If field, next to the italicized lowercase letter "a" (see Figure 3.11) to reveal attributes from which to choose. To navigate the list, simply click the dark arrow beside each row to reveal more options. Navigate to Attributes > Spaceship (the name of your current actor) > Position

and double-click X to select it. The self.position.x attribute appears in the If field and a new input field appears next to it.

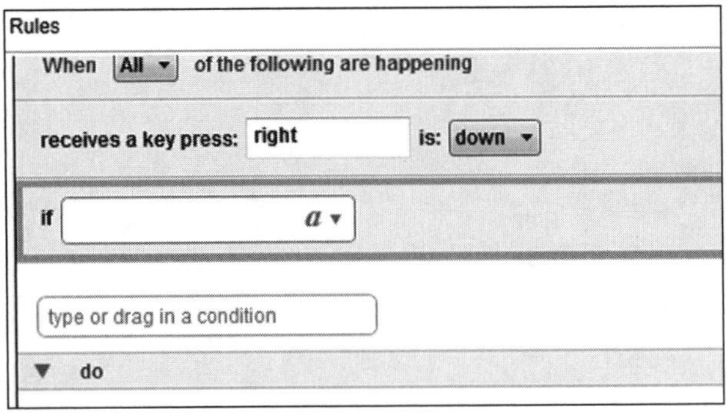

Figure 3.11
An if condition checks the validity of an attribute.
Source: The GameSalad Creator, © 2013 GameSalad®, Inc. All Rights Reserved.

5. Click the = (equals) drop-down list between the two input fields and choose < (less than).

6. In the new blank input field, type a number that is the width of your game's display minus half the width of your actor. For example, my screen is 480 pixels wide and the Spaceship actor is 120 pixels wide, so I subtract 60 (half the width of my actor) from 480 to get 420, as shown in Figure 3.12. Now when I preview my game, the Spaceship actor can go all the way to the right edge of the visible zone and then stops. This is what you want!

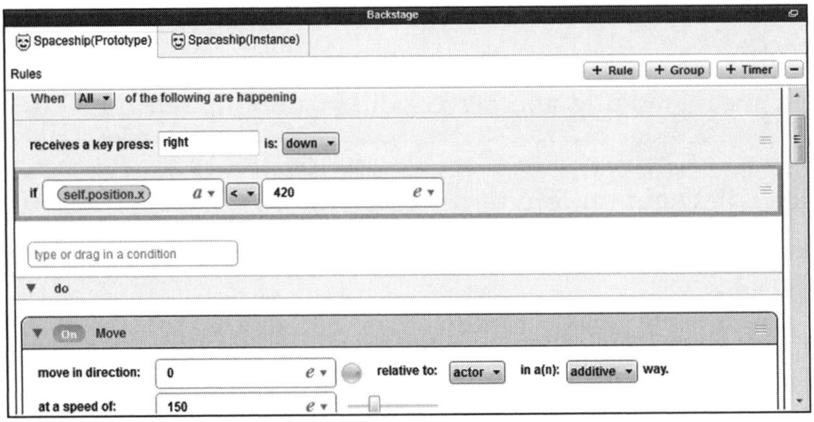

Figure 3.12
Set your if condition to check self.position.x to be less than the width of your display minus half the width of your actor.
Source: The GameSalad Creator, © 2013 GameSalad®, Inc. All Rights Reserved.

Tip

To find the width and height (which you'll need in a moment) of your game's display in Windows, open the Game tab in the Attributes panel, expand Display Size, and check the Width and Height values. Mac users choose screen resolution at the start but can review options by clicking the Home button, selecting the Project Info tab, and opening the Platform menu to see the different display sizes. Do not change the display size. Just record the height and width for calculating values as needed.

7. Now do the same for each of the other rules, starting with the up rule. For the up rule's attribute condition, set the attribute self.position.y to be less than (<) the height of your display (in my case, the display height is 320) minus half the height of the actor (in this example, the actor is 64 pixels high), which in my case would be 288. After previewing, I determined that 288 was not good enough and changed the value to 300. So my new condition reads if self.position.y < 300.

8. Set the down rule. In GameSalad Creator, display coordinates are measured in X and Y. X starts at zero (0) on the left and goes to the defined width on the right. Y starts at zero (0) at the bottom and goes up to the defined height at the top. That means for the down rule, you will want to set the if attribute to self.position.y and for it to be greater than or equal to (>=) zero (0). In other words, it should read if self.position.y >= 0. This says that as long as the ship is above the bottom of the screen, the player can continue to move it down the screen. Once the ship hits the bottom of the screen (or zero Y), it stops.

9. Set the left rule. The rule for moving the ship left will act similarly to the down rule but uses the self.position.x attribute instead of the self.position.y attribute. So the attribute condition should read if self.position.x >= 0. Half of the ship will disappear off screen if you leave the value at 0, which is fine. However, to keep the ship better in view, you can edit the self.position.x >= value to 32 (half the width of the ship).

10. Notice that each of the rules you created is simply named Rule. To rename a rule, double-click its title bar and type the new name. Using an evocative name such as Rule—Move Right (see Figure 3.13) ensures you and any subsequent developers who edit your work will be intimately familiar with the game logic each contains, which can save time hunting and scratching heads later on.

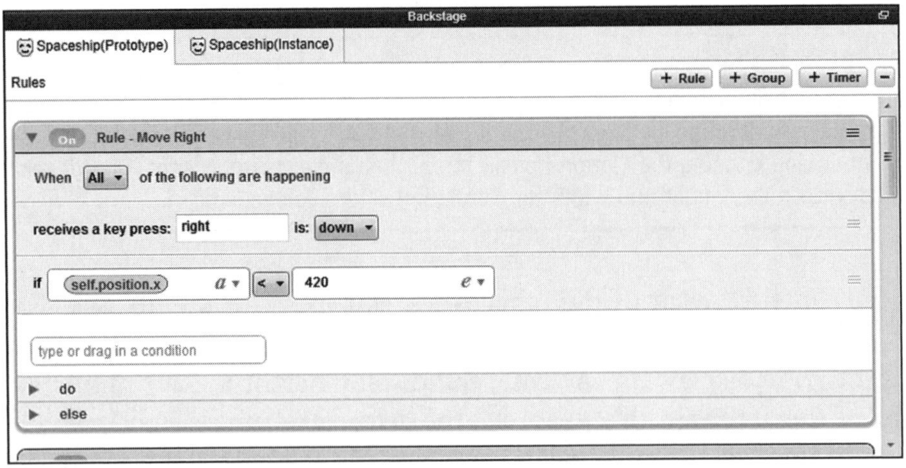

Figure 3.13
Give each of your rules a descriptive title.
Source: The GameSalad Creator, © 2013 GameSalad®, Inc. All Rights Reserved.

11. Save your work by going File > Save. Saving often will help you avoid the loss of hours of labor in the event of a power outage or accident that causes your program to quit working. Technology is fraught with "oops" moments, so it is best to back up your work whenever you think about it—and the more you think about it, the less stress you'll experience in your design process.

Weapons

Your player can move his ship around the scene, but simply moving objects does not in itself make a game. You have to provide unique challenges. To do so, you must add an enemy to fight against (in this case, an alien ship), a setting, and a method of defense. You must also edit the logic of the player's ship and the enemy's ship.

Creating the Enemy Actor

Before you can program weapon behaviors, you must create the enemy actor your player will fight against. Follow these steps:

1. Click the Actors tab in the Library panel and click the plus (+) icon to add a new actor.

2. Double-click the new actor's name, which defaults to Actor 1, and type Alien Ship.

3. In the Attributes panel's Actor tab, notice that the preview image for the Alien Ship actor reads "Drag an Image Here." Obey its command. Look in the

Library panel's Media or Images tab for the PNG file named boss (512×256); then drag and drop it to where it says "Drag an Image Here" in the Alien Ship's Attributes panel. When you release, the preview will update to show you the boss image, as shown in Figure 3.14.

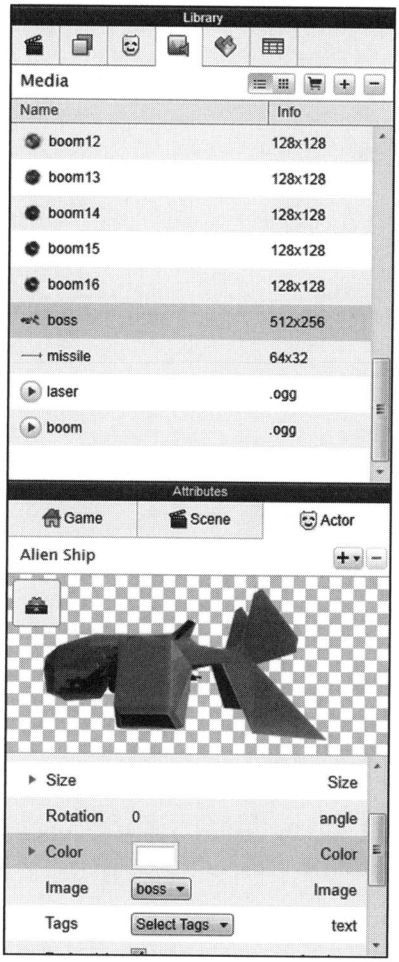

Figure 3.14
Give the Alien Ship actor the boss image for appearance.
Source: The GameSalad Creator, © 2013 GameSalad®, Inc. All Rights Reserved.

4. Don't like the dull gray of the Alien Ship actor? Change it! To alter how it looks, find the Color attribute in the Attributes panel's Actor tab and click the swatch to open the Color Swatch window. Then pick a color from the color wheel or type R, G, B, and A values if you know them. Alternatively, click the System Colors tab and scroll through your options there. I chose Spring Green. When

you have a color picked out, close the Color Swatch window. Your Alien Ship's preview will update to reveal the new tint, as shown in Figure 3.15.

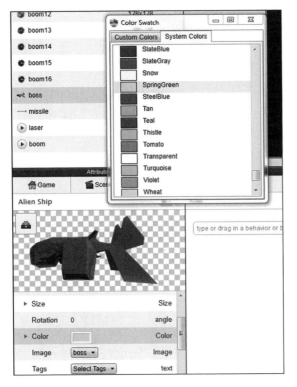

Figure 3.15
Give your Alien Ship actor a makeover by picking a unique color attribute.
Source: The GameSalad Creator, © 2013 GameSalad®, Inc. All Rights Reserved.

5. Drag the Alien Ship actor from the list of actors in the Library panel to the stage, but offset so it is hovering off the right side of the stage.

6. Note that the Alien Ship actor is too big for the current scene. To resize it, change the Width setting in the Attributes panel's Actor tab to 256 Width and the Height setting to 128. This is exactly half of its original size.

Creating the Setting

You could put just about anything your dear heart desires in the background of your scene. But there is an asset already waiting to be used in the current template, so for now you can place it in the background. Follow these steps:

1. Locate the Sunset actor at the top of the Actors list in the Library panel.

2. Drag and drop the Sunset actor onto your stage.

3. In the Attributes panel's Actor tab, expand the Position attributes and set X and Y to match your display size divided by two. For example, my display size is 480×320, so I set Position X to 240 and Position Y to 160. That centers my sunset perfectly within the stage.

4. Wait a minute! Now the sunset is covering up your Spaceship actor. This is easy to fix. Right-click the sunset and choose Send to Back from the menu that appears. This shifts the stacking order of your actors so that the sunset rests behind all the other objects. (See Figure 3.16.)

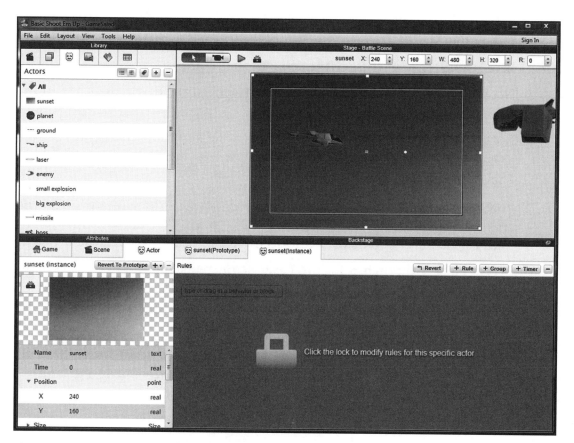

Figure 3.16
Center your sunset and move it to the back, behind your other actors.
Source: The GameSalad Creator, © 2013 GameSalad®, Inc. All Rights Reserved.

Armor

To incorporate armor into your player's ship, follow these steps to create it. (You'll learn how to apply it in a moment.)

1. In the Attributes panel's Game tab, click the plus (+) button twice and choose Integer each time to add two new integer game attributes.

2. Name one of the new game attributes Player Armor and the other Alien Armor.

3. Set each at a default value of 100. This will give the ships a measure of success or failure as they trade weapon fire.

Building Weapons

Rather than build the weapon fire from scratch, you can use existing laser and missile actors. However, you will need to edit them. Follow these steps:

1. Locate the Missile actor in the Actors list in the Library panel.

2. Drag an instance of the Missile actor to the stage.

3. Double-click the Missile actor to see its rules appear below the stage in the Backstage area.

4. Because this instance of the Missile actor is locked to its prototype, you'll need to edit the prototype's rules. To do so, click the Missile(Prototype) tab of Backstage.

5. Find the Actor Overlaps or Collides with Actor of Type Ship condition and replace Ship with Spaceship. That way, the system knows that when the missile touches the Spaceship actor in the scene, the missile should cause it damage.

6. Repeat steps 1 through 5 for the Laser actor, replacing the Actor Overlaps or Collides with Actor with Tag Enemy Targets condition with Actor Overlaps or Collides with Actor of Type Alien Ship so the laser causes damage to the Alien Ship actor when hit.

7. When you finish editing their rules, delete the objects from the scene. You will not need them on the stage because they will be spawned in-game later.

Editing the Spaceship Actor's Logic

Now you are going to edit the Spaceship actor's prototype's rules by adding a new rule below the others. This rule will specify that if the player presses the space bar, a Laser actor will be spawned. Follow these steps:

1. Double-click the Spaceship actor on the stage. Go to the Spaceship(Prototype) tab in the Backstage area.

2. Add a new rule below the others.

3. Double-click the rule's default name and type `Player Weapon Fire` to rename it.

4. In the Receives a Key Press field, press the space bar.

5. In the "do" area, type `Spawn Actor` and choose the Spawn Actor option that appears.

6. As mentioned, the actor you want spawned is the Laser. To specify this, click the Spawn Actor drop-down list and choose Laser.

7. In the first From Position field, type 35. In the second From Position field, type −5. (See Figure 3.17.)

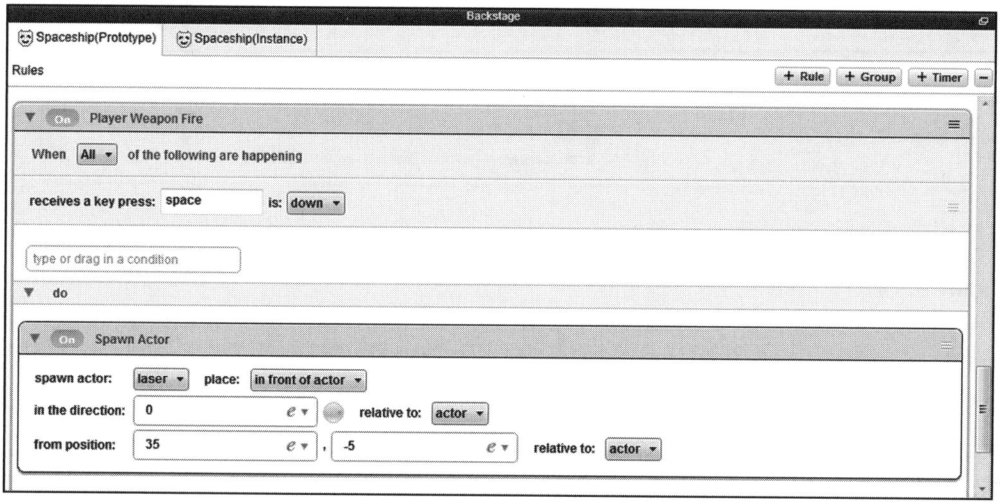

Figure 3.17
Add a new rule for the player's laser fire.
Source: The GameSalad Creator, © 2013 GameSalad®, Inc. All Rights Reserved.

8. Create another rule and call this one Player Take Damage.

9. Type `Collision` in the "condition" field and choose the Collision option that appears.

10. In the drop-down list, choose the Missile actor as the Actor Type.

11. In the "do" area, type `Change Attribute` and select that behavior from the pop-up options. Then specify that the attribute you want to change is Player

Armor. To do so, choose Attributes > Game (because that is where you created the attribute earlier). Then set the expression (the value you want it changed to) to Player Armor minus (-) 20 so that it will take five missile hits to destroy the player. (See Figure 3.18.)

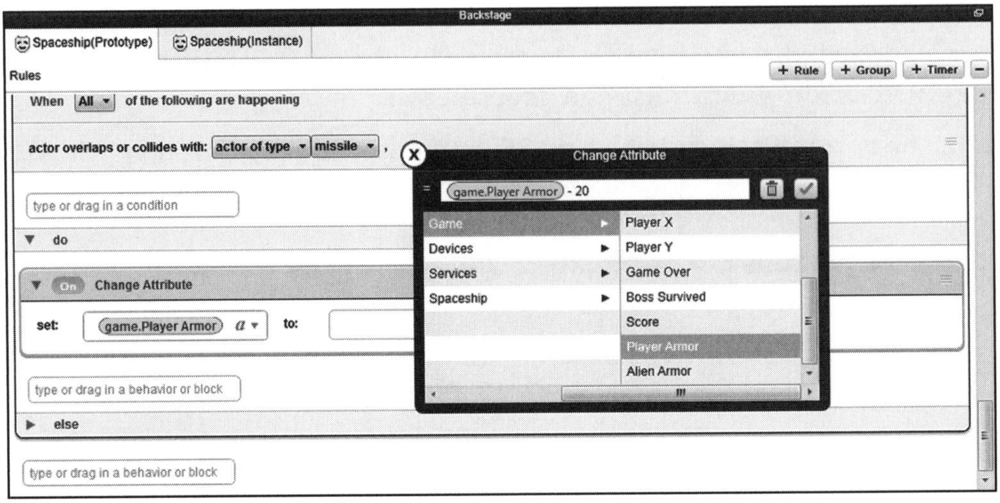

Figure 3.18
Set it where the player takes −20 Player Armor damage with each missile hit.
Source: The GameSalad Creator, © 2013 GameSalad®, Inc. All Rights Reserved.

12. What will happen when the player's armor reaches zero? Right now, nothing! Return to the Spaceship's prototype rules and add a new one. Name it Game Over and set its condition to Attribute. Next, choose the game attribute Player Armor and set it to equal 0.

13. In the "do" section, type Spawn Actor and select the Spawn Actor option when it appears. Choose the Small Explosion actor, which looks pretty combustive and has a timer embedded in its rules so it will not stay onscreen forever. Set its layer order to In Front of Actor and its position to 0 and 0 relative to the actor.

14. Add another behavior right after that one (within the same rule). For this one, type Change Attribute and select the Change Attribute option when it appears. Click the "a" drop-down list and choose Attributes > Spaceship > Color > Alpha; then set the Alpha attribute to 0. Now, when the player's armor reaches zero, the ship will disappear from the scene.

Editing the Alien Ship Actor's Logic

In this game, you want the Alien Ship actor to slowly move up and down the right side of the screen. You also want it to fire missiles once per second. The Spaceship actor is damaged by missiles, and the Alien Ship actor is damaged by lasers. Follow these steps:

1. Select the Alien Ship actor in your scene and navigate to the Alien Ship (Prototype) rules, of which there are currently none. You are going to add its logic here.

2. Start with weapon fire. Click the Add Timer button (located beside the Add Rule and Add Group buttons) to add a new timer. Name it Enemy Weapon Fire, set it to run every 1 second, and check the box next to Run to Completion to make sure it has finished running each time.

3. In the "do" area, add a new behavior. Type Spawn Actor and select the Spawn Actor option when it appears. Choose Missile in the Spawn Actor drop-down list. Set its From Position to −100 and −40, and choose Actor from the Relative To drop-down list. (See Figure 3.19.)

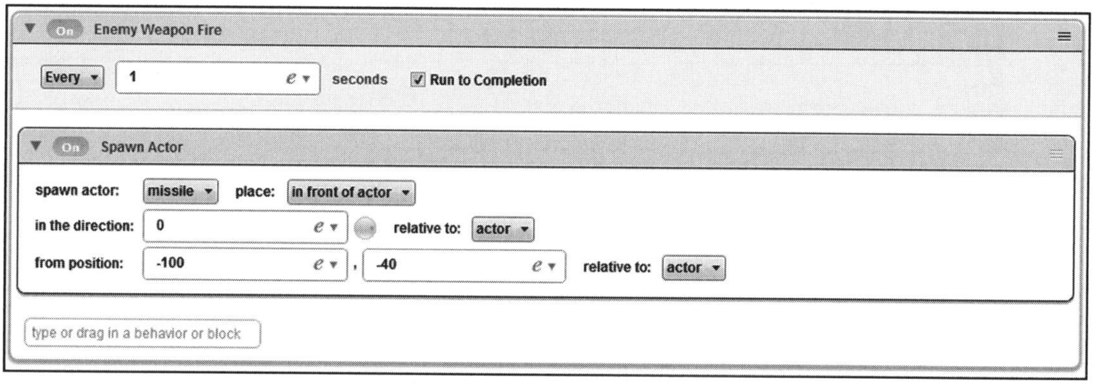

Figure 3.19
Have the Alien Ship actor shoot missiles once every second.
Source: The GameSalad Creator, © 2013 GameSalad®, Inc. All Rights Reserved.

4. Now that the Alien Ship actor is shooting missiles, you have to get it in motion. To do so, repeat step 2 to add a new timer. Name it Enemy Movement and set it to run every 1 second.

5. Add a Move To behavior and specify the exact X and Y coordinates (in that order) to which you want the Alien Ship actor to move. You can preview these coordinates by dragging the Alien Ship actor up or down within your scene. I set my initial Move To behavior to move the Alien Ship to position 450 and 58. Rename this behavior Move Down, as that is what it makes the Alien Ship actor do.

6. Add a second Move To behavior below the first one that moves the Alien Ship actor to the opposite edge of the screen. I chose the coordinates 450 and 280. Call this behavior Move Up.

7. Set both Move To behaviors to run all the way to completion and to move at a speed of 100. (See Figure 3.20.)

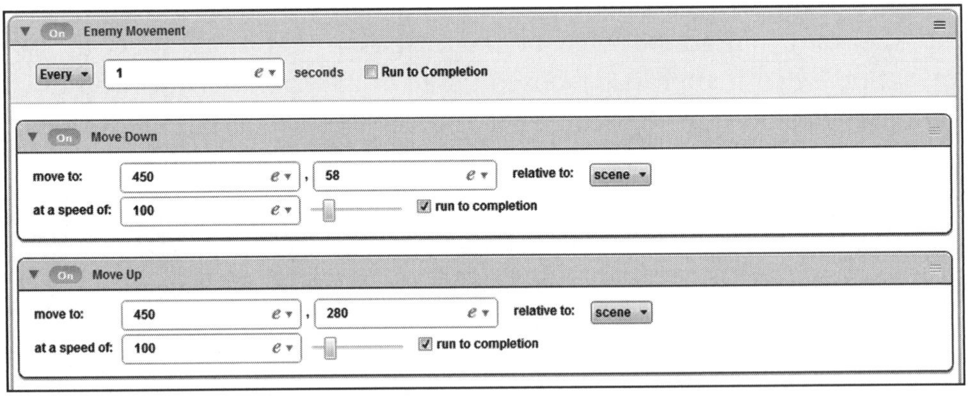

Figure 3.20
Have the Alien Ship actor shoot missiles once every second.
Source: The GameSalad Creator, © 2013 GameSalad®, Inc. All Rights Reserved.

8. Next you need to add the logic so the Alien Ship actor takes damage whenever shot by a laser. This logic is identical to the one you put on the Spaceship actor for missile hits. To begin, add a new rule and select Collision as the condition, with Laser selected as the Actor of Type.

9. What you want it to do is to change an attribute. In the "do" area, type Change Attribute and select the Change Attribute option when it appears. The attribute you want to change is Alien Armor, the game attribute you created earlier, and you want to change it to an expression of Alien Armor minus (–) 10. Do so now.

10. You'll set up the destruction of the Alien Ship actor if its armor reaches 0 in almost exactly the same way as you did the Spaceship actor. First, create a new rule and call it Enemy Destruction. Set its condition to Attribute. The attribute chosen will be game.Alien Armor = 0.

11. In the "do" area, add a Spawn Actor behavior to spawn a Big Explosion at position 0 and 0, relative to the actor. Then, use the Change Attribute behavior to change the Alien Ship actor's alpha color attribute to 0 so it will disappear from the scene. Do this the same way you did the Spaceship actor.

12. Save your project and test your game (see Figure 3.21). You can use the arrow keys to move the Spaceship actor in four directions and the spacebar to shoot lasers. Dodge the enemy missiles and shoot the Alien Ship actor until it combusts. Click the Reset button (it looks like a refresh icon above the preview window) to retry the game. This time, let the Alien Ship actor take you out so you can see how the Spaceship actor blows up. You have the start to an interesting shmup!

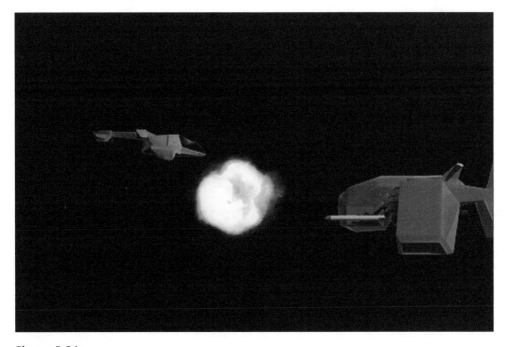

Figure 3.21
Test your game.
Source: The GameSalad Creator, © 2013 GameSalad®, Inc. All Rights Reserved.

Common Behaviors

There are 36 standard behaviors embedded in the GameSalad Creator. These behaviors are as follow:

- **Accelerate:** Use this to specify the rate and direction of acceleration for an actor. If the drag attribute or gravity is not also applied to an actor, acceleration will be continuously applied, increasing the actor's speed until it reaches the maximum defined speed, if any.

- **Accelerate Toward:** Use this to specify the rate of acceleration and the targeted location of an actor. You can specify a static or moving target position. If the drag attribute or gravity is not also applied to an actor, acceleration will be continuously applied, increasing the actor's speed until it reaches the maximum defined speed, if any. The actor will continue accelerating past the target location along the existing trajectory unless slowed through other behaviors or attributes.

- **Animate:** Drag and drop a sequence of images into this behavior from your project library. Once added, images can be reordered, and additional images can be inserted. The controls in this behavior allow you to specify the frame rate of the animation, up to 30 frames per second, regardless of whether the animation loops, stops at the last frame, or returns to the last image used before the animate behavior started.

- **Change Attribute:** This allows you to set, change, or increment a game, scene, or actor attribute. It can be used to change a numerical value, color, size, movement, acceleration, or any other value determined by an attribute.

- **Change Image:** Use this to specify an image to replace the current image on an actor. You can either drag the new image to this behavior or specify an image from the drop-down menu.

- **Change Scene:** This will stop the current scene and immediately move to the designated scene. It's best to place this behavior inside a rule that changes to the game credits scene, menu scene, or a new game level after certain objectives are met.

- **Change Size:** This changes an actor's size by a scale factor (use a negative number to shrink an actor). Note: The actor's original size will still determine its collision volume. To change this, use Change Attribute or Interpolate instead. Use a timer to specify the amount of time that the transformation should take to occur.

- **Change Velocity:** Specify the direction of movement for the actor at a constant designated speed. After the direction is specified, other influences on movement will begin to affect the actor, such as drag, gravity, or other movement behaviors.

- **Collide:** This controls which actors or groups of actors will collide with each other. A group of actors may be created by using a tag in the project editor.

- **Constrain Attribute:** This continuously updates the value of one attribute to match another attribute. This is particularly useful to keep two objects moving in sync, or to keep an actor tied to the movement of the mouse or touch.

- **Control Camera:** Add this to an actor and the scene's camera will scroll to follow. The tracking area for the camera can be changed in the Scene Editor using Camera Edit mode. Only one instance actor per scene can have this.

- **Destroy:** This immediately removes the actor from the scene.

■ **Display Text:** This will show the text entered in the box, and includes controls over the color, alignment, font, wrapping, and size of the text displayed. Wrapping will cause line breaks to keep all the text inside the actor.

■ **Group:** This is an organizational behavior, which allows you to group certain behaviors and rules together easily and clearly. It can also be created by clicking the Create Group button.

■ **Interpolate:** This allows you to change attributes from their existing value to a new value over a set period of time. Interpolate will use a constant rate of change over the designated time period. This can effect a rapid or gradual change in any game attribute, and cannot be obstructed or stopped by any other behavior.

■ **Load Attribute:** This loads the value stored with a custom key name using the Save Attribute behavior. A key is basically a storage location for a specific attribute. Use any key you want when saving an attribute, and then use the same key to load that same information later.

■ **Move:** Use this to move in a particular direction relative to the actor or the scene at a specified velocity. Additive movement allows multiple move behaviors to stack, or act on an actor simultaneously.

■ **Move To:** Use this to move toward a specific X/Y coordinate relative to the actor or to the scene. This movement will stop upon arrival at the designated coordinates unless the controlling conditions are no longer valid and the Run to Completion checkbox is not checked, in which case the movement behavior will cease as soon as the controlling conditions are no longer valid.

■ **Note:** This allows the developer to record reference notes explaining a rule, behavior, group, or other aspect. These will not be visible in or affect the operation of the game.

■ **Particles:** This spawns a designated number of particles from behind the actor. This includes options for color, size, lifetime, velocity, images, and more.

■ **Pause Game:** This will pause the current scene and display the scene selected in the behavior over the current scene. Using the Unpause Game behavior removes the scene and resumes the original scene.

■ **Pause Music:** This will pause the current music track, if one is playing. Use the Play Music behavior to resume the track.

■ **Play Music:** This causes the selected music file to start playing. Select Loop to cause the selected music to begin again after it has played through to the end.

■ **Play Sound:** This causes the selected sound file to start playing. Select Loop to cause the selected sound file to repeat each time it completes; select Run to Completion to prevent other behaviors from interrupting the sound before it has played through to the end. Positional Sound and Velocity Shift affect the volume and pitch of the sound as the actor controlling the sound effect moves through the scene.

■ **Replicate:** This creates duplicates of an actor without actually spawning additional actors into a scene, based on the value of an attribute. It is most commonly used to display the number of lives a player has left.

■ **Reset Game:** This resets the game and all the scenes in it. This will restore all the attribute values to their original state, but will not delete keys saved using the Save Attribute behavior.

■ **Reset Scene:** This resets the current scene and all the actors in it. If placed in the scene that appears during a pause, it will not reset the underlying paused scene.

■ **Rotate:** This causes the actor to spin clockwise or counter-clockwise at the speed specified in the Expression Editor. The Rotate to Angle and Rotate to Position behaviors perform similar but unique tasks.

■ **Rotate to Angle:** This causes the actor to spin clockwise or counter-clockwise at the speed specified until it reaches a particular angle, at which point rotation will cease. Unchecking Stops at Destination will cause this behavior to act similarly to the Rotate behavior.

■ **Rotate to Position:** This causes the actor to spin clockwise or counter-clockwise at the speed specified until it reaches the designated X/Y coordinate, at which point rotation will cease. Unchecking Stops on Destination will cause this behavior to act similarly to the Rotate behavior. Use Offset Angle to rotate to a position a designated number of degrees from the specified X/Y coordinate.

■ **Rule:** This creates a condition or set of conditions to check before activating an enclosed behavior. These conditions include player input (mouse clicks, touches, key presses) and attribute values. Rule also includes an "otherwise" section; behaviors placed here will trigger whenever the conditions in the rule are not true.

■ **Save Attribute:** This stores the value of an attribute with a custom key name. Any key name can be used; inputting the key name in the Load Attribute behavior will yield the stored value. Saving a new attribute value with a previously used key name will result in overwriting any existing saved data. Values stored using Save Attribute will remain accessible, even if the game or device is turned off.

■ **Spawn Actor:** This creates a new actor instance in the scene. Specify which actor to spawn and the directional and position of that actor relative to the scene or spawning actor. This allows any actor in a scene to spawn additional actors anywhere else in the same scene. Newly spawned actors will immediately begin following any movement or other behaviors associated with them.

■ **Stop Music:** This stops the current music track. Unlike the Pause Music behavior, this resets the track, so that a Play Music behavior acting afterward will start the music track from the beginning.

■ **Timer:** This allows you to activate behaviors or rules at specified intervals. All timer values are input in seconds. Within a timer, choosing the option After will trigger the behavior/rule once the given time period has passed. Choosing the option Every triggers the behavior repeatedly with the seconds given as a time delay between each. Choosing the option For keeps a behavior going for the duration of the time given.

■ **Unpause Game:** If the Pause Game behavior has activated and opened the pause scene, this behavior will remove the pause scene and resume the underlying paused scene.

CHAPTER 4

A MORE ADVANCED SHOOTER

You have a basic shooter game done, but it is still very plain. This chapter's purpose is to show you how you can enhance your shmup.

KEY DESIGN CONSIDERATIONS

When designing game scenes, there are various factors to consider. (If you are working on an establishing intellectual property [IP], there are likely to be additional guidelines.) These factors are as follows:

- **Reward:** When a player tackles any enterprise, subconsciously he or she expects a reward. This can take the form of an increased skill level, an in-game item (such as better weapons), a discovered secret, or simply the satisfaction of a challenging task being dealt with successfully. The reward must be something tangible for the player to feel a strong sense of achievement.

- **Risk:** The reward should match the risk involved to get it. If the player finds a secret chamber, battles past extreme ninja bunnies, and makes the perfect leap over rivers of lava, then you should reward him or her with something truly worthwhile. Otherwise, the player may feel the game is gratuitously challenging or even stupid. On the flip side, if the challenge is super easy to beat, the reward should not be nearly as valuable.

- **Challenge:** Players have come to expect games to pace them through a variety of difficulty levels. These levels of challenge are an important response to the types of players you may have. Some players might delight in being tested to the absolute limit, while others might want a simple distraction—something mildly challenging but not requiring a huge time investment to get through. The pace of the challenges is also important. Players appreciate the opportunity to start with an easy challenge to practice and train. After this, they can more readily accept an increasingly difficult challenge.

■ **Consistency:** Be consistent in the types of challenges you offer the player. Things that look the same should act the same, every time. For example, if a red barrel explodes when hit by bullets, then all red barrels should be explosive, not just a few. Inconsistencies will only serve to confuse or frustrate the player.

■ **Interest:** This concerns maintaining the player's engagement with the game. A game can have only so many game mechanics and will have only a limited number of opponents or challenges. It is the job of the designer to keep mixing and matching these factors to present an interesting variety of challenges to the player—to keep him or her glued to the screen and not putting the game down, bored by it.

IMPROVING THE BASIC SHOOT-EM-UP

Open the game you have been working on creating. You are going to make some improvements to it so that it operates more like a commercial video game and less like a starting coder's experiment. Of course, you can continue to improve upon the game; the more you put into it, the more satisfying the end product. These tips will help you move in that direction.

Change Scene

The first thing you will do is add a transition that takes the player to a new scene.

1. Press and hold down the Alt (Windows) or Option (Mac) key while dragging a copy of the Battle Scene from the Scenes tab in the Library panel and dropping it beside the original. By default, the duplicate will be called Battle Scene Copy 1; double-click on its name to rename it Swarm Scene.

2. Select the Alien Ship actor in the stage of your new scene and delete it.

3. Return to the Battle Scene. You must add a victory condition so that if the player beats the Alien Ship actor in battle, then he or she moves on to the Swarm Scene. Doing so is so simple, it is silly. In the Battle Scene stage, select the Alien Ship actor and go to the prototype's rules and behaviors (in the Backstage panel). Scroll down until you find the Enemy Destruction rule you created. Then add a new timer and drag it up right below the Spawn Actor and Change Attribute behaviors in the "do" section of the Enemy Destruction rule. (See Figure 4.1.)

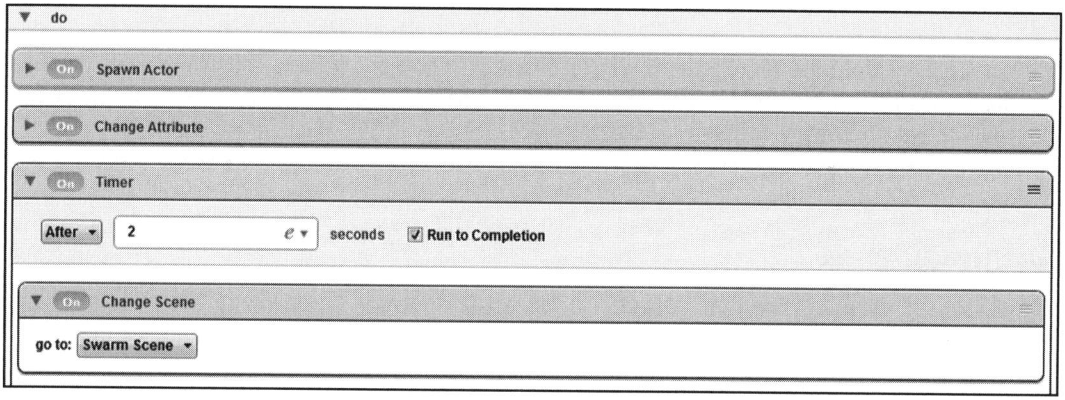

Figure 4.1
Add a new timer to the Enemy Destruction rule.

4. Instead of the default Every 5 Seconds setting, change it to After 2 Seconds and select the Run to Completion checkbox. Then, in the empty behavior field below, type Change Scene and select the Change Scene option. You will be asked what scene to go to; select the scene you just created, Swarm Scene. (See Figure 4.2.) Now, as soon as the Alien Ship actor is destroyed, the game will wait two seconds and then transport the player directly to the Swarm Scene.

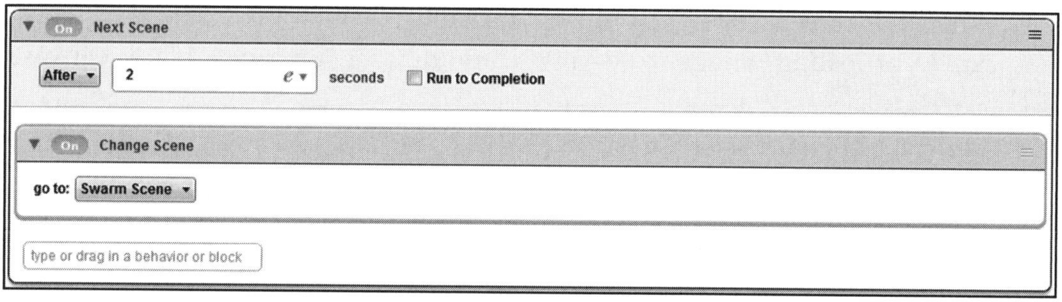

Figure 4.2
Have the game take the player to the Swarm Scene.

Note

> You could also choose to take the player to the next or previous scenes. This uses the order of scenes in the Scenes tab list to determine which scenes would be considered next or previous. Generally, however, you will want to define the exact scene.

Game Over

Wait! What happens if the player does not destroy the Alien Ship actor and gets blown up instead? Right now, nothing happens. The Spaceship actor will blow up and the game will continue without the player's interaction. This is less than satisfactory. The player needs immediate feedback to inform him or her of the consequences. You will need to build a scene for the "game over" condition and transition to it. To begin, create a new scene and name it Game Over. Leave this scene empty (black) for now.

Using Sumopaint to Design an Image

Leaving the GameSalad Creator briefly, open your Web browser and go to the following Web address: www.sumopaint.com. It's the main page for Sumopaint, a free online image editor that is similar in many ways to Adobe Photoshop. It offers filters and layer stacking—things many other image editors do not. Navigate to the app and choose the free version. When it loads in your Web browser, do the following:

1. When the screen comes up, it will ask you if you want to create a new blank canvas or load an image from your computer. Create a new blank canvas.

2. Choose Image > Canvas Size and change your canvas's size to match the display size of your game. As the Basic Shoot-Em-Up template's display size is 480×320 pixels, set your canvas's size to 480×320, as shown in Figure 4.3.

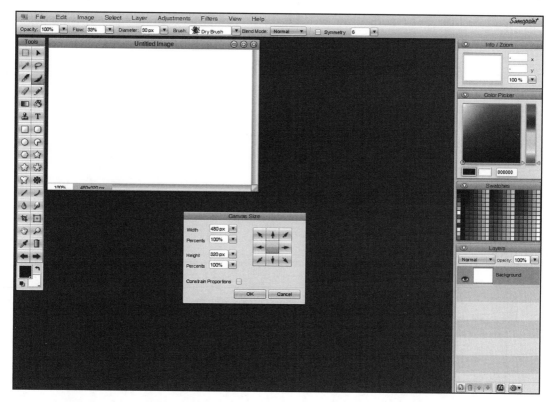

Figure 4.3
Change your canvas size to match your game's display size.
Source: Sumopaint, © 2013 Sumoing Ltd.® All Rights Reserved.

3. Insert a new layer. To do so, click the Add a New Layer button at the bottom of the Layers panel in the lower-right corner of the screen. (The Add a New Layer button looks like a piece of paper with the corner bent and a plus sign on it.) The new layer, called Layer 0 by default, appears above the existing one in the stacking order. Drag and drop it above the Background layer in the Layers panel.

4. For the moment, hide the Background layer by clicking the eyeball icon beside it in the Layers panel. When the eyeball icon is grayed out, it means that layer is hidden from view.

5. In the Tools panel on the left side of the screen, click the Text tool (its button is marked with the letter T). Notice that the row of options just below the main menu bar changes to contain text-related options. You can select your font, font color, alignment, and so on here. (The fonts displayed are not loaded from the Sumopaint program, but from your device fonts, so whatever fonts you have

installed on your computer will be displayed.) Choose an appropriate font for a "Game Over" message and choose red as the font color.

6. Click the stage in the Layer 0 layer. A box will appear. Type `Game Over`; the text will fill the box on the stage, as in Figure 4.4.

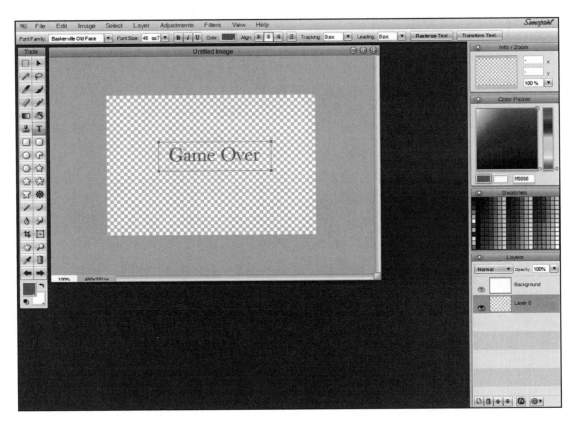

Figure 4.4
Write the words "Game Over" in red.
Source: Sumopaint, © 2013 Sumoing Ltd.® All Rights Reserved.

7. As long as the box is still selected on stage (you can tell it is selected by the square anchor points at each corner), you can edit its contents using the options above. This time, click the Center Alignment button to center-align the text. To change the font size, use your cursor to select the text in the box; click the drop-down arrow right of Font Size to display a slider and then drag the slider to resize your words, making them appear larger on the stage.

8. In the Tools panel, click the Move tool, marked by a black up arrow icon. With the Move tool, you can drag and drop your text in the center of the stage.

9. In the Layers panel, click the eyeball next to the Background layer to make it visible again.

10. Notice the two color swatches—one for the foreground color and one for the background color—at the bottom of the Tools panel. Click the top one (for the foreground color); a color picker window appears. In the color settings, set R (for red) to 21, G (for green) to 7, and B (for blue) to 93. The resulting color will be a dark blue, almost purple in its depth and intensity. Click OK to accept it.

11. In the Tools panel, click the Paint Bucket tool. It looks like a bucket tipping on its side. This tool can be used to fill color anywhere on the canvas. In this case, you will fill the entire Background layer with the dark blue color you just selected. Making sure you have the Background layer selected, click anywhere in the white area on the stage to paint it blue. (See Figure 4.5.)

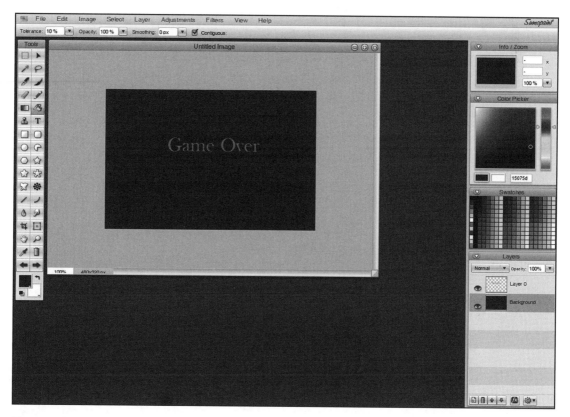

Figure 4.5
Fill the background with a dark blue color.

12. Select Layer 0 and click the Layer Effects button at the bottom of the Layers panel (marked with the lowercase letters "fx") to open the Layer Effects dialog box. In it, under Layer Style, select the Stroke option. Then, in the Stroke panel, make sure the Opacity option is set to 100 and that the Outer option button Stroke Position is selected. Then change the Size setting to 5. (See Figure 4.6.) Click OK when you are finished.

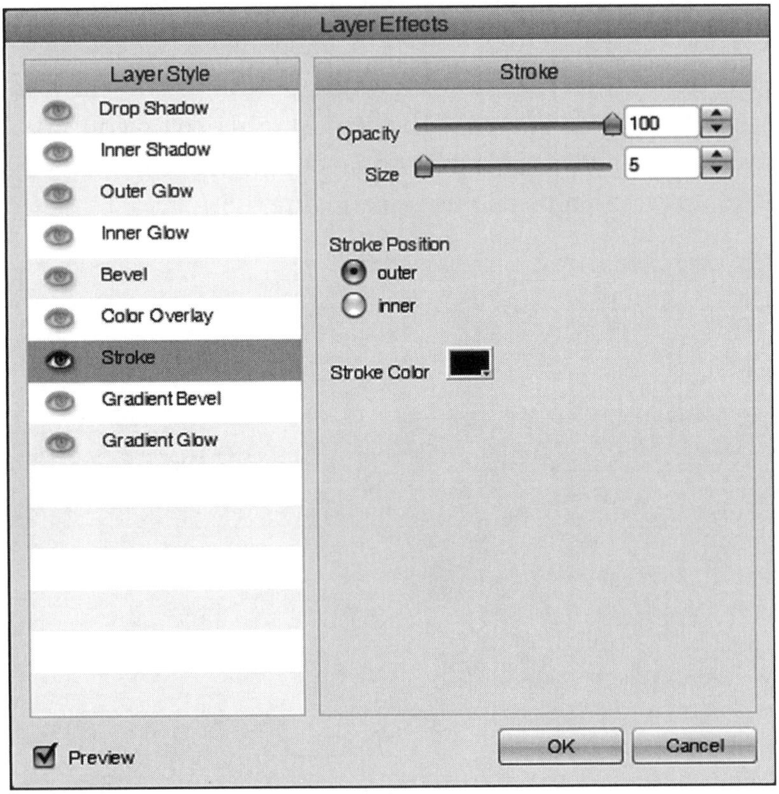

Figure 4.6
Set the Stroke options.

13. Create a new layer, select the Text tool, and type `Press SPACEBAR to retry`. Choose whatever font and font color you prefer. Move the text beneath the Game Over text and give it a black stroke layer effect. (I will explain how to incorporate the key press for spacebar to restart the game in a bit.)

14. Click the Background layer to select it. Then click the Brush tool in the Tools panel (it looks like the tip of a paintbrush) and choose a dark color such as forest green to stipple the background and provide some texture to it. I used a

combination of Dry Brush 1 and Brush 1 from the Brushes drop-down menu—
both resized to be really large—to paint with. I went over a few areas multiple
times to build up the texture and make it look more natural. You can see my
finished piece in Figure 4.7.

Figure 4.7
Stipple-paint the background green to add texture.
Source: Sumopaint, © 2013 Sumoing Ltd.® All Rights Reserved.

15. When you are satisfied with how your image looks, save it by choosing File >
    Save to My Computer. Select PNG as the file type and name it gameover.png.
    Save this PNG file to your projects folder, or wherever you are saving your game
    files. In the template Basic Shoot-Em-Up template, you have separate folders
    such as Actors, Behaviors, Images, Scenes, and so forth. You could, optionally,
    save your image in the Images subdirectory.

Importing New Media

Now it's time to import the art you created into GameSalad Creator. Follow these
steps:

1. Close Sumopaint and return to GameSalad Creator.

2. Click the Media tab in the Library panel and click the Add Media button, which features a plus sign (+). Locate and select the gameover.png file you just saved to load it to your Media tab list. It will appear close to the bottom of the list, just above the audio.

3. Click the Actors tab in the Library panel and add a new actor. Name it Gameover.

4. Click the Actor tab in the Attributes panel so you can see the preview image. Right now, it reads, "Drag an Image Here." Do just what it says. From the Media tab in the Library panel, drag the gameover file you just added to the preview window in the Attributes panel's Actor tab.

5. Switch to the Game Over scene (if you are not already there), drag the Gameover actor to the stage, and drop it.

6. In the Attributes panel's Actor tab, expand the Position group and set X and Y to match your display size divided in half. For example, my display size is 480 × 320, so I set X to 240 and Y to 160. That centers the Gameover actor perfectly on the stage. (See Figure 4.8.)

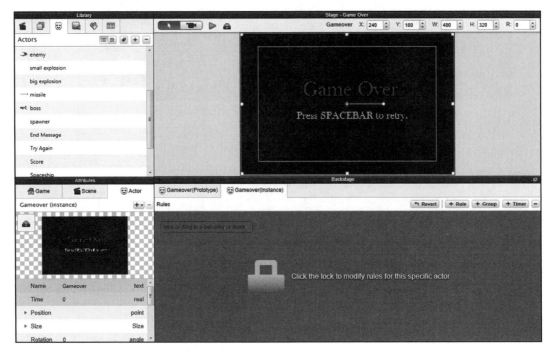

Figure 4.8
Center your Gameover actor on the stage.

Programming the Gameover Logic

To program the Gameover logic, follow these steps:

1. Backstage, open the Gameover (Prototype) rules, of which there are currently none.

2. Add a new rule and call it Restart Game. Set its condition for key press and set the key command to be the spacebar.

3. In the "do" area, type `Reset Game` and select the Reset Game option that appears. This will reset the game to starting attribute values. This includes repositioning the actors and giving them full armor. Essentially, whenever the game is over (the player's ship has blown up), the player can restart the game by pressing the spacebar, the same key command for shooting lasers.

4. To get the player to this scene when he dies, you have to input a change of scene upon the Spaceship actor's destruction. To start, switch to the Battle Scene and double-click the Spaceship actor.

5. Open the Spaceship (Prototype) rules and scroll to the Game Over rule you created. Right now, all that happens is that when the Player Armor reaches 0, a small explosion is spawned and the actor disappears from the scene (alpha = 0).

6. Add a new timer and drag it directly below the last behavior. Call this new timer End Game and set it so that after two seconds, it uses a Change Scene behavior to take the player to the Game Over scene. Make sure the Run to Completion checkbox is selected. (See Figure 4.9.)

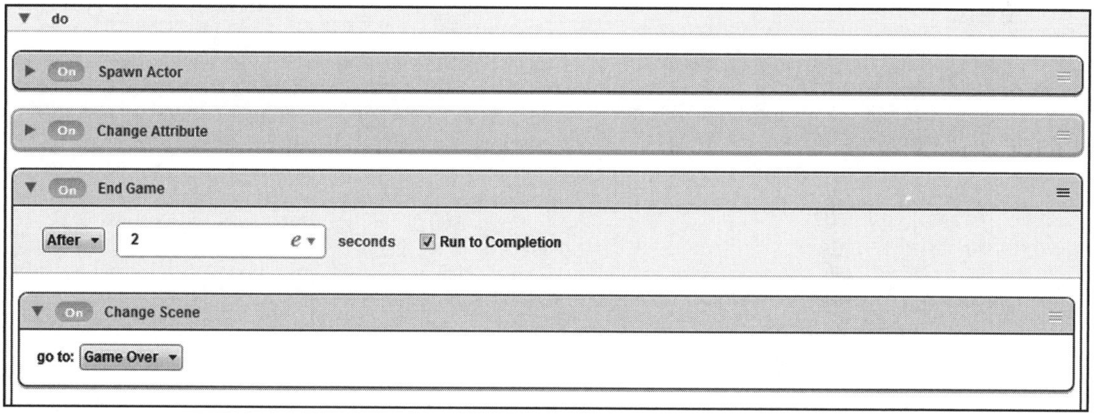

Figure 4.9
Create logic that is "game over" for the player.

Spawning More Enemies

Create a new actor in the Actors tab and name it Enemy Generator.

Using Sumopaint to Design an Image

Currently, the Enemy Generator does not have an image attached to it; it's just a white square. To fix this, you want to draw something that will serve as an enemy generator. My thought is to have an asteroid with an antenna or beacon atop it, which could draw enemies to your position. Follow these steps:

1. Return to Sumopaint.

2. Resize your Sumopaint canvas to 100×100 pixels. To do so, choose Edit > Canvas Size and change the Height and Width values accordingly. You can zoom in to get a better look at your drawing field by choosing View > Zoom In or pressing Ctrl++ (Windows) or Command++ (Mac). (See Figure 4.10.)

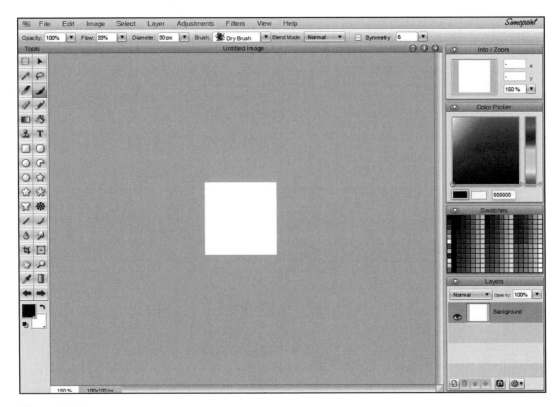

Figure 4.10
Create a 100 × 100 canvas and zoom in for a better look.

3. Add a new layer to draw on and hide the Background layer from view by clicking the eyeball icon beside it.

4. Click the Brush tool in the Tools panel. For the brush settings, choose Air Brush 5 with its parameter set to Ink for a smooth wet look. Set the Opacity and Flow to 100% and the Diameter to 2 pixels. Then draw a rough oval shape for the asteroid.

5. Click the Paint Bucket tool in the Tools panel and select a gray or brown color of your choice. If you set Smoothing to 4 pixels and the Tolerance to 40%, you can click a couple times in the center of your asteroid shape to create an interesting color fill. (See Figure 4.11).

Figure 4.11
Draw an asteroid shape.

6. Add a new layer and move it above the asteroid's layer. Using the Brush tool set to a blue or silver color with a diameter of 5 pixels, draw a shape for the beacon that goes on top. Do not just draw the outline; draw the entire shape.

Then, add a Stroke layer effect set to 3 pixels wide and a dark stroke color. The Stroke creates a thicker outside line around your paint. Also add a Drop Shadow layer effect with the Opacity set low (around 40%) to give the beacon an almost 3D effect, as shown in Figure 4.12. The Drop Shadow virtually drops a shadow underneath your paint, which makes it appear to pop out at the viewer. The Opacity defines how transluscent the shadow will appear. Opacity is rated 0% to 100%, with 0% being completely nonexistent (see-through) and 100% being completely opaque or filled in.

Figure 4.12
Draw the beacon on top of the asteroid.

7. Click the Default Colors button, located below the foreground and background swatch panels at the bottom of the Tools panel. (This button looks like a black and white color square overlapping one another.) This button returns your foreground and background swatch panels to their default black and white.

8. Click the Circle tool, marked with a circle, in the Tools panel. Notice in the options bar that appears below the main menu bar that its default fill shows a red and yellow gradient pattern. Click the Fill drop-down list to adjust some of

its parameters, setting Rotation to −32 and Focal Point to 0.6. Then click the Radial Gradient option in the Fill Type section. (See Figure 4.13).

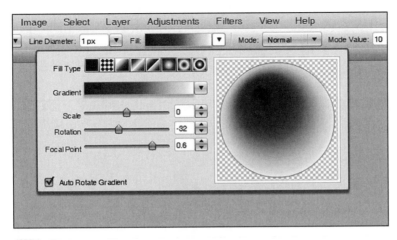

Figure 4.13
Set your fill for the Circle tool.
Source: Sumopaint, © 2013 Sumoing Ltd.® All Rights Reserved.

9. Click the Gradient drop-down list and, on the right, select the Reverse checkbox in the Gradient Options section, as shown in Figure 4.14.

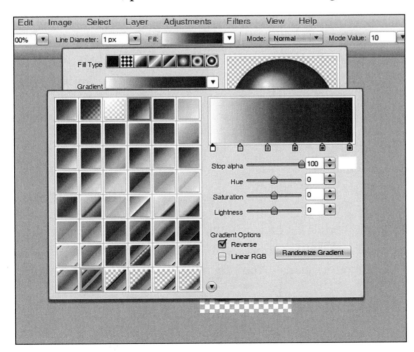

Figure 4.14
Reverse the gradient for a specular look.
Source: Sumopaint, © 2013 Sumoing Ltd.® All Rights Reserved.

10. Back in the editor, create a new layer above the others in the stacking order and use the Circle tool to draw a circle atop your beacon in the new layer. This gives you one bright, shiny orb. You can add more if you like, or even experiment with the gradient settings to make ones of different colors. You can also add layer effects such as the Outer Glow effect to make the lights stand out. (See Figure 4.15.)

Figure 4.15
Add the final touches to your asteroid.
Source: Sumopaint, © 2013 Sumoing Ltd.® All Rights Reserved.

11. Delete the default Background layer from the layer stacking order to leave the background behind the generator transparent. Finally, save the image (choose File > Save to My Computer) as asteroid.png with your other game project file images.

Importing the New Media

To import the image of the asteroid and associate it with the Enemy Generator actor, follow these steps:

1. Return to GameSalad Creator and click the Media tab in the Library panel.

2. Import the asteroid image.

3. Click the Enemy Generator actor in the Actors tab list in the Library panel.

4. Find and drag the newly imported asteroid image from the Media tab to the Actor tab in the Attributes panel, where it says, "Drag an Image Here." Watch it update to show your image. (See Figure 4.16.)

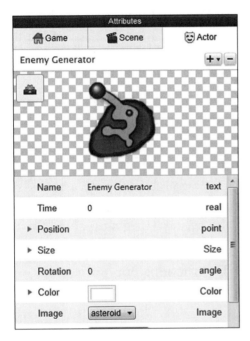

Figure 4.16
Give your Enemy Generator actor the asteroid image.
Source: The GameSalad Creator, © 2013 GameSalad®, Inc. All Rights Reserved.

Programming the Enemy Generator Logic

To program the Enemy Generator actor logic, follow these steps:

1. In the Attributes panel, create a new game attribute called Generator Health. It should be an integer attribute, set to 500 by default. Similar to the Player Armor and Alien Armor, the Enemy Generator will have Generator Health.

You put it five times higher than the Player Armor or Alien Armor, so that it takes longer to destroy it with weapon fire in-game.

2. Navigate to the Swarm Scene, if you are not already there. Drag and drop an instance of the Enemy Generator actor to the right of that scene's stage, lurking outside the visible area.

3. Double-click the actor and navigate to the prototype's rules and behaviors (of which there are currently none).

4. Add a new timer that uses Move To every two seconds to move the Enemy Generator actor to position 424,168 (relative to scene) at a speed of 50. Be sure to select the Run to Completion checkbox; otherwise, rather than moving all the way into position, it will just move a little bit and then stop. I selected 424 X and 168 Y by dragging the actor to the position in the scene where I wanted it to stop, recorded the numbers, and then dragged the actor back to its starting position. X/Y coordinates can be defined easily through experimentation.

5. Add another new timer, this one called Spawn Enemy. Set this timer to spawn the enemy actor every five seconds. Tell it to spawn this enemy from position 550, random (25,300) relative to the scene.

6. Add another new rule, this one called Take Damage. It should have a Collision condition that checks whether actor overlaps or collides with an actor of type laser. If it does, it should perform a Change Attribute behavior that reduces the game attribute Generator Health by −25. The actual expression should read as follows: game.Generator Health = game.Generator Health −25.

7. Create another new rule, this one called Destruction. For the condition, type Attribute and select Attribute option that appears. Select the game attribute you just created, Generator Health. For the operator, choose is (=) and set it to 0. What this condition says is, if Generator Health is zero, do this. What are you going to have it do? Explode and disappear, of course.

8. Spawn a big explosion actor in front of the actor, at position 0,0 relative to the actor. Then use Change Attribute to turn the Enemy Generator's color attribute of alpha to 0. This is similar to what you did earlier with the Alien Ship actor.

Testing the Enemy Generator

If you were to test your game now, you would have to start with the Battle Scene. To cheat on preview, click the Scenes tab in the Library panel and drag the Swarm Scene up to the top of the list. That way, it will be the first scene that starts on loading the preview. Next, go ahead and preview the game to make sure your rules and behaviors are working. You should have a moment of nothingness before the Enemy Generator hovers into place and enemy ships start drifting from right to left across the screen. As it stands, your lasers will pass right through the Enemy Generator (even though they do damage to it), and the enemy ships will not do any harm to you. Go back to the editor and fix these bugs.

1. In the Actors tab, select the laser and view its prototype rules and behaviors.

2. Scroll down to the very last rule, where if the laser actor overlaps or collides with the actor of type Alien Ship, it is removed. Just beneath that condition add a second Collision condition that checks whether the laser has overlapped or collided with the actor of type Enemy Generator. Then, click the All drop-down list where it says, "When ___ of the following are happening,"and choose Any, as shown in Figure 4.17.

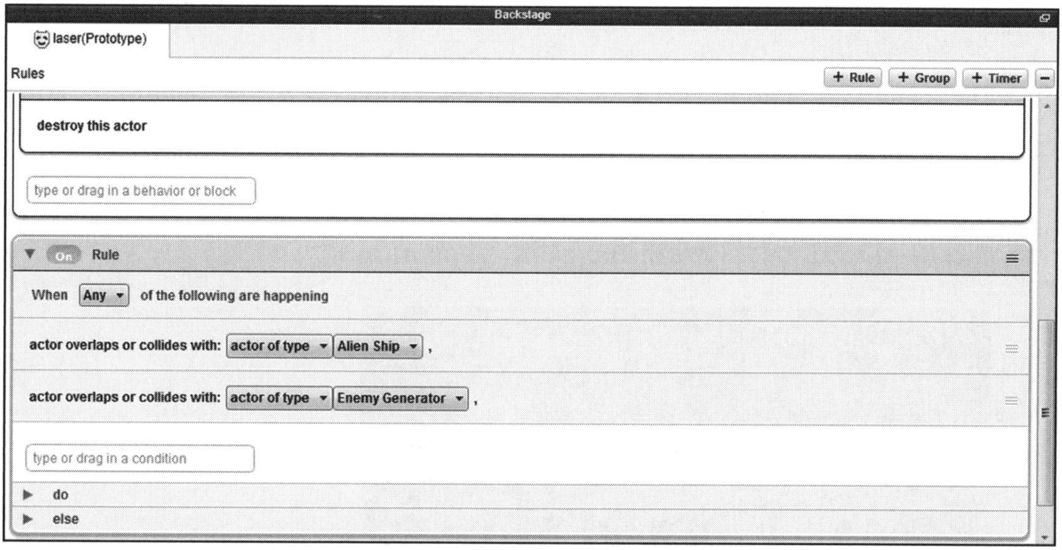

Figure 4.17
Add a second condition to the rule so the laser disappears after hitting either actor.
Source: The GameSalad Creator, © 2013 GameSalad®, Inc. All Rights Reserved.

3. Select the enemy actor from the Actors tab in the Library panel and view its prototype's rules and behaviors Backstage. The rule directly after the Move rule handles collisions with the laser, meaning that if the player shoots the enemy actor, the enemy actor blows up, and the player is given 10-point bonus in the Score game attribute. (You have not dealt with the Score game attribute yet, but you will soon.) Select the entire rule and, pressing down the Alt (Windows) or Option (Mac) key, drag and drop a duplicate of it below the original.

4. Rename the two rules. The first, on contact with laser fire, call Hit by Player. The second, which you are about to edit, call Hits Player.

5. In the Hits Player rule, change the actor of type collided with to Spaceship. In the "do" section, edit the Change Attribute behavior so that it reduces Player Armor by −10. The actual expression should say, set game.Player Armor to game.Player Armor −10.

Scoring

Right now, there is no way defined for the player to see how much damage they do to their enemies or how much damage is inflicted upon their own ship. There is a Score actor with predefined rules and behaviors that will help you here.

1. In the Actors tab, locate the Score actor. This is a simple text display that will show the player's current score. Drag and drop it in the lower-left area of the visible screen.

2. Play-test your game. You will be more satisfied with the results. If an enemy ship touches you, it blows up, but not before reducing your armor. You can also shoot these ships before they touch you to score points, as in Figure 4.18. If you destroy the Enemy Generator, it goes away, but nothing else changes. Go back to the editor to tweak the game some more.

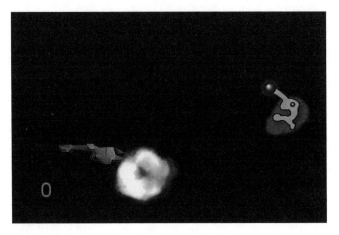

Figure 4.18
Test your game so far.
Source: The GameSalad Creator, © 2013 GameSalad®, Inc. All Rights Reserved.

3. While pressing the Alt (Windows) or Option (PC) key, drag and drop a duplicate of the Score actor in the Actors tab list. The duplicate, by default, will be titled Score Copy 1, but you can rename it to Player Armor.

4. Open its prototype rules and behaviors, change it to display the game attribute Player Armor (instead of Score), and change its inherent color to blue, as shown in Figure 4.19.

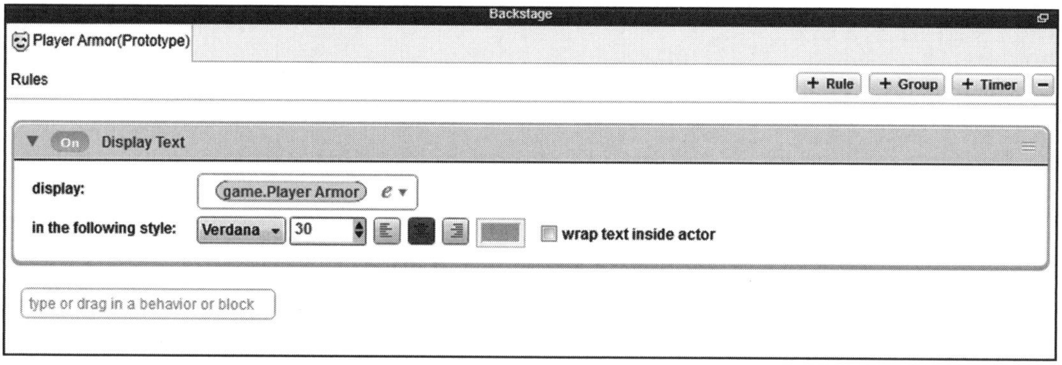

Figure 4.19
Add a score of Player Armor to your game screen.
Source: The GameSalad Creator, © 2013 GameSalad®, Inc. All Rights Reserved.

5. Drag the Player Armor actor to the upper-left corner of the stage. Now you can see your accurate Player Armor points when playing the game. However, these score cards (as they are) can only be witnessed within the Swarm Scene. To fix this, navigate to the Battle Scene and drag the Player Armor and Score actors into that scene, in the same exact positions. (You can edit their positions precisely within the Attributes panel. I placed my Player Armor at 50 X and 270 Y, and my Score at 52 X and 52 Y.)

6. Within the Battle Scene, select the Alien Ship actor and open its prototype rules and behaviors. Before the timer that takes the player to the Swarm Scene but after the self.color.alpha = 0 attribute change behavior, add a new Change Attribute behavior. Set the attribute to the Score game attribute and increase Score +25. (See Figure 4.20.)

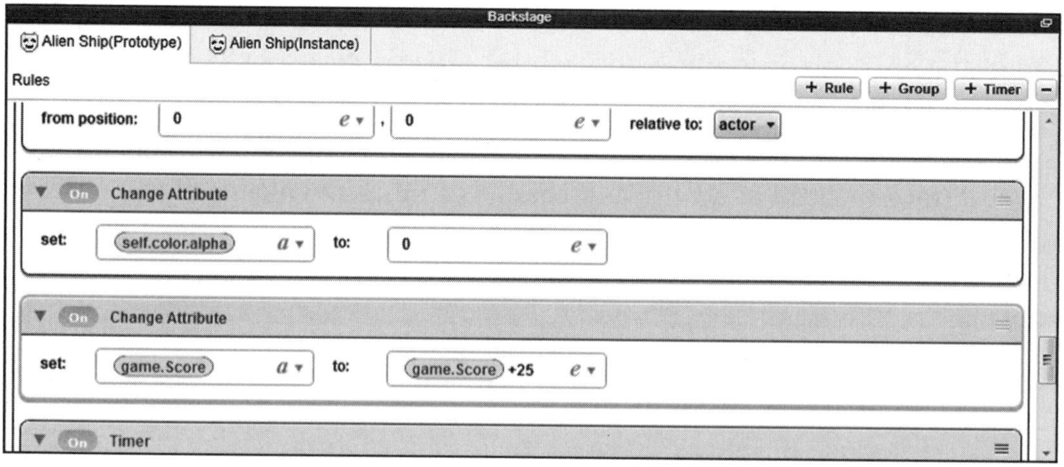

Figure 4.20
Raise the Score game attribute 25 points for demolishing the Alien Ship.
Source: The GameSalad Creator, © 2013 GameSalad®, Inc. All Rights Reserved.

Victory

Next, you need to create a victory screen. Follow these steps:

1. Using Sumopaint, create a victory screen that will fit your display size, which should be 480×320 since you are using the Basic Shoot-Em-Up template. This screen will be similar to the Game Over screen you made earlier, except it should congratulate the player for a job well done.

2. In GameSalad Creator, create a new actor named Victory and add it to the image you created in Sumopaint.

3. Create a new scene with the name Win and drag and drop your Victory actor into it, positioning the actor so it fills up the stage.

4. Open the rules for the Enemy Generator's prototype and add a new behavior to its Destruction rule for Change Scene, selecting the Win scene as the scene to which you want to take the player. That way, when players blow up the Enemy Generator, they are taken to the victory message you have prepared for them and know that they have beaten the game. You could even put an instance of the Score actor on the stage of the Win scene, with text on the image behind it saying something along the lines of, "Your final score:" This gives the player an indication where they stood as a player.

5. Optionally, copy the "Press SPACEBAR to Replay" text you placed on the Game Over screen to the Win screen (see Figure 4.21). Be sure to add the rules and behaviors you did for the Gameover actor to the Victory actor if you decide to

do so. It is only optional, but it will give the player the chance to retry for a higher score.

Figure 4.21
Add a Win scene for when the player beats the game.
Source: The GameSalad Creator, © 2013 GameSalad®, Inc. All Rights Reserved.

Pickup Items

Lastly, I believe it is crucial to give the player a reward. Currently, players exhaust their armor fighting against the Alien Ship and then a swarm of enemy ships brought on by an Enemy Generator. You should give players some method for regenerating their armor, especially now that they can see their Player Armor's current value on screen. To do this, I suggest having armor pickup items dropping from the top of the screen to the bottom. If the player touches one of them, his or her Player Armor will increase by +5.

1. Design or find an appealing shape for your power-up. The image I used was an animated atom GIF I found online for download, but your pickup item could look like anything as long as it gives the player some indication it would be beneficial to obtain. Once you settle on an image, use the Library panel's Media tab to import the image into GameSalad Creator. Then create an actor called Armor and give it the image you just imported.

Note

Be careful when downloading images from the web and using them within your own personal game projects. For one thing, other people's graphics are copyright protected by them, unless they expressly give you permission to use their images. Likewise, be wary about sites that profess to share royalty-free graphics, because some may still be copyright-protected by their original author, regardless where you discovered them. Even when graphics are free for grabs, it is always best policy to credit the author of them.

2. Open Armor's prototype rules and behaviors. Add a timer that every 0.15 seconds changes Armor's Rotation attribute +20 and changes Armor's Position Y attribute −10, as shown in Figure 4.22.

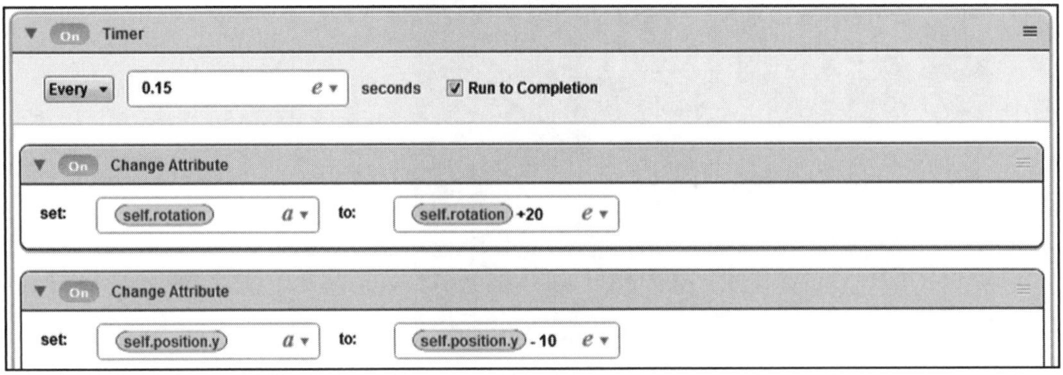

Figure 4.22
Adjust the Armor actor so it will drop and rotate at the same time.
Source: The GameSalad Creator, © 2013 GameSalad®, Inc. All Rights Reserved.

3. Create a rule that checks for a collision with the Spaceship actor. In the "do" section, add a Change Attribute behavior that adds +5 to Player Armor. After that, add a Destroy behavior that removes the Armor actor.

4. Add the spawner that will drop the Armor actors. To do so, create a new actor and call it Item Drop. It does not need a graphic (unless you prefer to give it one) because it will be above the stage, outside the visible area, and the player will never see it. Edit its rules and behaviors so that it moves left and right horizontally across the top of the screen, outside the stage. This will require a timer and Move To behavior like you used with the Alien Ship. I set my Item Drop actor to do the following: every 1 second, move to 0 X, 390 Y relative to scene at a speed of 100 (Run to Completion selected), and then move to 550 X, 390 Y relative to scene at a speed of 100 (Run to Completion selected). A second timer sets it to every 5 seconds spawn an Armor actor in front of actor in the direction 270 relative to actor. (See Figure 4.23.)

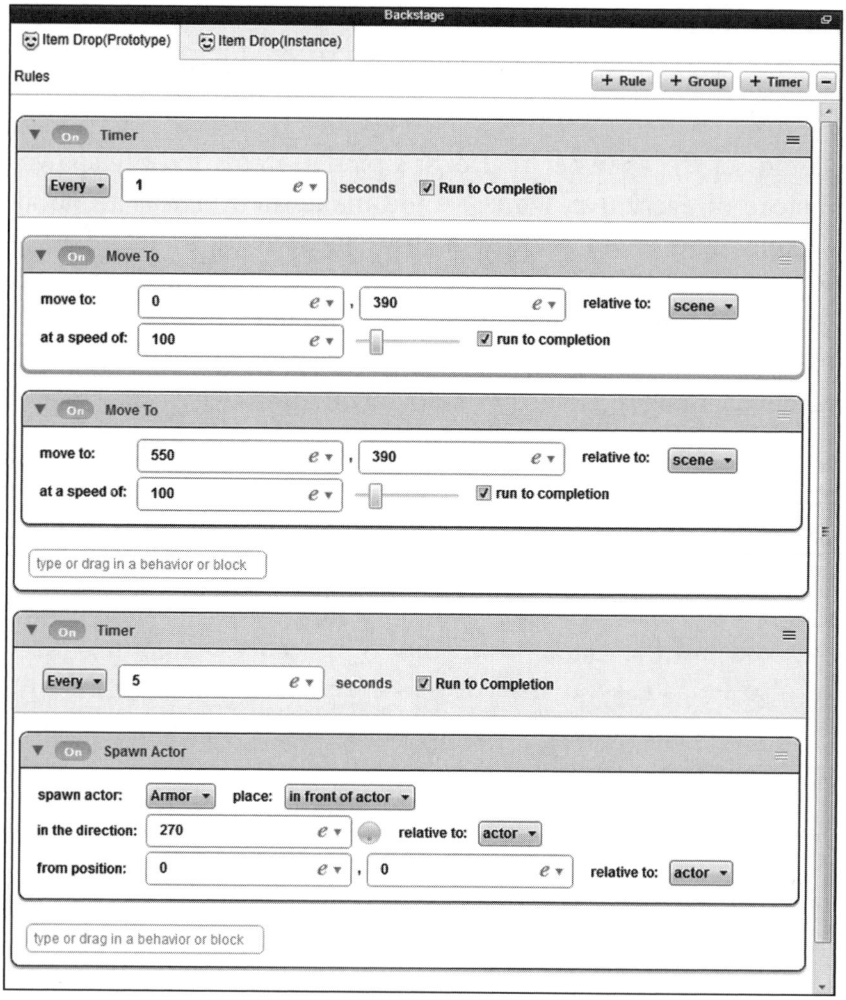

Figure 4.23
An example of the Item Drop's rules and behaviors.

5. Test your game. You should see your pickup items fall from the sky. If you catch them (while avoiding missiles or enemy ships), you will recover some of your lost armor. You will even go over the default value of 100, which you could limit by placing a rule within your rules and behaviors, but limiting Player Armor is not important for testing purposes.

FURTHER THOUGHTS

You could vary the pace of the game by going back and editing any of the values you have input for movement speed and timers in your game.

For instance, you could set the spawner that drops pickup items to only spawn them every 10 seconds instead of every five, which would make them harder to obtain and therefore more valuable. You could set the enemy ships to move faster across the screen, so they are practically whizzing past. You could increase the starting Enemy Generator Health or Alien Armor to make those foes tougher to beat. Making subtle changes to the Backstage values can completely alter the game flow, causing the effort involved in meeting its challenges to go up or down in complexity.

You could add more scenes to your existing list. Currently, the game starts with the Battle Scene, moves to the Swarm Scene, and ends with the Win scene. If the player loses all their armor, he or she is greeted with the Game Over scene and must reset the game. However, you could add a Title scene at the very beginning that shows the name of the game and a short description of how to play. You would construct this screen the same way you did the Game Over and Win scenes. Extending the length of the game should also be as easy as inserting new scenes, with more Enemy Generators or Alien Ships. Each new scene could ramp up in difficulty, making the shooter a strain to complete successfully.

CHAPTER 5

CREATING A BASIC PLATFORMER

In a platformer, also called a "run-and-jump" game, the player character typically moves from left to right across a scrolling landscape while jumping over chasms and onto moving platforms and avoiding dangerous obstacles.

This chapter will instruct you in how to build a basic platformer in GameSalad Creator. You will learn how to get an animated character to move left and right and to jump. In this chapter, I will also demonstrate the various settings in the Physics attributes for the main character and platform elements. With this knowledge, you can build your own amazing platformers like *Super Mario Bros.* or *Sonic the Hedgehog.*

SCENE SETUP AND MAKING A PLATFORM ACTOR

This chapter will look at creating a game for the iPad. To begin, you'll create a new file with a starting scene. Follow these steps:

1. Open the File menu in GameSalad Creator and choose New. The Create a New Project dialog box appears. Here, you choose a name for your project and the platform on which to publish it.

2. In the Title field, type Basic Platformer. In the Platform drop-down list, choose iPad Landscape. Then click the Resolution Independence checkbox to select it. (Resolution Independence enables you to build one project file using graphics optimized for the third-generation retina display iPad, including the iPad 3 and 4, and still publish game files for the iPad and iPad 2 platforms. When publishing for the iPhone, you have the same option.) Finally, click the Create Project button. See Figure 5.1.

Figure 5.1
Create a new project titled Basic Platformer.
Source: The GameSalad Creator, © 2013 GameSalad®, Inc. All Rights Reserved.

3. Next, create the base actors for this project. The first two actors will be the platform and the player character. In the Actors tab of the Library panel, click the plus (+) button in the upper-right corner to add a new actor. An empty Actor 1 is added to the Actors list.

4. Double-click Actor 1. The title becomes highlighted. Type Platform and press Enter to save your name change. You can name your actors anything you like, but as your project grows (which they always do), it helps to make things as straightforward and understandable as possible.

5. Drag and drop the Platform actor into the middle of the scene on the right. Of course, Platform is currently a white square 120×120 pixels.

6. Look in the Actor tab of the Attributes panel. Assuming the Platform actor selected in the Library panel, you can control the appearance and functionality of this actor in the Attributes panel. Click anywhere within the scene to deselect the actor, and then click Platform in the Actors list to select the prototype actor.

7. Without closing GameSalad Creator, open your Internet browser, visit www.noctua-graphics.de, and enter the language section for you. Click Download, click Textures, and then click Wall. Here, you can find Wall textures for download. These are royalty-free graphics, and although they are free, you should credit the author (Herbert Fahrnholz) if you use them in a commercial product. Select bricks 01 from the list of images you can download. Notice that this graphic's size is 512×512 and it is seamless, meaning you can repeatedly tile the image without any visible seams. Download bricks01.jpg to your computer.

Note

Tiling is quite common in two-dimensional (2D) game design. With tiling, you can use a smaller image to make up larger objects on screen by repeating patterns.

8. Back in GameSalad Creator, drag and drop the bricks01.jpg image you just downloaded to the Drag an Image Here area in the Attributes panel. Alternatively, import the graphic to the Media tab of the Library panel; then, in the Actor tab of the Attributes panel, scroll down until you find the Image attribute and set it to bricks 01. As shown in Figure 5.2, the Platform preview displays the image you just set.

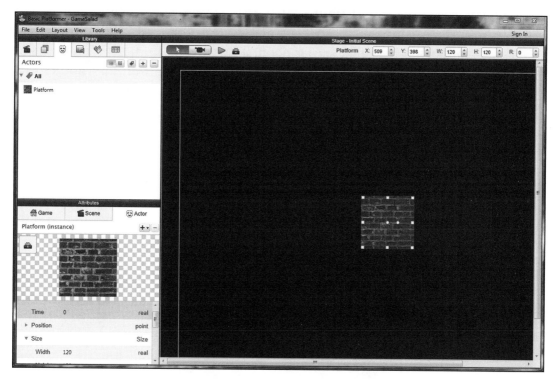

Figure 5.2
Add the bricks 01 image as your Platform actor's visual representation.
Source: The GameSalad Creator, © 2013 GameSalad®, Inc. All Rights Reserved.

9. Still in the Attributes panel, expand the Size attribute to show the Width and Height settings. Set the Width to 200 and the Height to 50. Notice as you do so that the actor in the scene automatically updates to those dimensions, and that the brick image stretches to fit, distorting the bricks (see Figure 5.3).

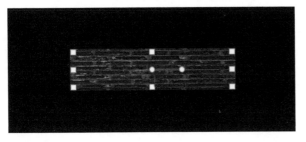

Figure 5.3
Resize your Platform actor.
Source: The GameSalad Creator, © 2013 GameSalad®, Inc. All Rights Reserved.

10. To fix the distortion, expand the Graphics attribute in the Attributes panel. Here, you will see sub-attributes such as Blending Mode, Horizontal Wrap, Vertical Wrap, Horizontal Anchor, Vertical Anchor, and more. From the drop-down options beside each, set Horizontal Wrap and Vertical Wrap to Tile. This would normally work, but as you can see, the graphic still does not look right. That is because the source file, bricks01.jpg, is still too big for the game.

11. You will need to fix the source image size. Returning to your Internet browser, visit www.resizeyourimage.com. This is a free online picture-resizing application. Click the Choose File button, then locate and select the bricks01.jpg image you downloaded to your computer to upload it to this application. Click the Zoom Out button 17 times, or until both the Width and Height settings are 150 pixels, as shown in Figure 5.4.

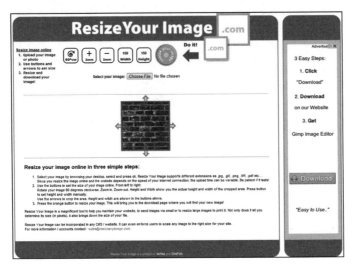

Figure 5.4
Change the size of your bricks01.jpg image.
Source: The GameSalad Creator, © 2013 GameSalad®, Inc. All Rights Reserved.

12. Click the Resize Your Image button at the top of the screen and save the image as a PNG file. Then, to save the file to your computer, click the brick01.001.png link. (See Figure 5.5.) Save your image to the Images folder of your game project.

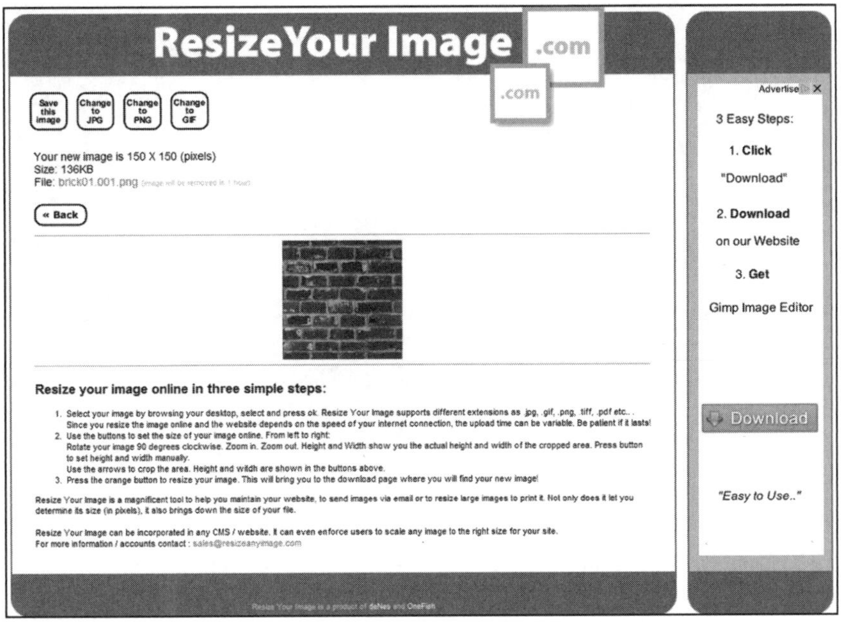

Figure 5.5
Download the new sized image to your computer.
Source: The GameSalad Creator, © 2013 GameSalad®, Inc. All Rights Reserved.

13. Back in GameSalad Creator, import your new image and attach it to your prototype Platform actor. Again, you can do this by dragging and dropping the graphic directly onto the preview of the actor in the Attributes panel or by importing the graphic to the Media tab of the Library panel and then attaching it to the Image attribute of the Platform actor in the Attributes panel. Now, the Platform actor should look a whole lot better.

14. In the Attributes panel, change the actor's Horizontal Anchor setting to Center and the Vertical Anchor setting to Top. This will change the origin of the image to middle top. (See Figure 5.6.)

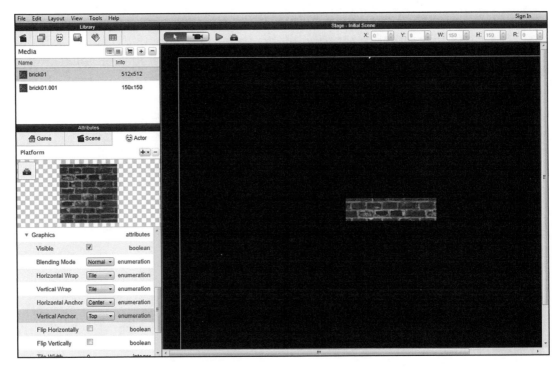

Figure 5.6
Adjust the anchors horizontally and vertically to change the placement of your bricks.
Source: The GameSalad Creator, © 2013 GameSalad®, Inc. All Rights Reserved.

15. Expand Physics in the actor's Attributes panel to display all the attributes available. As you can see, there are several options here. Deselect the Movable checkbox, about half-way down the list. This makes it so the GameSalad physics engine does not move this actor, even if another actor were to collide or interact with in any way. This also helps with overall game performance, enabling the game to run faster than it would otherwise. If you know in advance an actor will not need to be moved, it is smart to turn Movable off.

MAKE A PLAYER CHARACTER

Now you need to generate the onscreen avatar with which the player will be able to interact. Follow these steps:

1. In the Actors tab of the Library panel, add a new actor. Name this one Player. The companion site for this book has an image you can download called freaky.png. It is Freaky, the oblong head of a green goblin with one red eye (see Figure 5.7). Alternatively, you can create your own player character image in the

image-creation app of your choice. For the sake of this lesson, keep your image dimensions less than 150×150 pixels. Any bigger, and you may experience some lag. In fact, since our next step after import is to resize the image to 75×75, you could set it at that before saving your image. This will also help decrease memory usage. It is always best to be frugal with memory usage, especially if publishing to mobile devices.

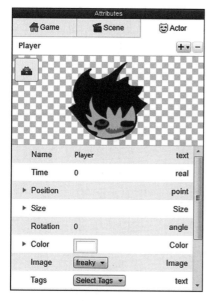

Figure 5.7
Freaky, a freakish goblin head.
Source: The GameSalad Creator, © 2013 GameSalad®, Inc. All Rights Reserved.

2. After saving freaky.png to your machine, import it into GameSalad Creator. Set it as the image for the prototype Player actor. With the Player actor selected, expand the Size settings in the Attributes panel. Adjust the Width and Height attributes to 75 pixels each. This will shrink the prototype from the original source image's size. If you note any distortion, you can play with the values (raising the numbers up or down) until you feel comfortable with the size and look of your actor.

3. Expand the Physics settings and select the Fixed Rotation checkbox. Leave Movable selected. Because you are leaving Movable on, this actor will be able to move around the scene. By turning Fixed Rotation on, you ensure this actor will not fall over on its side when the player bumps into other objects or falls off platforms. In this way, the Player actor will always land on its feet, so to speak.

4. Drag and drop an instance of the Player actor into your scene. Because Freaky's hair is black, he blends into the scene's background color, which (by default) is black. To fix this, change the background color to a color other than black. To do so, click Scene tab in the Attributes panel and click the rectangular thumbnail image next to the Color attribute to open the Color Swatch dialog box, where you can select a color for your background. To pick a sky blue color, type 150 in the R field, 200 in the G field, 255 in the B field, and 255 in the A field at the bottom of the Color Swatch dialog box. Close the Color Swatch dialog box; the scene updates automatically, as shown in Figure 5.8. That is better.

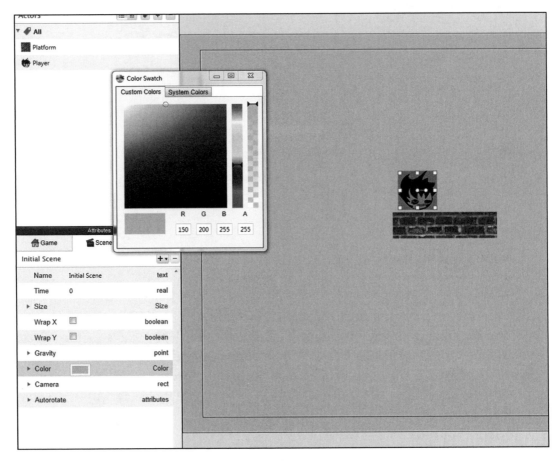

Figure 5.8
Change the background color so Freaky stands out from it.
Source: The GameSalad Creator, © 2013 GameSalad®, Inc. All Rights Reserved.

BUILD YOUR SCENE

With multiple Platform actors, construct a scene to test game physics. Follow these steps:

1. Drag and drop several instances of the Platform actor into your scene and arrange them as floors, walls, a ceiling, and shelves in between. Your placement is entirely of your own devising, however you think the scene needs to look. The more platformers you have played, the more intuitive placement will seem for you. If you are uncertain where to start, you can always make yours look like Figure 5.9.

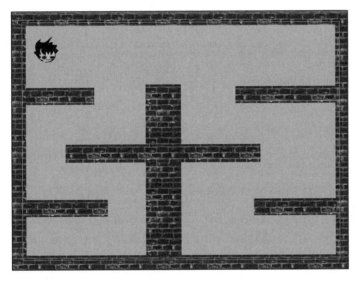

Figure 5.9
One example of a scene's layout.
Source: The GameSalad Creator, © 2013 GameSalad®, Inc. All Rights Reserved.

Note

When you click an instance of the Platform actor, you'll see resize handles at all four corners and sides and a rotation handle in the middle. You can play with these if you want to see what they all do. As you can see in Figure 5.9, I stretched out one block to be the ceiling. Then I pressed the Alt/Option key and drag-and-dropped a duplicate copy of it out beside it, which I then dragged to the bottom of the scene for a floor. I then stretched a block vertically to be one side's wall and did the same duplication maneuver to move a copy to the opposite side. Each platform that rested against another, I nudged until the mortar between the bricks lined up so that the placement would look more natural and less separate. As you place the sides, floor, and ceiling, you should bear in mind that the white inner and outer outlines of the scene define the margins of the iPad screen. Whatever you place outside the outer white outline will not be visible in the final game.

2. Move your Player actor to an empty space in the upper-left corner of your scene, above a platform. Make sure the Player actor is not touching or overlapping any of the Platform actors.

3. Save your project and click Preview to see what your game looks like so far. Unfortunately, nothing much happens. You can see how the preview clips the edges of your scene to match the iPad's screen resolution, but that is about all you will see. Click Back to Editor to return to the Scene Editor so you can start adding functionality.

GAME LOGIC

You have the major components of the game collected and imported, but without some behaviors or rules attached to them, the actors cannot do anything on their own. This section will show you what behaviors and rules you need to attach to the actors to turn this from a boring diorama into a vivacious video game.

Physics

The default physics for your actors do not work well for a platformer. First, you will need to give the Player actor gravity so it can fall down. Then, you need to add a behavior for collision and make that collision believable. Follow these steps:

1. Double-click the Player actor in the Actors tab of the Library panel to open the rules and behaviors for the prototype Player actor in the Backstage panel. (If the Backstage panel does not appear in the lower right, you can reveal it by clicking the Toggle Backstage button, which is beside the Preview button.) In the Library panel, switch to the Behaviors tab and scroll down the list until you see the Accelerate behavior. Drag and drop the Accelerate behavior from this list to the Player actor's rules and behaviors, where it says, "Type or Drag in a Behavior Block Here."

2. Set Accelerate in Direction to 270 by typing 270 directly into the Accelerate in Direction field or clicking the direction indicator beside it. This tells the physics engine in which direction the actor should fall. Set this direction relative to the scene, not the actor.

3. Set With Acceleration to 275. Figure 5.10 shows this behavior's setup. This tells the physics engine how fast the actor should fall. Note that the way the physics engine interprets this value means the actor will start falling and continue to fall right off the virtual screen. This is not precisely what you want, as the Player actor does not interact with the Platform actors. You have to add a behavior for that, too.

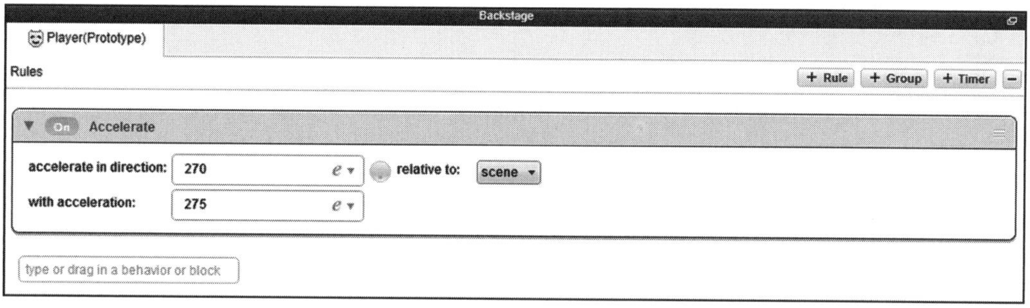

Figure 5.10
Mocking gravity by use of an Accelerate behavior.

Source: The GameSalad Creator, © 2013 GameSalad®, Inc. All Rights Reserved.

Note

There is an option in GameSalad's Scene attributes to set gravity for your entire game. However, I find doing the gravity like this, on an actor-by-actor basis, to be not only more flexible, but also better in terms of the end result. Not every actor having motion should have the same downward acceleration, based on your imagined concept of their mass. To change the game's overall gravity setting within the Scene Editor, go to the Scene tab in the Attributes panel and set both the X and Y attributes under Gravity to 0. For now, though, you should use the Accelerate behavior to fake gravity on an actor-by-actor basis.

4. From the Library panel's Behaviors list, drag and drop Collide under Accelerate in the Player actor's rules and behaviors. Make sure the Bounce When Colliding With drop-down lists read Actor of Type and that Platform is selected. This behavior does exactly as it says: When the Player actor collides with the Platform actor, the Player will bounce. It won't just bounce once, though! It will be very bouncy—too bouncy for what you want. To fix this, you must edit some of the Physics attributes of both the Player and Platform actors.

5. Select the Platform actor in the Actors tab in the Library panel. In the Actor tab in the Attributes panel, expand the Physics settings. The third attribute under Physics is Bounciness. This controls how bouncy this actor appears in-game. Older versions of GameSalad called this attribute Restitution. Change the value here from 1 to 0, so the Platform actor will not be the least bit bouncy.

6. Select the Player actor from the Actors tab in the Library panel and expand the Physics options in that actor's Attributes panel. Change the Bounciness setting from 1 to 0.5. This leaves the Player actor just bouncy enough to appear natural, not wooden or robotic in how it comes to rest when striking the Platform actors. Depending on the character you are developing, you might want it more or less bouncy.

Movement Controls

Now that you have better physics and solid platforms, it is time to add movement controls to put the Player actor in the player's hands. Follow these steps:

1. With the prototype Player actor still selected, go to the Backstage area and click the Create Rule button to add a new rule just below the current behaviors. Make sure right under the rule's title bar that the When All Conditions Are Valid option is set to All and not Any. Any implies that if one or another of the following conditions are met, then the behavior will be carried out. All implies that every single one of the following conditions must be met before the behavior can be executed.

2. For the condition, type Collision and select that option when it appears. In the first Actor Overlaps or Collides With drop-down list, choose Actor of Type. In the second drop-down list, choose Platform.

3. Just below that condition, add another. Type Key and select that option when it appears. The key press you want mapped to this condition is the right-arrow key.

4. Now that both conditions of your rule have been added, add the action. In the "do" area just below the "condition" area, type Accelerate and select that option when it appears. Alternatively, find the Accelerate behavior block in the Behaviors list of the Library panel and drag and drop it into the "do" section of your new rule. You do not need to edit any of the default values for this behavior.

5. Preview your game. When Freaky falls and finishes bouncing on a platform, you can press the right-arrow key to move Freaky to the right along the platform. Move Freaky off the edge of a platform and watch him fall to the next platform. That takes care of moving him to the right.

6. Return to the editor. Rename your right movement rule Move Right.

7. Highlight the Move Right rule and, pressing the Alt/Option key, drag and drop a duplicate copy of it just below. Rename this copy Move Left. Modify the second condition of the rule so the key press is the left-arrow key instead of the right-arrow key. In the Accelerate behavior, modify the Accelerate in Direction value to 180 (the game direction for left).

8. Save your project and preview your game to check that you have left and right control over the Freaky character. If something does not work correctly, simply go back to the editor and proofread your behaviors. They should look like Figure 5.11.

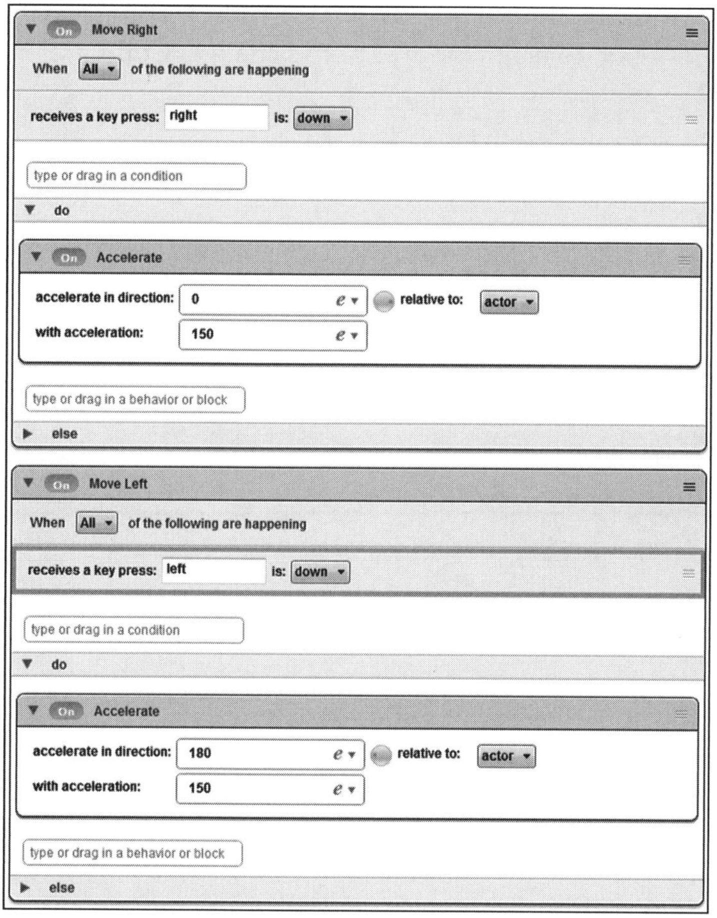

Figure 5.11
The Player actor behaviors, including movement controls.
Source: The GameSalad Creator, © 2013 GameSalad®, Inc. All Rights Reserved.

Jump Control

Finally, you need to add a jump control to complete the player interaction. Follow these steps:

1. Duplicate either the Move Left or Move Right rule. Call the new rule Jump.

2. Change the key mapped to this action to be the spacebar. Select the Accelerate behavior in the "do" area and press Delete on your keyboard to remove it. Type Change Velocity and select this option when it appears in the Accelerate behavior's place. Set the Change Movement to Go in Direction field to 90 (straight up) relative to the scene, not the actor. You can alter the At a Speed Of value to 350 or thereabouts. The layout of your scene may need higher or farther

jumps made—or, conversely, shorter, simpler jumps made. Adding or subtracting the speed of your Change Velocity behavior affects the change. Compare your behavior to Figure 5.12.

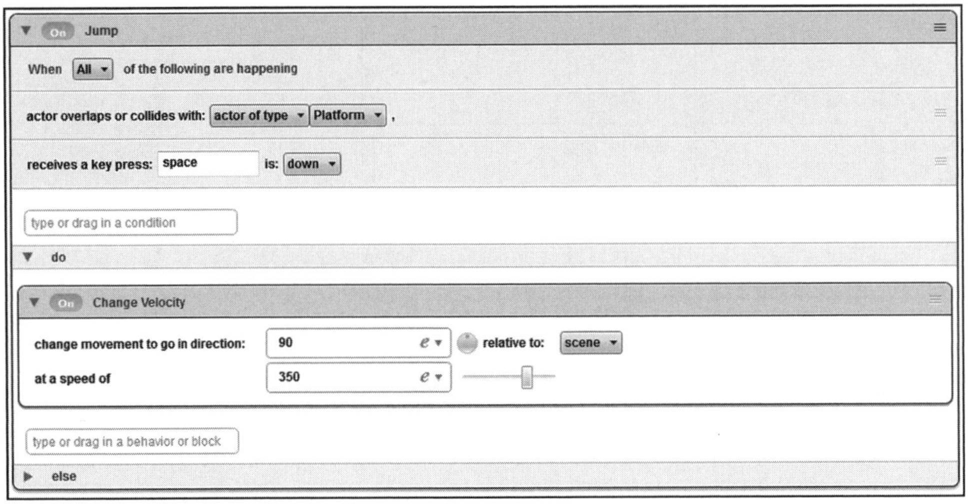

Figure 5.12
The Player actor's Jump behavior.
Source: The GameSalad Creator, © 2013 GameSalad®, Inc. All Rights Reserved.

3. To make some of the jumps easier, because Freaky is just a round head, go to the actor's attributes in the Attributes panel and, in the Physics attributes, change the Collision Shape setting from Rectangle to Circle. This will place an invisible circular bounding margin around Freaky instead of a rectangular one, which is the default.

4. Preview your jump motion in the game. Try bouncing from platform to platform, both left and right. Go all the way down to the floor and then attempt to jump back up to the top platform. See how springy Freaky acts now? This is a lot of fun, but when you add dangerous obstacles for Freaky to overcome, the challenge will be in avoiding them precisely—something the super-bouncy Freaky will not handle well. To reduce his elasticity, return to the editor, go to the actor's attributes in the Attributes panel, and change the Bounciness value (in the Physics attributes) to 0.25 rather than 0.5.

5. Save your project and preview it again. Notice how Freaky is not nearly as springy as he was before, but that jumping is still a lot of fun? This is much improved. The player can face challenges while hopping around, but the jumps will not be nearly as uncontrolled as they were before.

A Few Minor Tweaks

Right now, Freaky is looking pretty good. However, whether moving left or right or jumping up or down, he always looks the same. You can change that. Follow these steps:

1. First, in the Backstage area, with the Player prototype selected, go to the Move Right command. In the "do" area, immediately after the Accelerate behavior, type `Change Attribute` and select that option when it appears. Click the "a" button and select Attributes > Player > Graphics > Flip Horizontally. Finally, set the expression to be false, as shown in Figure 5.13.

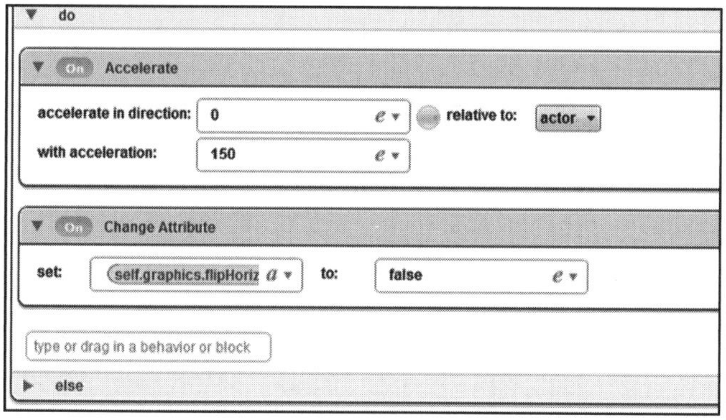

Figure 5.13
Set the Player's Flip Horizontally attribute to false.
Source: The GameSalad Creator, © 2013 GameSalad®, Inc. All Rights Reserved.

2. Add a duplicate of this Change Attribute behavior to the Move Left command, just after its Accelerate behavior in its "do" area. (To create a duplicate, press Alt/Option while selecting, dragging, and dropping the behavior.) Change the expression to true instead of false.

3. Preview your game to test out your edits. Now, when you move right, Freaky turns to face right, and when you move left, Freaky turns to face left. This is much more natural to the player and therefore more desirable.

4. Return to the editor and add a new rule. Name it Reset Size. Set the condition to Collision for when the Player actor touches the Platform actor. In the "do" area, add two Change Attribute behaviors. The first should change the Player actor's Size > Width to 75. The second should change the Player actor's Size > Height to 75. Your image of Freaky, remember, was 75×75 pixels, so really all this rule does is say that if the Freaky hits the bricks, he should return to his original size.

5. Go to the Jump command. Below the Change Velocity behavior in its "do" area, add two Change Attribute behaviors. Set the first one so it changes the Player actor's Size > Width to 65 and the other changes the Player actor's Size > Height to 90. (See Figure 5.14.)

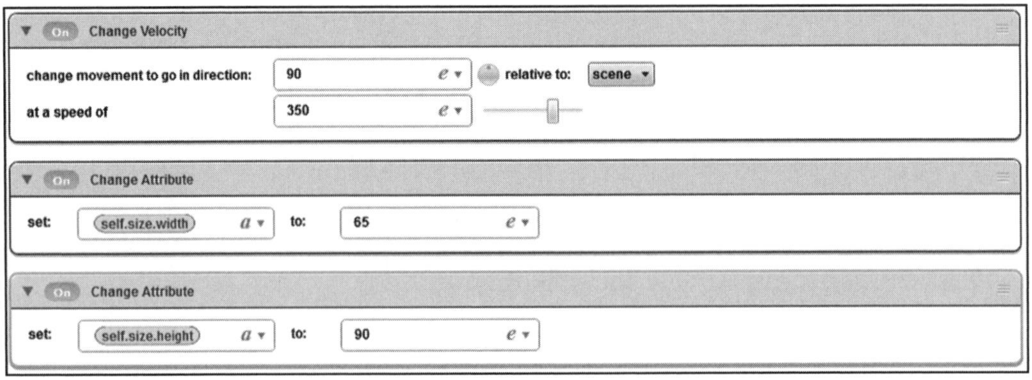

Figure 5.14
Stretch the actor vertically and squash it horizontally by adding these two Change Attribute behaviors.
Source: The GameSalad Creator, © 2013 GameSalad®, Inc. All Rights Reserved.

6. Preview your game. Note that whenever you jump, Freaky stretches out slightly. When he comes back to the ground, he straightens back out. For a truly cartoon animation, you would have him return to normal in mid-arc, before he begins falling back to the floor, but this is good enough for now. You might also see that when Freaky touches the ceiling or walls in the middle of his jump, that he changes back to his regular size.

7. Save your project.

CREATING A GAME INTERFACE

You will want to expand the game a little by adding a game interface. A game interface is the encapsulating menu screens that you come to before, during, and after a game, where the game's action stops and options are presented to the player. The most common interface screens are the start/intro screen and the pause screen, which you will add to your platformer now. Follow these steps:

1. Open the Scenes tab in the Library panel. You currently have only the Initial Scene entry in the list. Double-click this entry to select it and type Main to rename it.

2. Add a new scene by clicking the plus (+) button. Name this new scene Start. In the list, click and drag it up above the Main scene.

3. Add another scene by clicking the plus button again. Call this scene Pause. As it shows up at the bottom of the list, it is alright to leave it there.

Painting a Start Screen in Sumopaint

Using an image-editing application, create an image for the Start scene. Make sure the size of the image you design is 1,024×768 pixels, because that is the display size for the iPad Landscape resolution you have set for this platformer game. If you decide to use the free version of the Sumopaint app (www.sumopaint.com/app/), you can follow these instructions:

1. Create a new blank canvas.

2. Choose Image > Image Size. Set Width to 1,024, set the Height to 768, and click OK.

3. Choose View > Zoom Out so you can see the whole canvas as you work.

4. Use the Color Picker or Swatches panel on the right to select a color for your background. Then select the Paint Bucket tool from the Tools panel on the left and fill your canvas with your chosen color.

5. Add a new layer in the Layers panel by clicking the Add a New Layer button. (It looks like a page with one corner folded down.) The layer will be added above your Background layer.

6. Select the Text tool from the Tools panel. Click where you want to add type on your canvas and type Freaky in Bricktown. Then select the text and, in the toolbar above, just below the main menu bar, select an appealing option from the Font Family and Font Size drop-down lists. Choose a color that is opposite in tone from the one you used for the background. For instance, if you selected a dark color for the background, use a lighter color for the text, or vice versa. You can see your changes on the fly and adapt them until you are satisfied with the result.

Note

If you ever need or want more device fonts on your Windows PC, visit www.dafont.com. Dafont.com offers hundreds of free fonts for download. You can browse fonts by category and preview text displayed in them before you download. After you download, you will need a decompression program like WinZip or WinRAR to unzip the files. Copy the TTF font file to your C:/Windows/Fonts directory on your Windows PC and wait for it to install. Then, whenever you open a program that uses device fonts, such as Microsoft Word or Sumopaint, your new font will be ready and available.

7. When you are finished with the title, select the Free Transform/Rotate tool from the Tools panel. (Its icon looks like a square with smaller squares in the corners and center of it.) Click and drag a selection square completely around the title you just typed. When you let go, you will have sides and anchors in the corners by which you can scale, stretch, and rotate your words around the canvas. You can see how I positioned my title in Figure 5.15.

Figure 5.15
Resize, reposition, and rotate your title until you are satisfied with the way it looks.
Source: Sumopaint, © 2013 Sumoing Ltd.® All Rights Reserved.

8. Add a new layer above the last one. Select the Rounded Rectangle tool from the Tools panel. In the toolbar above, click the Fill red-to-orange sample to open the Fill dialog box. There, click the Gradient sample and choose from one of the predefined gradients. I picked Glossy Fill Green.

9. Use the Rounded Rectangle tool to draw a button somewhere off-center, close to the bottom of your canvas, like in Figure 5.16.

Figure 5.16
Place a button on your canvas.

10. Add a new layer above the last one. Select the Text tool again. With a smaller Font Size setting, type `Click to Start` over the top of your rectangular button. Use the Move tool to position it as close to center over that button as possible. Make sure it is small enough that none of the words hang outside the button. If they do, simply use the Free Transform/Rotate tool to shrink the text down. (See Figure 5.17.)

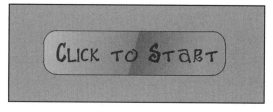

Figure 5.17
Add "Click to Start" inside the button.

11. Add another layer above the rest. Then choose File > Import to Layer > From My Computer (see Figure 5.18). Browse to your character image file (freaky.png) and import it to your Sumopaint canvas inside the new layer. Use the Free Transform/Rotate tool to transform and position the image wherever you think best. Be forewarned, though, about enlarging him too much; raster graphics like this, which are composed of tiny pixels, tend to become blurry to the eye when you scale them up. That is why it is generally best to start big and shrink

images down as needed. However, it is okay to make Freaky a little larger than his source file here, as long as he does not look too blurry. (See Figure 5.19.)

Figure 5.18
Go to File > Import to Layer > From My Computer to import remote graphics.
Source: Sumopaint, © 2013 Sumoing Ltd.® All Rights Reserved.

Figure 5.19
Resize and even flip Freaky if you want, as long as you do not make him look too blurry.
Source: Sumopaint, © 2013 Sumoing Ltd.® All Rights Reserved.

12. You can add more to your image, but that is enough for this exercise. Go to File > Save to My Computer As and save the image as Start.png to your computer.

Building a Start Interface

Return to GameSalad Creator. Here, you will import your Start.png file and attach it to a new actor that will fill the Start scene. Follow these steps:

1. Click the Media tab in the Library panel and click the plus (+) button in the upper-right corner. Browse until you find the Start.png file you just saved to your computer and import it.

2. Switch to the Actors tab. Add a new actor by clicking the plus (+) button. Name your new actor Start.

3. In the Actor tab of the Attributes panel, scroll down to Image and, from the drop-down list, select Start. Watch the preview update to show your image.

4. In the Attributes panel, under Size, change the Width setting to 1,024 and the Height setting to 768. Check your work against Figure 5.20.

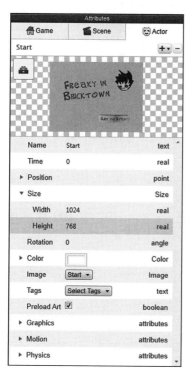

Figure 5.20
Set your Start actor to match the Start image's dimensions.

5. Drag and drop an instance of your Start actor into your Start scene on the right. With the instance selected, look in the Attributes panel for the Position settings. Change the X position setting to 512 and the Y position setting to 384. X and Y correspond directly to width and height, in that order, and these values are half of each, so your Start actor will be centered to the Start scene, as shown in Figure 5.21.

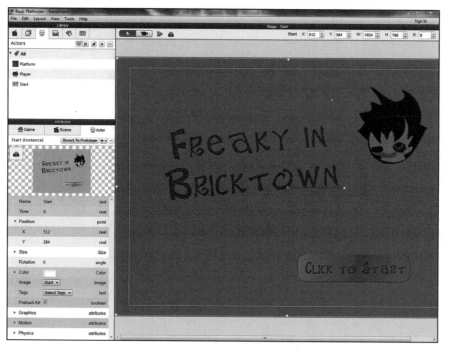

Figure 5.21
Center your Start actor in the Start scene.
Source: The GameSalad Creator, © 2013 GameSalad®, Inc. All Rights Reserved.

6. Select the prototype actor from the Actors tab list in the Library panel. Then go to the Backstage area to add rules and behaviors. Add a new rule. For the condition, type `Mouse Button` and select that option when it appears. Once selected, you do not have to edit it; what this condition says is, if the player clicks with his or her mouse, then do this.

7. In the "do" area, type `Change Scene` and select that option when it appears. For the specific scene, choose Main. Your Start scene is all set to go. Now, when the game begins, the player merely clicks to begin play.

8. Save your project.

Building a Pause Interface

Adding a pause screen will be a little different. You could do it the same way you did the intro screen, but in this case, I want you to experiment with some of GameSalad Creator's built-in functions. Follow these steps:

1. Select the Player actor in the Actors tab in the Library panel. Go to the prototype actor's rules and behaviors in the Backstage area and add a new rule. Call your new rule Pause Game.

2. For the condition, set it to whenever the player presses the Esc key.

3. In the "do" area, type Pause Game and choose that option when it appears. Select the Pause scene to be shown.

4. Go to the Pause scene by clicking it in the Scenes tab in the Library panel. Currently, it is completely black with nothing in it.

5. In the Actors tab in the Library panel, add a new actor and name it Pause Menu.

6. In the Actor tab in the Attributes panel, click the color swatch thumbnail beside the Color setting. In the Color Swatch dialog box that appears, type 0 in the R, G, B, and A fields (see Figure 5.22). This sets the actor's background color to completely transparent.

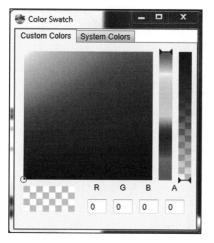

Figure 5.22
Set your color to all zeroes to make it see-through.

7. In the Backstage area, type Display Text and choose that option when it appears. In the box where it says "Hello world!" highlight the text and type

GAME PAUSED. Select the Wrap Text Inside Actor checkbox so the words will fit within your Pause Menu actor. Your behavior should look like Figure 5.23.

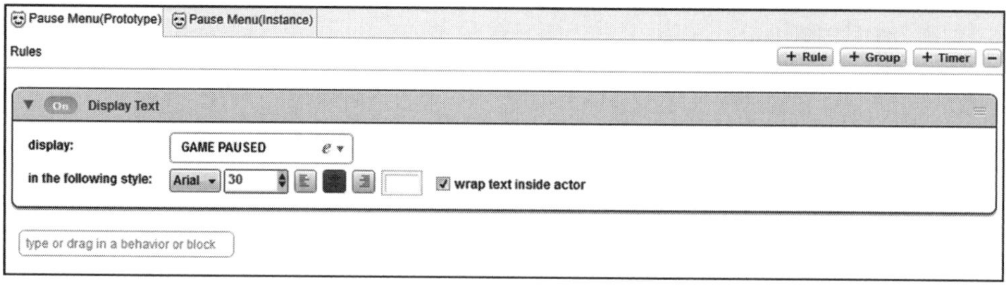

Figure 5.23
Add text to your Pause Menu actor through the Display Text behavior.
Source: The GameSalad Creator, © 2013 GameSalad®, Inc. All Rights Reserved.

8. Drag and drop an instance of the Pause Menu actor in the Pause scene on the right. Center it to the scene by editing its Position X and Y attributes in the Attributes panel to 512 and 385. Still in the Attributes panel, resize the actor's Size > Width setting to 300 and the Size > Height setting to 150.

9. Preview your game. When the game has started, press the Esc key to pause the game. The words GAME PAUSED will cover your screen, as shown in Figure 5.24. However, once the game is paused, you are stuck, because there is no way to unpause the game.

Figure 5.24
Pausing your game with the Esc key.
Source: The GameSalad Creator, © 2013 GameSalad®, Inc. All Rights Reserved.

10. Go back to the editor. Select the prototype Pause Menu actor and add a new rule to it in the Backstage area. Call this new rule Resume Game. Just as you did to pause the game, set the condition to the Esc key, but instead of adding a Pause Game behavior, type `Unpause Game` and choose that option when it appears.

11. Save and preview your game. Now you can pause and resume your game any time by pressing the Esc key.

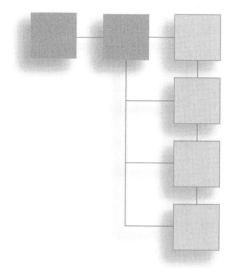

CHAPTER 6

A MORE ADVANCED PLATFORMER

Right now, you have the start of the makings of a great game, but it lacks several key components. Currently, your players can hurtle their avatar around the scene, up and down platforms. Yet there is no main objective, or goal, for them to reach—and nothing hindering them from accomplishing their objective even if there were one. Having an aim to strive for and challenges to overcome are integral to making a great game. Without these, the player will get bored very quickly. This chapter will show you a quick and clever way to set up motivation and obstacles. You can expand on these ideas to make as many levels as you like.

SETTING UP A GOAL

First, you are going to give the player something visual to strive to reach. For a visual aid, how about you use an exit door? The player will not know if the door takes them to another level, also fraught with peril, or out of the game successfully, but they will attempt to reach it due to sheer curiosity. However, the door must not be too easy to reach. One technique (popularized by the game *Super Mario 64*) is to have the player collect a specified number of stars before he or she can open each door. You could place stars around your level that the player has to capture; when the player has them, he or she can open the door and see what is on the other side. This is easier than it sounds, trust me.

A Star for Motivation

You will need to set up an attribute to tell whether the door is locked. Then, based on that information, the door will either open, taking the player to another scene, or won't open, but will demonstrate to the player that he or she does not have enough stars to open it yet. Follow these steps:

1. With your Basic Platformer project open in GameSalad Creator, click the Game tab in the Attributes panel and click the plus (+) button to add a new integer attribute. Name this attribute Stars, and set its default value to 0. This number will keep track of the number of stars the player has picked up. See Figure 6.1.

Figure 6.1
Add a game attribute called Stars.
Source: The GameSalad Creator, © 2013 GameSalad®, Inc. All Rights Reserved.

2. In the Actors tab of the Library panel, click the plus (+) button to add a new actor. Name it Star. In the Actor tab of the Attributes panel, with the Star actor selected, expand the Physics attributes and turn all of them off. If the attribute is an integer, change it to 0, and if it is a checkbox, deselect it. You do not need the Star actor to be movable or any of these other options, as it will be a fixed image that the player can pick up. Change this actor's Collision Shape setting from Rectangle to Circle. See Figure 6.2.

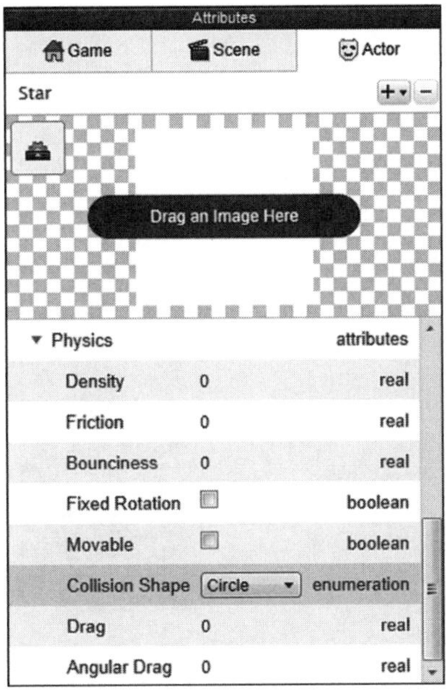

Figure 6.2
Edit your Star actor's attributes.
Source: The GameSalad Creator, © 2013 GameSalad®, Inc. All Rights Reserved.

Designing a Star

Now it's time to design the star. The following instructions are for using Sumopaint.

1. Open Sumopaint or whatever image-editing app you prefer.

2. Create a new blank canvas. Then choose Image > Image Size and change the size to 100 × 100 pixels. Select a yellow or orange color from the Swatches or Color Picker panels. I chose #FFCC00, which is hexadecimal code for an orange-ish yellow.

Note

Image-editing programs love to use hexadecimal color codes, which are six-character strings of letters and numbers that represent a color in a digital color palette. It is not necessary to memorize hexadecimals. If you ever need to look one up, visit www.color-hex.com.

3. Choose the Star tool from the Tools panel. Add a new layer to your Layers panel and, with this new blank layer selected, click in the middle of the stage and begin dragging. Do not let go of the mouse button prematurely. Move and rotate your mouse, watching the shape of your star change on the screen. The yellow color you chose will form the outline of the star, and a gradient (determined by

the Fill setting in the options area above) will fill in the star. Keep rotating until you get a shape similar to the one in Figure 6.3.

Figure 6.3
Make a star with the Star tool.
Source: Sumopaint, © 2013 Sumoing Ltd.® All Rights Reserved.

4. Hide the Background layer by clicking the eyeball icon beside it in the Layers panel. The white fill will disappear, leaving only the gray-and-white checked pattern that represents transparency. Select the Free Transform/Rotate tool from the Tools panel and drag a selection box around your star. Then move your cursor slightly outside the selection box, close to one of the corners, until your cursor changes into a semi-circular arrow shape. This indicates that if you click and drag, you will rotate the object. Do so now. Rotate the star until it stands upright. Finally, click the Apply Transformation button, in the upper-left area of your screen, to save your changes.

5. Use the Free Transform/Rotate tool again, this time clicking and dragging on the anchors and sides of your selection box, until your star image fills the canvas, the corners of the star touching each edge. See Figure 6.4.

Figure 6.4
The finished star.

6. Choose File > Save to My Computer As and save the image as Star.png in the Images folder of your Basic Platformer project.

Making the Star Functional

The star you just made will be part of a key to open doors. The player will need to collect three of them to open one door. Follow these steps:

1. Return to GameSalad Creator. Click the Media tab in the Library panel and click the plus (+) button to import your Star.png file. Switch to the Actors tab in the Library panel and select your Star actor. In the Actor tab of the Attributes panel, go to Image and select Star from the drop-down options. Then go to the Size attributes and change both the Width and Height settings to 35 pixels. Of course, you could have saved your star image to 35 × 35 before importing it, as well. I prefer working with images larger than what I need, but not too large to foster memory loss. If you are concerned about output lag, you may want to be more frugal about resource file size and quality. Now,

your Star actor is ready! Drag and drop three instances of it into your Main scene. Place them in the bottom left, middle, and right corners, as shown in Figure 6.5.

Figure 6.5
Place instances of your Star actor in the Main scene.
Source: The GameSalad Creator, © 2013 GameSalad®, Inc. All Rights Reserved.

2. Select the Star prototype actor and go to the Backstage area to set up its rules and behaviors. Create a new rule named Pick Up Star. You want the Star to check for a collision; the actor you want the Star to check for a collision will be the Player actor. In the "do" area, add a Change Attribute behavior. Search for the new attribute you created (choose Attributes > Game > Stars). For the expression, you want it to say game.Stars +1, so that when the Player actor touches a Star actor, the system adds +1 to the current Stars counter.

3. Add a Destroy behavior directly after the Change Attribute one. Otherwise, when the player touches the star, it will not go away. It will just sit there, allowing the player to hit it as many times as he wants, getting more stars each time. The Destroy behavior removes the current instance of the star after the player has touched it. See Figure 6.6.

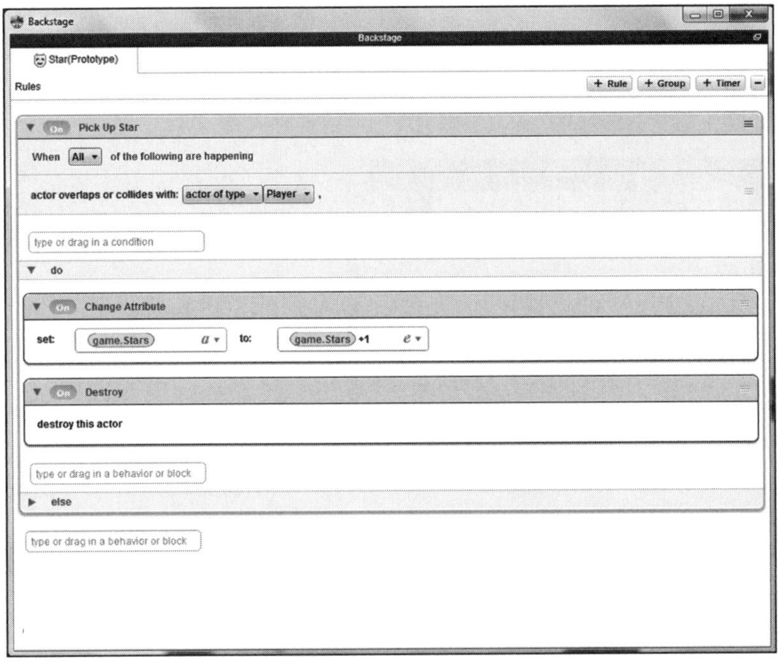

Figure 6.6
Behaviors of the Star actor.
Source: The GameSalad Creator, © 2013 GameSalad®, Inc. All Rights Reserved.

4. Add another actor to your game. Call this one Star Display. This will be a visual counter, so the player can see how many stars he has collected so far. Go to the actor's attributes and expand the Color attributes. Set Alpha to 0, so the background will be transparent. Then expand the Physics attributes and turn all of them off. (You do not need the game engine keeping track of physics for a text display object such as this one.)

5. With the Star Display actor still selected, go the Backstage area and add a Display Text behavior. In the input box for the display, enter the following: `"Stars:" + game.Stars` (see Figure 6.7). This means this text box will show the current number of stars collected. Set the style of text to Verdana, size 24, and left justified. Pick a color close to the one you used for your star's outline. Mine is an orange-ish shade of yellow.

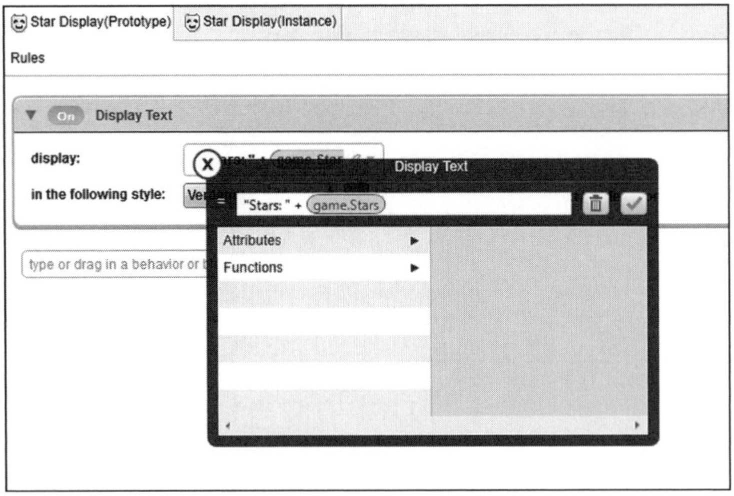

Figure 6.7
The correct expression for the Display Text behavior.
Source: The GameSalad Creator, © 2013 GameSalad®, Inc. All Rights Reserved.

6. Drag and drop an instance of the Star Display actor into your Main scene. Move it up near the top-right corner of the scene. Preview your game to check for placement and that your displayed expression is the correct one. If you do not like the position of your text block, you can always return to the editor and move it until you are satisfied. In your preview, move Freaky over the Star actors you placed in your scene. The Star actors should disappear and the Stars Display actor should increment +1 each time a Star actor is picked up (see Figure 6.8). If not, there might be something wrong with your behaviors, and you should go back to the editor and proofread them carefully.

Figure 6.8
The counter keeps track of how many Star actors the Player actor picks up.
Source: The GameSalad Creator, © 2013 GameSalad®, Inc. All Rights Reserved.

Designing a Door

Now to create a door. Again, I will use Sumopaint, but you can use whatever image-editing app you choose. The instructions that follow are for Sumopaint.

1. In Sumopaint, create a blank canvas. Choose Image > Image Size and change the size to 100×200 pixels. Add a new layer above the Background layer and hide the Background layer by clicking the eyeball icon next to it. The Background layer is arbitrarily added by the program and filled with white, and you do not want the white to show.

2. Select the Brush tool from the Tools panel. In the options above, change the Flow setting to 100% and the Diameter setting to 5 pixels. Click the drop-down arrow next to Brush and choose the Circle brush type from the options that appear. Select the Ink checkbox. On the stage, draw a line across the bottom and then an arched door above, being sure to touch the top and side edges. See Figure 6.9.

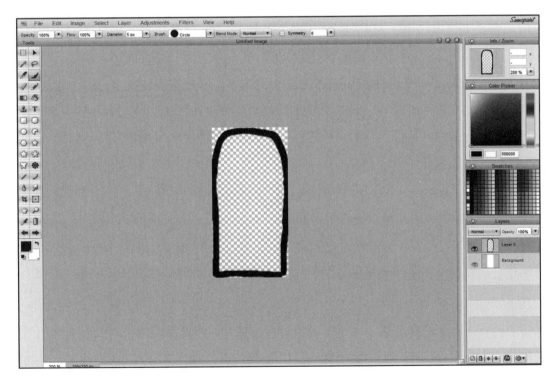

Figure 6.9
Draw an outline of a door that fills your canvas.
Source: Sumopaint, © 2013 Sumoing Ltd.® All Rights Reserved.

3. Change your Brush tool's Diameter setting to 2 pixels and draw a circle on your door for the doorknob. Then click the Paint Bucket button in the Tools panel. Set the Tolerance option (in the options above) to 50%, select a brown color from the Swatches or Color Picker panels, and click inside the door to color it brown. Next, select a gray color and fill the inside of the doorknob.

4. Add a new layer above this one in the Layers panel. Click the Star tool in the Tools panel and draw a smaller version of the star you made earlier. After drawing it, use the Free Transform/Rotate tool to rotate it until it stands upright. Then select the Lasso tool and drag a large circular border around the star, encapsulating the entire star with it. When you let go of the mouse button, the star will be selected. Press Ctrl+C (PC) or Command+C (Mac) to copy the star and press Ctrl+V (PC) or Command+V (Mac) to paste it. It will paste over itself in the exact same location it was in before, so you might not see it readily; if you look in the Layers panel, however, you will see that Sumopaint automatically generated a new layer for you with a second star image in it. Use the Move tool to place this second star beside the other. Paste again to create a third star, and move it to the opposite side of the first, so the stars are arranged in a pyramid. See Figure 6.10.

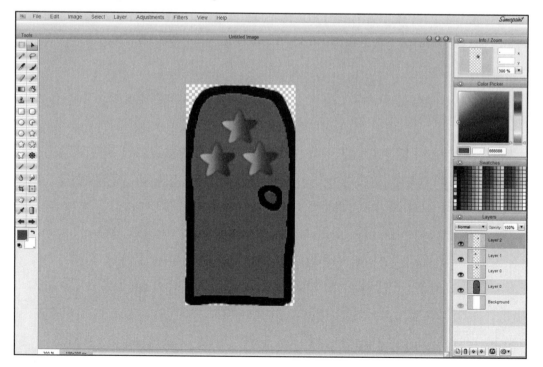

Figure 6.10
The finished door.

5. Save your image to your game project's Images folder. Name the image Exit.png. Before leaving Sumopaint, choose Adjustments > Brightness/Contrast and drag the slider to the left, all the way to 0, for Brightness. This turns the door completely black. Save a copy of this image as ExitOpen.png in the same folder as the other.

Making the Door Functional

Once you have images to serve as the door as it appears closed and open, you are ready to set it up in GameSalad to act like a door.

1. Return to GameSalad Creator and import both Exit.png and ExitOpen.png. Create a new actor and name it Exit. Attach the Exit.png file as the image for the Exit actor. In the Physics attributes for the Exit actor, deselect the Movable checkbox. Drag and drop an instance of the Exit actor into the Main scene, positioning it on a topmost platform in the upper-right area. Make sure it appears to touch the top of the platform, and that there is not a gap between the two. Right-click it and choose Send to Back from the menu that appears.

2. Go to the prototype Exit actor's rules and behaviors, of which you have none yet. Add a new rule that checks to see if the game's attribute Stars equals 3 or greater. If so, you want it to perform a Change Image behavior and select the ExitOpen image you imported. Your rule should look like Figure 6.11. This will turn the door completely black if the player gets three or more Star actors.

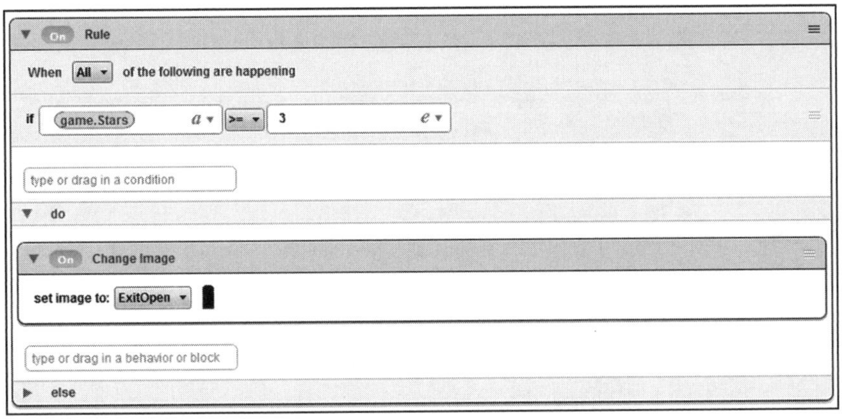

Figure 6.11
The Exit actor's behaviors.

Source: The GameSalad Creator, © 2013 GameSalad®, Inc. All Rights Reserved.

3. Rename that rule Open Door. Then add a new rule and name it Next Scene. In this rule, you want two conditions to be valid. The first condition will be if the game's attribute Stars equals 3 or greater. The second condition is if there is a collision with the Player actor. In the "do" area, set a Change Scene behavior that takes the player to Next Scene.

4. Go to the Scenes tab in the Library panel. While pressing the Alt key (PC) or Option key (Mac), drag and drop a duplicate of the Main scene between Main and Pause. Rename this copy Level 2. As Level 2 is right after Main in the Scenes list, it will be the next scene loaded based on the Change Scene behavior of the Exit actor. You can use the Exit actor repeatedly, because the Next Scene renders whatever the next scene is in order each time.

5. Of course, when the player is taken to Level 2, he or she starts with three Star actors. To modify this, place a Change Attribute behavior before the Change Scene behavior and have the Change Attribute behavior change the game attribute Stars back to 0. You can see the final behaviors for the Exit actor in Figure 6.12.

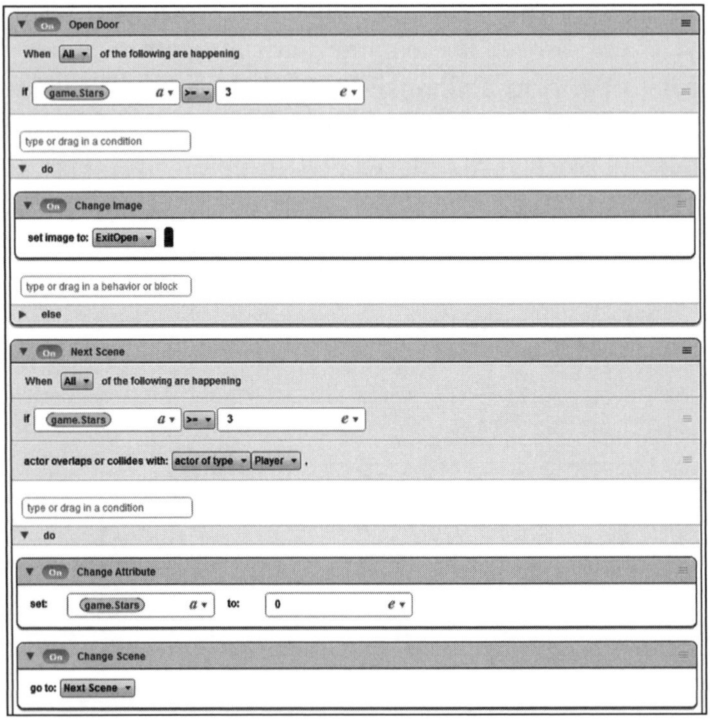

Figure 6.12
The Exit actor's finished behaviors.
Source: The GameSalad Creator, © 2013 GameSalad®, Inc. All Rights Reserved.

CREATING OBSTACLES

Now that the player is motivated, you need to put something that stands in his or her way. You do not want to outright thwart the player or frustrate him or her into quitting. You just want to provide more entertainment by increasing the challenge the player faces.

Pit Spikes

The first obstacle in the player's path includes pit spikes, the kind where one wrong touch can mean end game for the player. You do not want to actually kill the player, but to reset the current scene upon impact. That way, the player will have to redo the scene until he or she avoids the pit spikes. Follow these steps:

1. In Sumopaint (or the image-editing program of your choice), draw an image of four short gray triangles (like the ones in Figure 6.13) that is 100×50 pixels. Save your image in your game project's Images folder as Spikes.png with a transparent background.

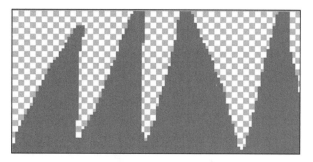

Figure 6.13
An example of pit spikes.
Source: Sumopaint, © 2013 Sumoing Ltd.® All Rights Reserved.

2. Return to GameSalad Creator and import the Spikes.png file into the Media tab of the Library panel. Switch to the Actors tab and add a new actor. Call this actor Spikes, and set the Spikes.png image as the image for the actor. Make sure the Spikes actor's size is 100×50 pixels and that the Movable checkbox is deselected.

3. Now it is time to set up the collision between the Spikes actor and the Player actor. Select the Player actor from the Actors list in the Library panel; then go to the Backstage area, to its growing list of rules and behaviors. Type Collide and select that option when it appears. Move this new Collide

command up beneath the other one. Change the Actor Overlaps or Collides With setting to Actor of Type > Spikes. Now, when the Player actor hits the Spikes actor, it will bounce off them. With the Bounciness setting in place, the Player actor will not only hit the Spikes actor, but also appear to rebound off them, which is even more believable!

4. Still within the Player actor's behaviors, add a rule and name it Hit Spikes. Set the condition to check for collision with Spikes. In the "do" section, type `Interpolate` and select that option when it appears. For the attribute to interpolate, find Attributes > Player > Color > Red, and the expression to interpolate it to should be 180 over 0.5 seconds. This turns the Player actor red in half a second.

5. Add a timer and drag it up beneath the Interpolate behavior. Set your timer to run for 0.5 seconds and select the Run to Completion checkbox. Then input a Reset Scene behavior. Now, after half a second (the same amount of time it takes the Player actor to turn red), the scene will reset. Your finished Hit Spikes rule should look similar to Figure 6.14.

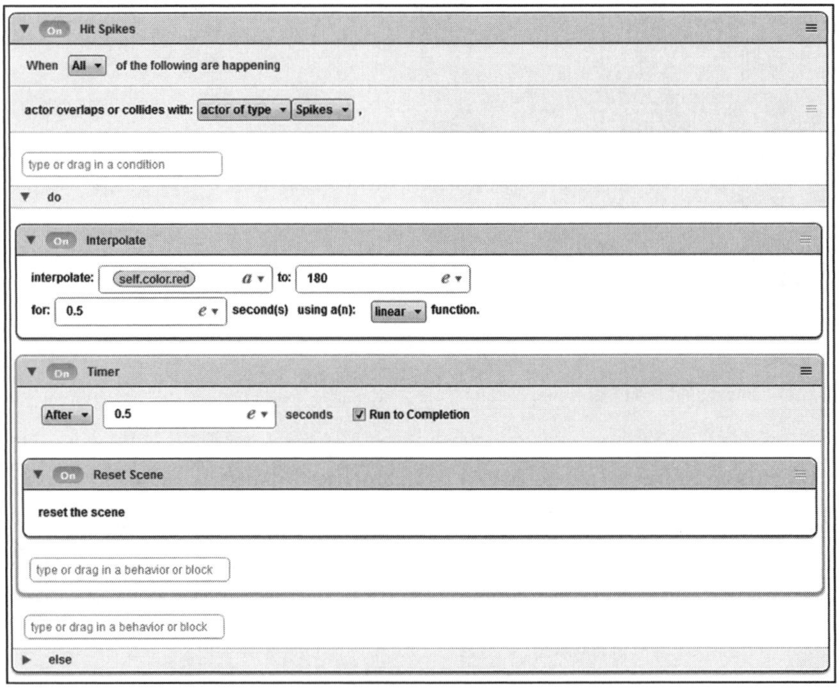

Figure 6.14
The finished Hit Spikes rule for the Player actor.
Source: The GameSalad Creator, © 2013 GameSalad®, Inc. All Rights Reserved.

6. To test the Spikes actor, select the Level 2 scene in the Scenes list of the Library panel and, within that scene, rearrange your Platform instances to look like Figure 6.15. Place a row of Spikes actors, one beside the other, at the bottom. Right-click each one and choose Send to Back so they will appear to disappear behind the brick floor. Preview your game. When you get to Level 2, walk Freaky right off a platform so he hits the spikes, observing what happens to him when he does. Then, jump the platforms to seize the stars and sling wide the door. Of course, the next scene the exit teleports you to will be the Pause scene.

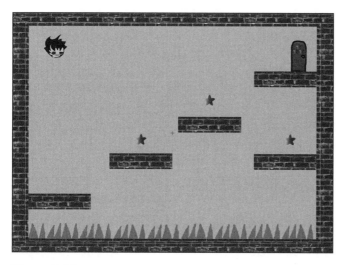

Figure 6.15
Rearrange your Level 2 scene like so.
Source: The GameSalad Creator, © 2013 GameSalad®, Inc. All Rights Reserved.

Monsters

You can make monsters similar to the way you made pit spikes. Instead of being immovable, however, monsters creep all around the place, and it is their motion that makes them tougher and less predictable.

1. On the companion site for this book, you will find another image in the data files where you found Freaky. This one is ghost.png, which you can see in Figure 6.16. Copy the ghost.png file to your game project's Images folder and import it into your current project through the Media tab of the Library panel. Alternatively, you could use an image-editing program to draw your own monster to use instead.

Figure 6.16
The ghost.png image.
Source: The GameSalad Creator, © 2013 GameSalad®, Inc. All Rights Reserved.

2. Create a new actor named Monster. Attach the ghost image to your Monster actor as its visual representation. In the Attributes panel, set its size to 50×50 pixels and its Alpha to 0.75 (to make it slightly transparent, like a ghost would be). With the Monster actor selected, go to the Backstage area to set up some basic behaviors.

3. First, you want to make the Monster actor patrol an area. That means you want it to move back and forth, as if searching for prey. You can do this by hard-coding specific X and Y coordinates you want the Monster to traverse. To begin, insert a new timer (by clicking the Add Timer button in the Backstage panel). Set this new timer to run every 0.5 seconds. Inside the timer, add a Move To command that tells the Monster actor to move to 585×422 relative to the scene at a speed of 75 pixels and select the Run to Completion checkbox. Duplicate this Move To command, but set the coordinates to 730×422. This will make the Monster actor move back and forth between 585 X and 730 X, just above the Platform actor you placed at 654.5×366 in a duplicate of the Main scene you rename Level 3. In the Scenes list in the Library panel, make sure your Level 3 comes after Level 2 and before Pause.

4. Preview your Level 3 scene. During the preview, click the thumbnail image for Level 3 beneath your preview area to go directly to that scene. This is a shortcut for navigating between scenes while previewing. You should see your ghost drift back and forth in your scene. Currently, it will not harm the player if Freaky touches it.

5. Return to the editor. If you left the behavior as is, you would have to set up a separate timer for each instance of the Monster actor that you want in your level. An easier approach is, well, to cheat. In the Backstage area, in your timer,

edit the Move To commands. Set the first one to -75×0 and the second one to $+75 \times 0$, with both of them to be relative to actor, not relative to scene. Preview again and you will see the ghost flit back and forth in a straight line, in a somewhat random pattern. He may cross over the brick walls, but since he is a ghost, this is acceptable. Now you can make as many instances of the Monster actor you like without having to edit each instance, and the ghost will still patrol.

6. Select the Player actor from the Actors tab in the Library panel and go to the Backstage area. Duplicate the Hit Spikes command, calling this duplicate Hit Monster. Set the object of collision for this rule to be Monster. Preview your game. Now, as shown in Figure 6.17, whenever Freaky touches the Monster actor in-game, he will turn red and the scene will reset itself.

7. Save your platformer project.

Figure 6.17
Freaky tagged by a ghost.
Source: The GameSalad Creator, © 2013 GameSalad®, Inc. All Rights Reserved.

SOUND EFFECTS

Your game is really coming together. However, you are missing one key component that will be a glaring fault if you were to forget about it: the aural experience. Humans can perceive auditory signals from many different directions at once and separate the sounds based on where they come from. Sound forms at least a full fifth of the way we perceive our environment, and we innately use sound as a means of survival. Being capable of telling when a noisy ambush predator like a cougar snuck up behind our ancestors helped our ancestors stay alive. Today, we use sound to listen to the latest pop hits on our MP3 players.

Sound makes everything come alive. It stamps the heartbeat for our culture and provides us with an aural experience. It can support the story of a game and shape the soundtrack. Try playing a video game with the TV or computer speakers on mute. Watch a YouTube video without headphones or a speaker, and realize just how disappointing the experience quickly becomes. In this section, you are going to look at how you use sound in GameSalad Creator.

Artificial Sound

You may not realize it, but most film and TV sound for your entertainment pleasure does not come from the original recorded sound. Sounds you hear in cinema are rarely accurate representations of real sounds. Instead, engineers construct the sound in post-production, utilizing many pieces of sound they mix together in software programs to create a seamless whole. These professionals often take separate pieces from sound-effects libraries and from custom recordings done in studios, what's called *Foley sound*. Foley artists record custom sound effects that emphasize sounds that *should* be heard in context. For instance, a Foley artist might shake a sheet of metal to simulate thunder or squash melons to represent a character getting squished by a falling anvil. When creating a game, every piece of sound has to be manipulated by the game programmer. The piece of sound used can be hyper-real, placing emphasis that subtly influences the game's players.

Sound Licensing

You probably already know this, but you can get in trouble for using music or sound effects intended for private home use in a for-profit production, even if it is a video game. If you pay special attention when watching a movie, there is usually a message warning that comes up at the beginning, noting that "unauthorized duplication or presentation, even without monetary gain" is punishable by law. That means even though you might be legit and not intending to make any money, even if you own an original copy of the product, or you are just making an unauthorized copy for your own personal use, you can still be fined or jailed.

For educational or private use, it might be okay to use an MP3 of your favorite band, be it One Direction or Paramore, but you won't be able to show it to anyone without special permission or a usage license from the artist. You can write to the band and tell them what the music is for and ask if it would okay to use it; if you get signed written permission from them, you are okay.

Gaining permissions has helped me countless times in the past, covering my rear, and I have often been amazed at how helpful other artists have been. For instance, when I started my first game, I contacted three rock bands to see if I could use their music in my game, and two out of the three eagerly agreed, sent me free CDs, and ultimately joined my group of close acquaintants! This shows it never hurts to try. Most often, however, artists have their lawyers draw up a single-user license and charge you a fee or percentage in royalties for using their creation.

Royalty-Free Sound Effects

On the other hand, you could use royalty-free music or sound effects. *Royalty-free* means that once you pay a set price for a CD or download, you're done paying for it and can use it in any productions you want to make.

Be sure, if you go this route, to carefully read your licensing agreement with the creators of the royalty-free tunes or sound effects, as there will occasionally be stipulations written into the fine print. For instance, some royalty-free providers want you to advertise or credit them in your finished product (which is fair, as they are still saving you money and time having to make all that stuff yourself).

Some popular sites you might look at that have royalty-free music or sound effects include the following:

- **deusX:** www.deusx.com/studio.html
- **Flash Kit:** www.flashkit.com
- **FlashSound.com:** www.flashsound.com
- **Looperman:** www.looperman.com
- **The Music Bakery:** www.musicbakery.com
- **Shockwave-Sound.com:** www.shockwave-sound.com
- **Sound-Ideas:** www.sound-ideas.com
- **Sound Rangers:** www.soundrangers.com

Sound Effects in GameSalad Creator

There are lots of apps out there for sound recording and editing that you can use to make your sound effects for use in GameSalad Creator. Here are some of the more spectacular apps you should investigate:

- **Audacity:** http://audacity.sourceforge.net/
- **Audio Expert:** www.audioexpert.com/

- **ClubCreate:** http://remixer.clubcreate.com/v2/musiclab/launch.html
- **Musicshake:** http://eng.musicshake.com/create/
- **Soundation:** http://soundation.com/

There are some sounds included on this book's companion website that you can use for the following exercise. Download them now and add them to your game project's Sounds folder.

1. In GameSalad Creator, click the Media tab in the Library panel and import the sounds you downloaded from the companion website for this book: bounce.ogg, door_open.ogg, ghostLaugh.ogg, ow.ogg, teleport.ogg, and win.ogg (see Figure 6.18).

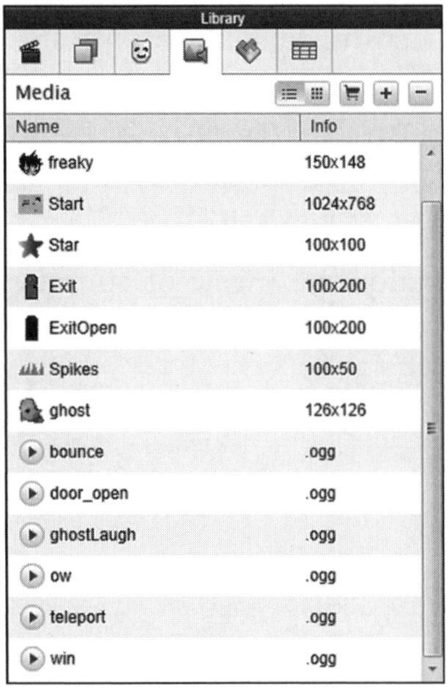

Figure 6.18
Import the sound files.
Source: The GameSalad Creator, © 2013 GameSalad®, Inc. All Rights Reserved.

2. Select the Player actor in the Actors tab in the Library panel; then go to the Backstage area to edit its rules and behaviors. Scroll down until you find the Jump rule and expand it (if necessary) to see the actions within the "do" section. Add a new behavior immediately after the final Change Attribute behavior. Type Play Sound and select that option when it appears. Then select the bounce.ogg sound from the drop-down list. Make sure the Run to Completion and Velocity Shift checkboxes are selected. See Figure 6.19.

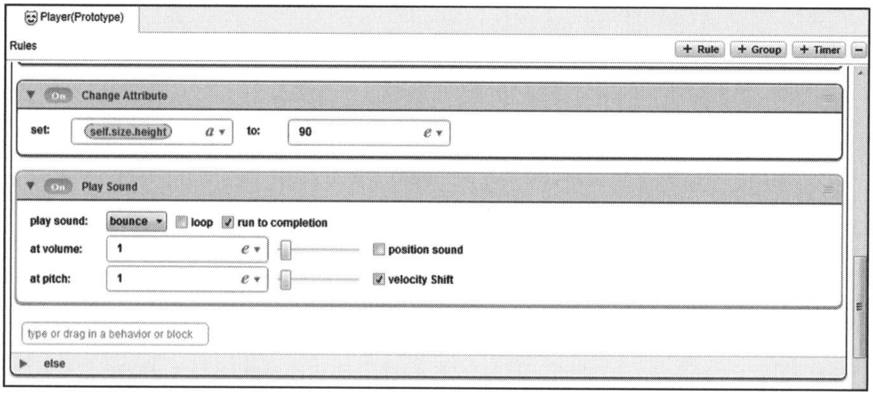

Figure 6.19
Insert a Play Sound behavior.
Source: The GameSalad Creator, © 2013 GameSalad®, Inc. All Rights Reserved.

3. Preview your game. When you jump, Freaky will utter a comical spring noise. If it is too loud, you can return to the editor and lower the volume and/or pitch of the sound played.

4. Go to the "do" section of the Hit Spikes rule and add a Play Sound behavior that plays the ow.wav sound. Add another Play Sound behavior to the "do" section of the Hit Monster rule and have it play the ghostLaugh.ogg sound.

5. Select the Exit actor in the Actors tab in the Library panel and go to the Backstage area to edit its rules and behaviors. In the Open Door rule, immediately after the Change Image action in the "do" area, add a Play Sound behavior that plays door_open.ogg. In the Next Scene rule, add a Play Sound behavior between the Change Attribute and Change Scene behaviors in the "do" section. Have this Play Sound behavior play the teleport.ogg sound.

6. Last but not least, go the Star (prototype) and edit the Pick Up Star rule so that, in its "do" area, you have a Play Sound behavior between the Change Attribute and Destroy behaviors. This Play Sound behavior should play win.ogg.

7. Save your game project and preview it. Your game is no longer one long, quiet affair, is it? You might want to bounce around, pick up stars, and open the door in the Main scene so you can hear those three sounds, and then fall on the spikes a couple times to hear that noise. Finally, meet up with the Monster actor in Level 3 and hear him laugh when he gets you.

There is another behavior, Play Music, that enables you to play a song. You can loop it so it plays repeatedly during the course of the game. I will let you have fun with that on your own.

CHAPTER 7

TOSSING AN ADVENTURE GAMESALAD

This chapter shows you how to use GameSalad Creator to design a fun adventure game. All you need to know how to construct your own adventure games can be found herein.

WHAT IS AN ADVENTURE GAME?

An adventure game, by broad definition, is any video game in which the player assumes the role of a hero in an interactive story. Adventure games are driven by exploring environments and solving puzzles instead of physical or reflex-based challenges. This sets an adventure game apart from action games. The genre's heavy focus on story enables it to draw from other narrative-based media such as written fiction and popular film, thus encompassing a huge variety of genres and styles.

Note

The genre title "adventure game" comes from the 1970s computer game *Adventure*, which pioneered the style of gameplay that has been widely imitated ever since. Since the game industry refers to its genre definitions based on gameplay and not the subject material, as the literary genre does, adventure games were called so because they were similar to the game *Adventure*.

Combat and action challenges are limited or totally absent from adventure games. Instead, the main elements of an adventure game include storytelling, exploration, and puzzle solving. Adventure games have often been described as puzzles embedded in a narrative framework. In other words, in an adventure game, the story plot is unlocked piece by piece, just like a puzzle coming together.

In the book *Andrew Rollings and Ernest Adams on Game Design*, the authors state that "this [loss of combat action] doesn't mean that there is no conflict in adventure games…only that combat is not the primary activity." You might be wondering, how can conflict exist without combat? The answer is easy. Conflict can arise through dramatic tension. If you have ever watched a movie and have been on the edge of your seat, eager to see what happens next, then you have felt that tension. This translates well into video games, including adventure games.

Nearly all adventure games are designed for a single player, not to be played online through cooperative (co-op) or competitive (player-versus-player, or PvP) play. This is because the hefty concentration on narrative and character portrayal makes a multiplayer format tough to design.

Adventure Games in America and Japan

In America, the adventure-game genre's popularity peaked around the late 1980s or the early 1990s, although it has persisted as a niche market with a steady following even today. However, in Asia—especially Japan—adventure games continue to be very popular. In Japan, they make up approximately 70 percent of all PC games sold. The majority of these adventure games are visual novels.

A visual novel is an adventure game featuring mostly static graphics, usually with animé-style art. As the name suggests, they resemble mixed-media novels or interactive stage plays. They are rarely produced for video game consoles and are usually distributed online or for PC users.

Japanese adventure games like these are driven by narrative, focusing almost exclusively on character interaction in a structure similar to a *Choose Your Own Adventure* story. Visual novels in that country frequently feature romantic storylines in which the main character may end up with one of several possible mates. Some of them, called crying games, attempt to make the player feel so strongly for the characters that they cry due to emotional scenes. These games often begin with a comedic first half, feature a heart-warming middle followed by tragedy, and end with an emotional reunion.

After completing his stealth game *Metal Gear*, Hideo Kojima released his first visual story in 1988. It was titled *Snatcher* and was an ambitious cyberpunk detective novel graphic adventure that was highly regarded at the time for pushing the boundaries of video game storytelling. It featured a post-apocalyptic science-fiction setting, an amnesiac protagonist, and some cinematic cut scenes with voice acting comparable to a film or radio drama. *Snatcher* was for a long time the only major visual novel game to be released in America, where it, despite its mature rating limiting accessibility, gained quite a cult following. Another acclaimed visual novel is Key's *Clannad* (2005), with a story revolving around the central theme of the importance of family.

SCUMM Games

In 1987, programmers Ron Gilbert and Aric Wilmunder, working for Lucasfilm Games (later LucasArts), developed SCUMM, which stands for Script Creation Utility for *Maniac Mansion*. It was a scripting language to make the development of the graphical adventure game *Maniac Mansion* easier to advance. Before SCUMM, most adventure games, including the popular *Zork*, required players to type command words to progress through the game.

For instance, if players found an woodcutter's axe leaning against a tree in a forest, they had to type "PICK UP AXE" to pick up the axe and add it to their inventory. If they later discovered an evil troll guarding a bridge, they had to type "USE AXE ON TROLL" to attack the troll with the axe. The adventure game's syntax analyzer had to determine whether the words the player used were the correct ones to execute an action. When the analyzer failed, or the player misspelled a word (which happened more often than not), the game came to a standstill.

SCUMM offered players a point-and-click interface instead. Instead of having to type in words, players could now click on text icons. To interact with the environment, a player could click an order, click an icon representing an inventory object, or click part of the scene or image.

SCUMM was first used for the game *Maniac Mansion*, but it would be used to great effect over several more games that followed it, including *Zak McKracken and the Alien Mindbenders* (1988), *The Secret of Monkey Island* (1990), *Day of the Tentacle* (1993), *Sam & Max Hit the Road* (1995), and *Full Throttle* (1995).

In 1998, the SCUMM style of adventure games would be replaced with a more first- or third-person shooter camera style in LucasArts' game *Grim Fandango*. After that, attempts at developing 3D games led to LucasArts abandoning SCUMM for good. Also, by the mid-1990s, the popularity of adventure games in America had begun to flounder as action arcade games picked up.

Later adventure games built in the SCUMM style, such as *Full Throttle*, replaced the text icons with universal symbol icons. Interactive options within the player's graphic menu often featured a fist for "use," "pick up," or "hit"; eyes for "look at" or "examine"; a mouth or tongue for "speak," "talk to," or "taste"; and a boot or shoe for "kick," "walk," or "run." After the menu appeared, the player selected one of these icons for the desired interaction.

Hidden-Puzzle Games

Another sub-genre of the adventure game is the hidden-puzzle game, which offers more obvious puzzles in lieu of stronger storylines. These games often include multiple scenes in which specific objects are hidden among other objects; the only way the player can progress is to find and click the objects they need without clicking anywhere else. Sometimes, a timer accompanies these hidden-objects scenarios. After the player completes a mini-game like this, a new item is added to his or her character's inventory to open another area in the game.

Like a salad, a hidden-puzzle game can be heavy on a single ingredient, such as more character development or better-looking settings, or it can have more exploration and graphic interaction menus akin to SCUMM games. However, it comes together, the main ingredient is always the hidden-object scenes.

The Future of Adventure Games

Some of the more recent adventure games feature 3D third-person character controls, such as those in Konami's *Shadows of Memories* (2001), Irem's *Disaster Report* (2002), and Quantum Dream's *Omikron: Nomad Soul* (1991), *Fahrenheit: Indigo Prophecy* (2005), and *Heavy Rain* (2010). Meanwhile, Frictional Games went another route, with first-person character controls, which you can witness in its *Penumbra* series (2007–2008) and *Amnesia: The Dark Descent* (2010).

LucasArts and Telltale Games worked together to release five episodic adventure games between July and December 2009 under the title *Tales of Monkey Island*, featuring characters and settings popularized by the original *The Secret of Monkey Island*. Telltale Games went on to produce a more commercially successful game called *Back to the Future: The Game*. That game's success helped springboard an even cleverer project, the adventure game adaptation of *The Walking Dead* television series.

Telltale's *The Walking Dead* focused more on story and characters than puzzles and inventory, and was a huge critical success for both the studio and adventure games in general. The zombie-crawling video game was named one of the best games of 2012 from several outlets and won numerous awards, including those from the Game Developers Choice Awards, the Spike Video Game Awards, and the DICE Interactive Achievement Awards. Ron Gilbert, co-creator of SCUMM, noted that *The Walking Dead*'s approach to appeal to the mass market could make adventure games as relevant as any other genre to larger publishers.

Double Fine Productions was created by Tim Schafer shortly after his departure from LucasArts, and most of his development team included former LucasArts adventure game programmers. Double Fine's first two games, *Psychonauts* and *Brutal Legend*, were praised critically by game journalists but were not considered financial successes for the game company.

Double Fine ran a Kickstarter campaign in early 2012 to develop a new adventure game, tentatively titled *Double Fine Adventure* and now officially named *Broken Age*. Schafer had seen the Kickstarter model as ideal for pitching a new adventure title directly to those who would buy it, as he found that publishers refused to consider the idea of publishing adventure games at that time. Double Fine set a modest goal of $300,000 to $400,000 to develop the game with a budget comparable to most mobile games, and the remainder for a documentary of the development created by 2 Player Productions.

Note

Kickstarter (www.kickstarter.com) is an American-based, private, for-profit company that provides tools to raise funds for all sorts of creative projects via the crowd-funding model. It is online or website based. Crowd funding describes the collective efforts of many individuals who network and pool together their money via the Internet to support efforts initiated by other people. Kickstarter includes fundraising for a diverse assortment of creative endeavors, including indie films, music albums, video games, and food products. People who back projects are rewarded with such things as a personal note of thanks, customized T-shirts, dinner with the designer, or an initial production run of the new product.

The initial funding amount was met within only a few hours going live, and the Kickstarter campaign ended with $3.45 million, far exceeding Double Fine's expectations. The company used additional funds to expand the platforms and languages available, to include professional voice acting, and for other improvements from their initial plans. The successful funding led other developers to explore the Kickstarter market to promote adventure games, including a successful fundraising for a high-definition remake of *Leisure Suit Larry in the Land of the Lounge Lizards* and a new game in the *Tex Murphy* series.

THE ELEMENTS OF AN ADVENTURE GAME

Some of the main elements of adventure games are as follows:

- Puzzle solving
- Inventories
- Narrative
- Dialogue

Puzzle Solving

Adventure games contain a wide variety of puzzles. These can include decoding messages, finding and using items, opening locked doors, and/or finding and exploring new locations. Solving a puzzle often unlocks access to a new area of the game world and/or reveals more of the game story.

Some puzzles are criticized for the obscurity of their solutions, such as the combination of a clothesline, clamp, and deflated rubber duck used to gather an item in *The Longest Journey*, which exists outside the game's narrative and ends up frustrating most players. Frustration is not good. This is why running your game by some testers is crucial to make sure your game does not have any serious bottlenecks such as this.

The primary goal in adventure games is the completion of a quest the player character undertakes. Early adventure games had high scores and some, such as *Zork*, assigned the player a rank, or a description based on the player's score. High scores provided players a secondary goal and served as an indicator of progression. While high scores are less common, external award systems such as Xbox Live's achievements perform a similar role.

Inventories

Most adventure games make use of a simple inventory management screen as part of gameplay. By "simple," I mean the inventory screen does not offer complex interactions with the inventory items as a role-playing game (which has internal economies to manipulate) does.

Players can pick up only certain objects throughout the adventure game, so the player knows if an item can be picked up that it must be important. Because there is no way to count or track the number of important items to be picked up, players will often scour every single scene for items. This is ideal in some ways because it encourages further exploration, but it can frustrate some players who are more used to the faster pace of action gaming. Some adventure games try to prevent player frustration by highlighting items that can be picked up or by snapping the player's cursor to the item.

Most inventory items come in handy for solving puzzles in an adventure game. There is seldom any time pressure for such puzzles, targeting player reasoning rather than quick-thinking reflexes. Players must apply lateral-thinking techniques, where they apply real-world knowledge about how objects work. For example, a key might be stuck down a drain. If the player found a magnet earlier in the game, he or she might infer that the magnet, which attracts metal objects, could be used to pick up the key lost in the drain.

Occasionally, the inventory management might allow for a combination of multiple items to make a stronger or more desirable one—especially to help solve one of the puzzles. For example, the player could figure out that combining kerosene fuel with an empty lantern would result in a lit lamp, or that combining a bottle of spirits, an old rag, and a lighter would create a Molotov cocktail.

Narrative

Adventure games are notoriously single-player experiences that are story- or character-driven. More than any other game genre, adventure games depend on their narrative to create a compelling experience. They are typically set in a beautiful, immersive environment and try to vary the setting from area to area to add novelty and player interest.

Because adventure games focus so much on storytelling, character development usually follows literary conventions of personal/emotional growth rather than new skills or abilities that affect gameplay (as you would see in a role-playing game). The player character often embarks on a quest in a strange world or must unravel a mystery in a maze-like place. Story events unfold as the player completes challenges or puzzles.

Dialogue

Because adventure games focus so strongly on storytelling, a major component of storytelling is done through significant dialogue. Sometimes the game's designers will make effective use of recorded dialogue or narration by professional voice actors.

If done through text only, conversation trees represent the dialogue. Players can engage with non-player characters by choosing a line of pre-written dialogue from a menu of options. The player's choice triggers a response from the game character. These conversations are often designed as a branching tree, with players deciding between each branch of dialogue to pursue until they come to a conclusion. There is a finite number of branches to pursue because of the design limitations of the game.

Conversing with game characters can reveal clues about how to solve puzzles. It can also offer plot exposition—the portion of a story that introduces important background information to the audience such as events that have occurred before the main plot, character back stories, and information about the setting.

ADVENTURE GAME DEVELOPMENT

The following instructions will show you how to make a short adventure game. The artwork will be mostly stand-in for something fancier you can add in later.

The concepts shown here are more vital than the art; when you have the concepts down pat, you can build your own adventure games based on them.

Building a Scenario

You will have the player character pose as an android that has come "online," or awake, after months of being in suspended animation. The android exists aboard an interstellar space vessel. The computer guidance system is offline and needs repairs or else the spaceship will float aimlessly through the vacuum of space. This is the player's quest. After you impart this information, the player can explore parts of the space vessel and solve the puzzle to fix the guidance system.

For this game, you will create one character (named Yuki) the player dialogues with; Yuki will brief the player on what he or she needs to do. You will also create two rooms, each including four directions to look in, so that the player can explore. You will also need to design some objects the player can interact with and inventory items he or she can pick up. Rather than letting the player move directly from the first room to the second, you will place a locked door between the two. This means the player will have to find a key to unlock the door. Second, before the player can fix the computer guidance system and get the space vessel back on track, he or she will have to find a tool in order to make repairs. Therefore, the two inventory items needed for this game are a key (in the guise of an electronic pass card) and a tool to fix the computer guidance system.

1. Open GameSalad Creator. Create a new project by choosing File > New. For the title, type Basic Adventure. Make sure Platform is set to iPad Landscape and that the Resolution Independence option is selected. Click Create Project to create it.

2. Click the Scenes tab in the Library panel. Double-click the Initial Scene and type Start to rename it. Click the plus (+) icon to add the following new scenes.

   ■ Start

   ■ Room A

   ■ Room B

   ■ Room C

   ■ Room D

   ■ Lab A

   ■ Lab B

   ■ Lab C

- Lab D
- Inventory

Compare your Scenes tab to the one shown in Figure 7.1.

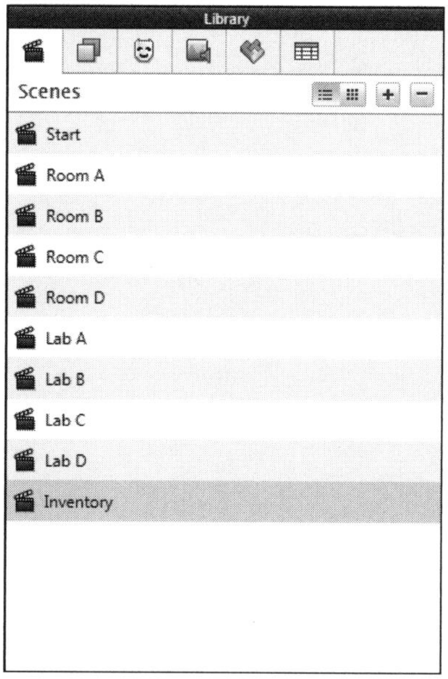

Figure 7.1
Create the scenes indicated.
Source: The GameSalad Creator, © 2013 GameSalad®, Inc. All Rights Reserved.

3. Click the Actors tab in the Library panel. Then click the plus (+) icon to add the following new actors.

- Start
- Room A
- Room B
- Room C
- Room D
- Lab A
- Lab B
- Lab C
- Lab D
- Inventory Frame

- Yuki

- Pass Card

- Panel

- Selection

- Screwdriver

- CGS

- Arrow

Compare your Actors tab to the one shown in Figure 7.2.

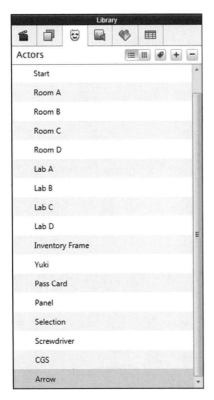

Figure 7.2
Create the actors indicated.

4. Save your Basic Adventure project by choosing File > Save As. Place it in the same general location as your other game projects, to keep them together. When you save, GameSalad will create a Basic Adventure subdirectory automatically. This subdirectory will include all your project files related to Basic Adventure, including Images and Sounds folders.

5. Open a Web browser and go to http://lovelymoro.web.fc2.com/moromagalabo .html. Shown in Figure 7.3, this is an excellent animé-style face generator. I cannot read Japanese. If you cannot read Japanese either, then working within the interface may be difficult—but it is not impossible. Google Chrome will automatically detect a page with a language that is not your native one and will offer to translate it for you. If you are not using Google Chrome, you can use Google translator

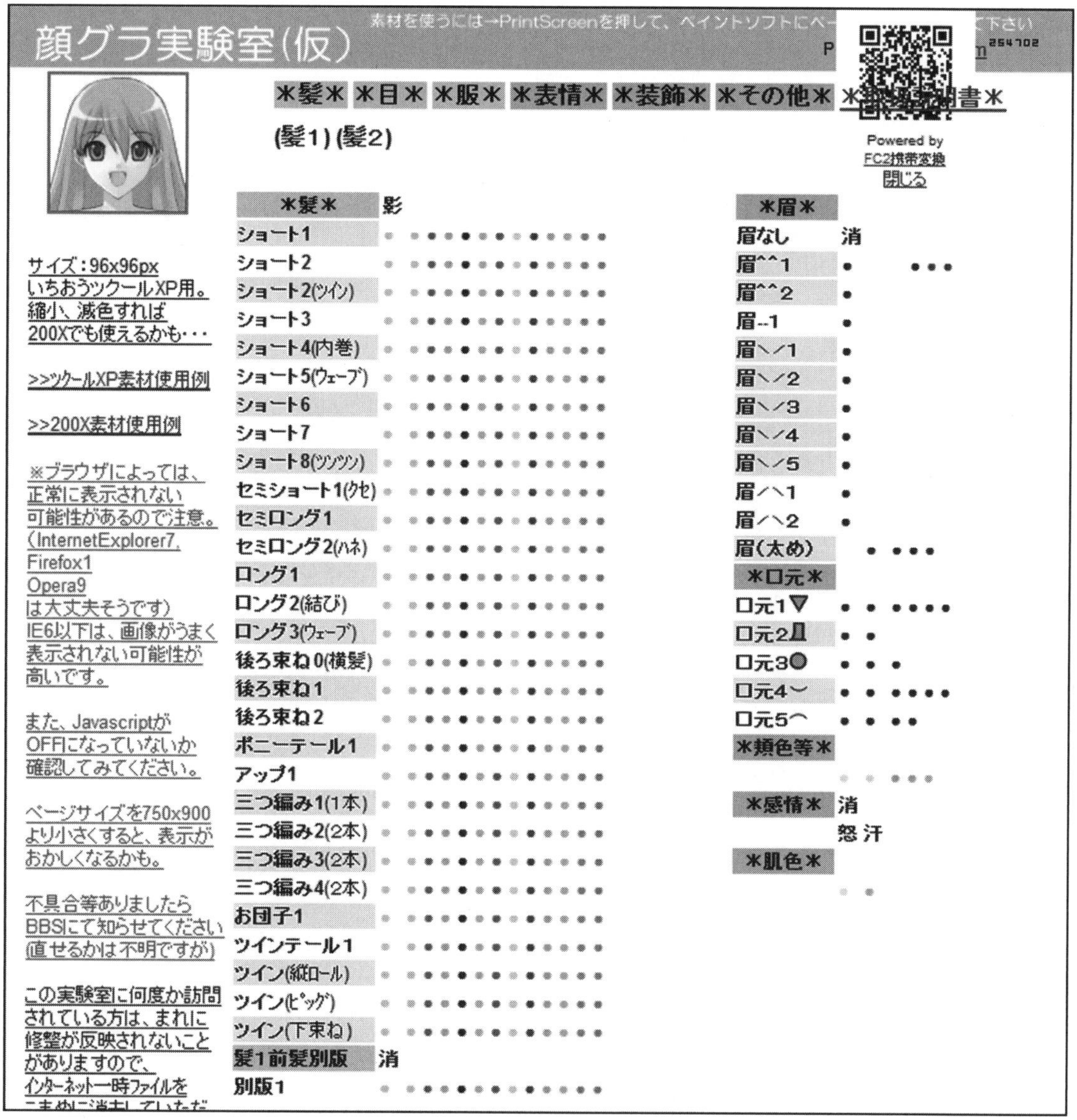

Figure 7.3
The Moromagalabo Face Generator.
Source: Moromagalabo Face Generator, © 2013 MOROMAGA. All Rights Reserved.

to translate the webpage. To do so, first type the following Web address in your Web browser's Address bar: www.translate.google.com/translate?sl=ja&tl=en& u=http%3A%2F%2Flovelymoro.web.fc2.com%2Fmoromagalabo.html. Unfortunately, using the Google translator will break the links, so changing the character's features will not work. If you have two tabs or windows open, you can instead choose to refer to the translated version of the site (see Figure 7.4) while working in the original site.

Figure 7.4
The Moromagalabo Face Generator in English.

Note

6. The tabs at the top can help you sort between hair, eyes, clothes, look, decorative accessories, and others. The displayed list of style options are what are available to pick from. Click a color dot to apply that style with that color tint used. Some styles do not have more than one color dot to choose from, often because there are no further color options. For the eyes, the numbers 1 through 14 are the styles, but you are able to choose each eye to look different. Each style has two blocks to it, the first being for the left eye and the second for the right eye.

7. Experiment within the Face Generator to create an agreeable (to you) face for the non-player character Yuki. Once you have a face you enjoy, you can export it by pressing the Print Screen key on your keyboard to copy your screen's display. Alternatively, if you have Windows OS version 7, you can use the Snipping tool (which you can find by choosing Start > All Programs > Accessories). After you have taken a screen capture of your 96×96 face, go into the image editor of your choice and paste it onto a new canvas. Then, crop the image so that only the square containing the face shows. This can take time and effort to perfect.

8. You will need two faces of the same character. One should have a smile and the other a frown. An example of each is shown in Figure 7.5. This is because you will show Yuki unhappy at first and then cheerier later, based entirely on parameters in-game.

Figure 7.5
Two versions of the completed Yuki face.
Source: The GameSalad Creator, © 2013 GameSalad®, Inc.
© Michael Duggan.

Tip

If you have trouble making your face in the Face Generator, you can use the ones made for this book. They are Yuki_01.png and Yuki_02.png, and can be found for download from the companion website at www.cengageptr.com/downloads.

9. There are four room actors and four lab actors. You will use them so the player can turn around in a complete circle and see all four walls of each room. Each wall will need an image designed in your image editor of preference. Each image should be the same resolution as your game's display size (in this case, 1,024×768 pixels) so it takes up the whole screen. That means you need to draw four walls. Each wall can be a scene unto itself, with furniture, decorations, and so forth. You can make your setting as elaborate or as modest as you like. For the purpose of this instruction, the walls can be simple constructs that you can replace later. The only requirements are that the wall for Room A will have a door and a video intercom beside it and the wall for Lab B will have a computer bank taking up most of it. The Figures 7.6 through 7.13 show examples of each. These graphics can be found in the resource materials for this book, if you would like to use them.

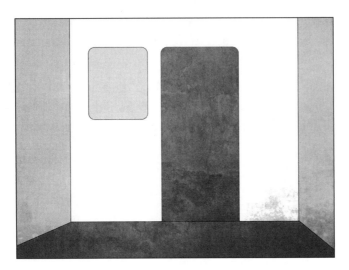

Figure 7.6
Room A.
Source: The GameSalad Creator, © 2013 GameSalad®, Inc.
© Michael Duggan.

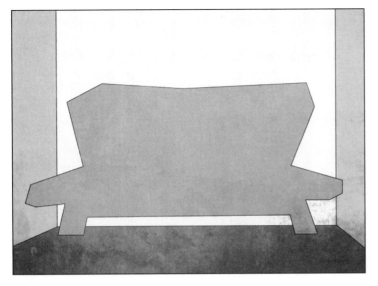

Figure 7.7
Room B.

Source: The GameSalad Creator, © 2013 GameSalad®, Inc.
© Michael Duggan.

Figure 7.8
Room C.

Source: The GameSalad Creator, © 2013 GameSalad®, Inc.
© Michael Duggan.

Figure 7.9
Room D.

Source: The GameSalad Creator, © 2013 GameSalad®, Inc.
© Michael Duggan.

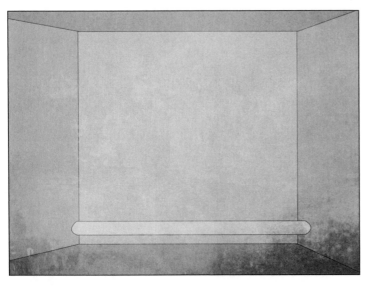

Figure 7.10
Lab A.

Source: The GameSalad Creator, © 2013 GameSalad®, Inc.
© Michael Duggan.

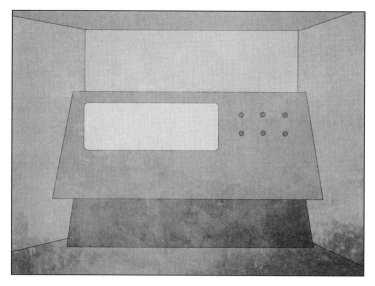

Figure 7.11
Lab B.

Source: The GameSalad Creator, © 2013 GameSalad®, Inc.
© Michael Duggan.

Figure 7.12
Lab C.

Source: The GameSalad Creator, © 2013 GameSalad®, Inc.
© Michael Duggan.

Figure 7.13
Lab D.

Source: The GameSalad Creator, © 2013 GameSalad®, Inc.
© Michael Duggan.

10. After you have the rooms designed, you have the interactive elements to draw. These include an arrow (for navigation), a pass card (an ID badge), a panel where the player can swipe the pass card to gain entry to the lab, a computer guidance system (a computer panel), a screwdriver, and a board with tools hanging on it. Figures 7.14 through 7.20 show each. Again, if you have difficulties drawing these items yourself in your preferred image editor, you can use the graphics found on the companion site.

Figure 7.14
Arrow.

Source: The GameSalad Creator, © 2013 GameSalad®, Inc.
© Michael Duggan.

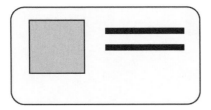

Figure 7.15
Pass card.

Source: The GameSalad Creator, © 2013 GameSalad®, Inc.
© Michael Duggan.

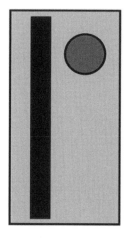

Figure 7.16
Access panel.

Source: The GameSalad Creator, © 2013 GameSalad®, Inc.
© Michael Duggan.

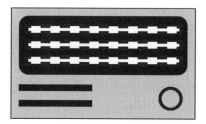

Figure 7.17
Computer guidance system.

Source: The GameSalad Creator, © 2013 GameSalad®, Inc.
© Michael Duggan.

Figure 7.18
Screwdriver.

Source: The GameSalad Creator, © 2013 GameSalad®, Inc.
© Michael Duggan.

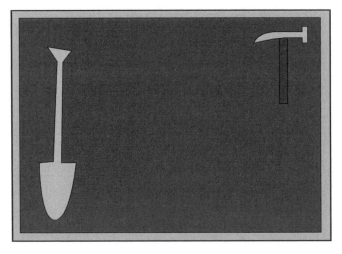

Figure 7.19
Tools.

Source: The GameSalad Creator, © 2013 GameSalad®, Inc.
© Michael Duggan.

11. The last graphic you have to draw is the inventory frame. This will overlay the current scene—whatever the current scene is—and will display the items the player has picked up so far. The graphic must be 1,024×768 to match the game's display size, with the middle cut out for alpha transparency. Figure 7.20 shows you one example, although you might want your inventory frame to be more decorative.

Figure 7.20
Inventory frame.

Source: The GameSalad Creator, © 2013 GameSalad®, Inc.
© Michael Duggan.

12. Return to the GameSalad Creator. Set your actors so they display the corresponding images. (See Table 7.1.)

Table 7.1   Actors and Their Corresponding Images

Actor	Image	Size
Arrow	arrowpng	142×80
CGS	CGSpng	130×80
InventoryFrame	inventorypng	1024×768
LabA	labApng	1024×768
LabB	labBpng	1024×768
LabC	labCpng	1024×768
LabD	labDpng	1024×768
Panel	accessPanelpng	35×95
PassCard	passCardpng	175×90
RoomA	roomApng	1024×768
RoomB	roomBpng	1024×768
RoomC	roomCpng	1024×768
RoomD	roomDpng	1024×768
Screwdriver	screwdriverpng	18×102
Selection	toolspng	305×220
Yuki	Yuki_01png	150×150

© Michael Duggan.

13. For the room and lab scenes, drag and drop each of the matching actors into the scene and edit its position to be 512×384, so the instance is centered to the scene. Do the same for the Inventory Frame actor in the Inventory scene.

14. In the scene Room A, drag and drop an instance of Yuki and position it in the video intercom panel (see Figure 7.21).

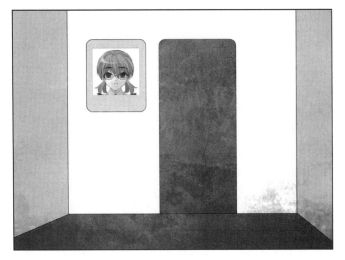

Figure 7.21
Add Yuki to Room A.

Source: The GameSalad Creator, © 2013 GameSalad®, Inc.
© Michael Duggan.

15. In the scene Room B, drag and drop an instance of Pass Card and position it beside the furniture. Resize the instance by clicking and dragging one of the corner anchors so it appears smaller in this scene, as you see in Figure 7.22.

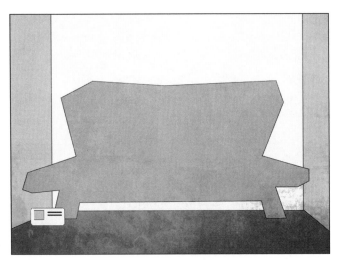

Figure 7.22
Add Pass Card to Room B.

Source: The GameSalad Creator, © 2013 GameSalad®, Inc.
© Michael Duggan.

16. In the scene Lab B, drag and drop an instance of CGS and position it on the computer bank somewhere, like in Figure 7.23.

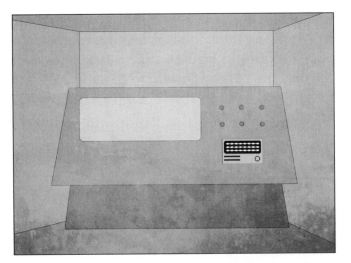

Figure 7.23
Add CGS to Lab B.

Source: The GameSalad Creator, © 2013 GameSalad®, Inc.
© Michael Duggan.

17. In the scene Lab C, drag and drop an instance of Selection. Hang it on the wall somewhere. Then, drag and drop an instance of Screwdriver. Position it over the top of Selection so it appears to be part of the rest of the tools, as you see in Figure 7.24.

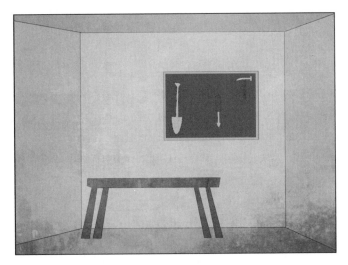

Figure 7.24
Add Selection and Screwdriver to Lab C.

Source: The GameSalad Creator, © 2013 GameSalad®, Inc.
© Michael Duggan.

18. Lastly, in scene Inventory, drag and drop instances of both the Pass Card and Screwdriver actors. Arrange them along the bottom panel of the Inventory Frame, below the cut-out area, as shown in Figure 7.25. You can move your cursor over one of the middle anchors of the Screwdriver instance. When your cursor becomes a circular arrow, you can drag and rotate the actor, which is what I did with the Screwdriver in Figure 7.25.

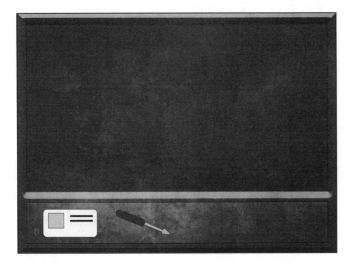

Figure 7.25
Add Pass Card and Screwdriver to Inventory.
Source: The GameSalad Creator, © 2013 GameSalad®, Inc.
© Michael Duggan.

Adding Navigation Controls

You have the basic scenes set up, but right now there is no way for the player to move between each room and lab area. You are going to use the Arrow actor multiple times, changing the behavior of the instances each time, to help the player navigate the setting.

1. In Room A, drag and drop two instances of the Arrow actor. Click the Actor tab in the Attributes panel and set the Position of one Arrow actor to 912×70 and

the other to 113×70. For the Arrow actor at 113×70, in the Attributes panel, set its Rotation to −180, which flips the arrow around horizontally. Compare your Room A to the one in Figure 7.26.

Figure 7.26
Add Arrow instances to Room A.
Source: The GameSalad Creator, © 2013 GameSalad®, Inc.
© Michael Duggan.

2. Select the Arrow actor at 113×70 (the left Arrow). Go to the Backstage panel. In the Arrow (Instance) tab, click the lock to unlock this instance so you can modify rules for the specific actor. Add a new rule by clicking the + Rule button. Set the first condition to Touch > Pressed and the second to Touch > Inside so the player has to click the arrow to enact this rule. For the behavior, set it to Change Scene and pick Room B as the target scene. (See Figure 7.27.)

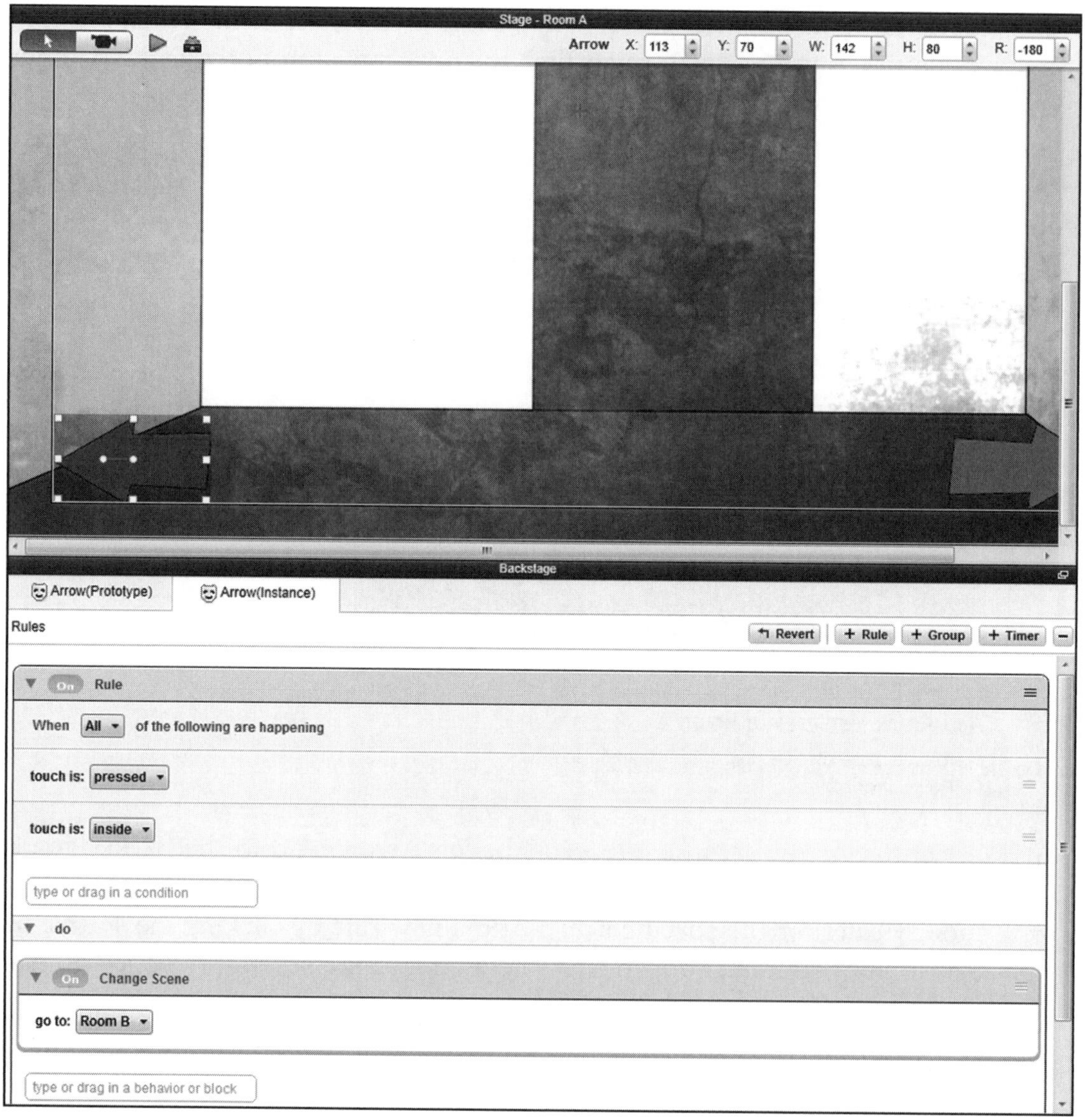

Figure 7.27
Set a rule on the Arrow actor that takes the player to another scene upon touch.
Source: The GameSalad Creator, © 2013 GameSalad®, Inc.
© Michael Duggan.

3. Select the other Arrow instance in Room A and unlock it. Add a rule similar to the preceding one, but have it point to Room D instead.

4. In the Library panel, click the Scenes tab and then click Room B. Add Arrow actors, both left and right, the same as you did for Room A. Have the left-pointing Arrow actor point to Room C and the right-pointing Arrow actor point to Room A. Go to Room C and set it so that a left-pointing Arrow actor points

to Room D and right-pointing Arrow actor point to Room B. Go to Room D and set it so that a left-pointing Arrow actor points to Room A and right-pointing Arrow actor points to Room C.

5. Save your project and preview it to test your Arrow actors. Start at Room A. The arrows should allow you to turn completely around, 360 degrees, going both left and right. If you find you cannot access a wall correctly, or the wrong wall comes up when you click an arrow, return to the Editor and fix the behaviors until you have them working splendidly.

6. Use the same technique for the walls in the lab. Start at Lab A and have a left-pointing Arrow actor that points to Lab B and a right-pointing Arrow actor pointing to Lab D. Go to Lab B and have a left-pointing Arrow actor that points to Lab C and a right-pointing Arrow actor pointing to Lab A. Go to Lab C and have a left-pointing Arrow actor that points to Lab D and a right-pointing Arrow actor pointing to Lab B. Go to Lab D and have a left-pointing Arrow actor pointing to Lab A and a right-pointing Arrow actor pointing to Lab C. Save your project and preview it again, this time starting at the Lab A scene and working your way around by clicking the arrows.

Inputting Player Interactions

The player does not know what is going on. In fact, you have a Start scene you have not developed. Also, the player cannot go between the room and the lab because there is a closed door in the way. To finish developing this adventure game, you will need to input the player interactions.

Rigging the Goal

First, convey the player's quest to him or her and provide dialogue from Yuki.

1. In the Editor, click the Actors tab in the Library panel. Create two new actors. Name the first one Title and the second one Instruction. Selecting each in turn, go to the Actor tab in the Attributes panel and set their Color attribute to R (Red) 0, G (Green) 0, B (Blue) 0, and A (Alpha) 0. This way, they are transparent actors.

2. Click the Scenes tab in the Library panel and select the Start scene. In the Scene tab of the Attributes panel, change the Color attribute to R 1, G 125, B 180, and A 255. This changes the Start scene's background color to a dark aquamarine blue.

3. Drag an instance of Title into the Start scene. Change its Position setting to X 512 and Y 600. In the Backstage panel, click the Title (Prototype) tab and

enter a Display Text behavior. Have it display the text "Basic Adventure" (minus the quotation marks) with a font style of Trebuchet MS, 72 point, centered. For the font color, set it to R 255, G 240, B 0, and A 255; you will get a bright yellow. See Figure 7.28.

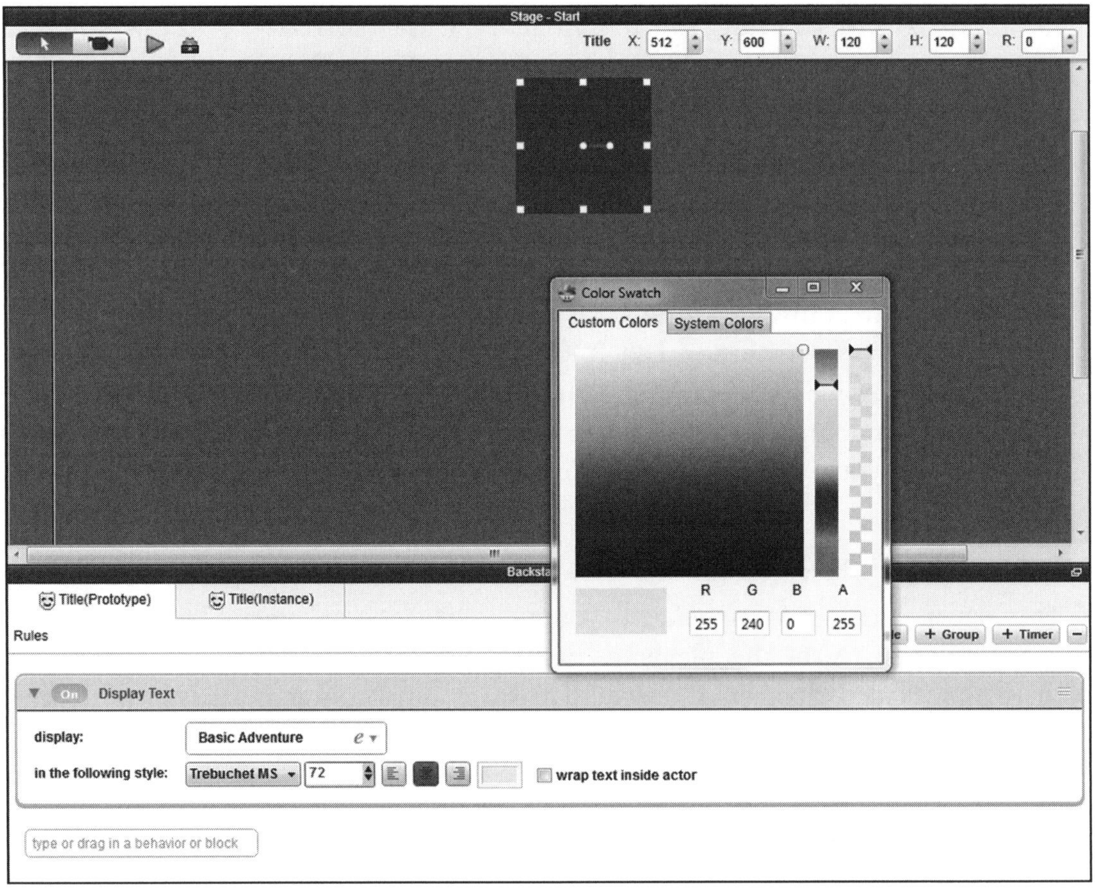

Figure 7.28
Set the title text color to yellow.
Source: The GameSalad Creator, © 2013 GameSalad®, Inc.
© Michael Duggan.

4. Drag an instance of Instruction into the Start scene. Change its Position setting to X 512 and Y 335. Change its Width setting to 650. Add a Display Text behavior to this actor, too. Have it say, "You awaken from suspended animation. Your senses come online, and you see a sterile room aboard a space vessel. You are a service android. Why you have been awakened, you know not." Set it to Arial, 24 point, centered. The default white color is okay. Be sure to select the Wrap Text Inside Actor option for this actor.

5. Add a timer to Instruction (Prototype) by clicking the + Timer button. Set it so that after 15 seconds, it will change the scene to Room A. Select the Run to Completion option.

6. Preview, and you will see your text appear on screen during the Start scene. After 15 seconds, the Start scene disappears and Room A takes its place. You could, if you decide to later on, add a Skip button to the Start scene, but the timer will work fine for starters.

7. Back in the Editor, go to Room A. Click the Game tab in the Attributes panel. Add two Boolean attributes by clicking the plus (+) button. Name the first one Has Pass Card and the second one Has Screwdriver. Leave both of these attributes deselected, or false, by default. See Figure 7.29.

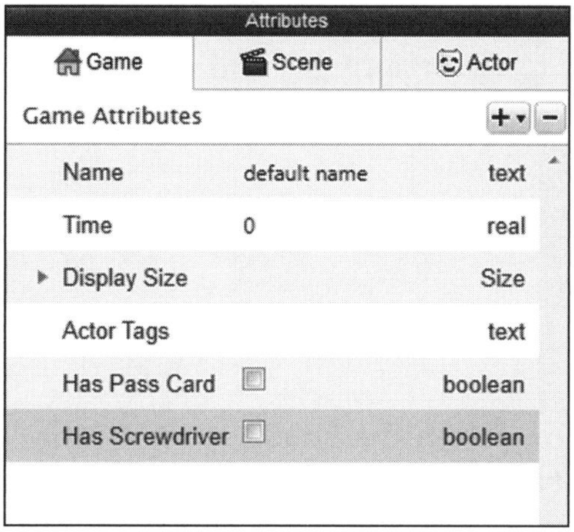

Figure 7.29
Add two new game attributes.
Source: The GameSalad Creator, © 2013 GameSalad®, Inc. All Rights Reserved.

8. Click the Actors tab in the Library panel and add a new actor called Dialogue. Set its Color attribute (in the Actor tab of the Attributes panel) to R 255, G 255, B 255, and A 100, so it is white but see-through. Change its Size > Width setting to 600. Drag and drop an instance of the Dialogue actor into the Room A scene. Position it at X 512 and Y 300.

9. With the Dialogue actor selected, go to the Backstage panel and add a new rule to Dialogue (Prototype). For the condition, type Attribute and select that option when it appears. Set the attribute of choice to the Has Pass Card game attribute you just created. Have it check to see if this attribute is false.

10. In the "do" area, add a Display Text command. Have the Display Text say: "YUKI: Oh, good. You're up. Our spaceship's guidance system is offline. I need you to fix it. You will find it in the next room, along with the tools to fix it. But the door here is locked. You'll need a pass card. I think I left mine in the room there by accident. Can you find it?" Set the font style to Arial, 18 point, centered, and black. Also, select the Wrap Text Inside Actor option.

11. Pressing and holding down the Alt/Option key, drag and drop a copy of the Display Text behavior you just added to the else area of this rule. Edit the text of this Display Text to say the following: "YUKI: You found my pass card! That's super. Use it to unlock the door and go in. You can fix the guidance system with a screwdriver, if memory serves me."

12. Still in Room A, select the Yuki actor. In the Yuki (Prototype) tab of the Backstage panel, add a rule that checks to see if the Has Pass Card game attribute is true. In the "do" area of this rule, set it to Change Image and choose the Yuki_02 graphic as your image. This will make Yuki look happy when she sees the player has obtained the pass card.

Unlocking a Door

Now you need to allow the player to pass through the door after getting the pass card.

1. Select the Pass Card actor from the Actors tab in the Library panel. In the Backstage panel, go to the Pass Card (Prototype) tab and add a new rule. For the condition, type Attribute and select that option when it appears. Set the attribute of choice to if the Has Pass Card is false.

2. Add another rule and drag it to the "do" area of the first. Set the first condition to Touch > Pressed and the second to Touch > Inside. In the "do" section, choose Change Attribute; for the attribute, choose the Has Pass Card game attribute, and set it to true. This way, when the Pass Card actor is touched, it will change the game attribute. See Figure 7.30.

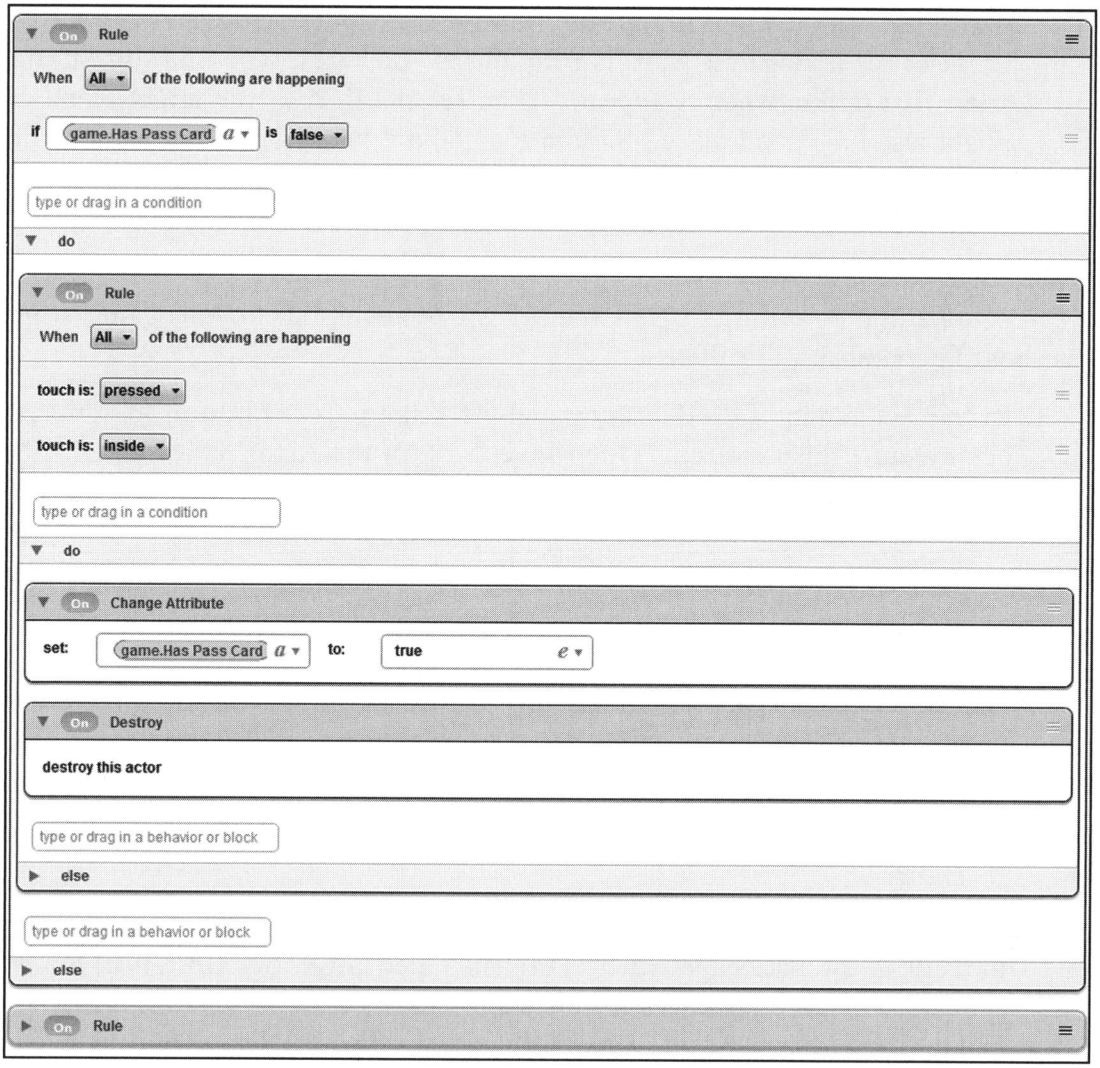

Figure 7.30
If the pass card is picked up, have it change the Has Pass Card attribute to true.

3. After the Change Attribute behavior, add a Destroy behavior so the pass card will disappear from the scene after being picked up. Add another rule below the first that checks to see if the attribute Has Pass Card is true, and if so, set it to Destroy.

4. Drag and drop the Panel actor into the Room A scene and position it at X 750 and Y 500. In the Backstage panel, go to the Panel (Prototype) tab and add a new rule by clicking the + Rule button. For the condition, type Attribute and

select that option when it appears. As to the attribute being checked, have it check to see if Has Pass Card is true. In the "do" area, type Change Scene and select that option when it appears. Then select Lab A as the target scene. This might also be a good place to add a Play Sound behavior, if you want to find or record a sound effect of the card reader beeping or the door sliding open.

Displaying the Inventory

You could add a button that opens the inventory menu, but for this game, using the keyboard's spacebar will suffice.

1. In the Actors tab of the Library panel, click the plus (+) button to add a new actor. Name this new actor Open Inventory. In the Actor tab of the Attributes panel, with Open Inventory selected, set its Color attribute to R 0, G 0, B 0, and A 0. This will make the actor completely invisible.

2. In the Backstage panel, with Open Inventory selected, go to the Open Inventory (Prototype) tab and click the + Rule button to add a new rule. For this rule's condition, type Key and select this option when it appears. For the key of choice, select the spacebar. In the "do" area, type Pause Game and select this option when it appears. For the scene to be shown, select the Inventory scene from the drop-down list.

3. Drag and drop instances of Open Inventory into every scene except Start and Inventory.

4. Go to the Inventory scene. Drag and drop an instance of Open Inventory here, too, but in the Backstage panel, go to the Open Inventory (Instance) tab and click the lock to unlock this instance and edit its rules separately. Delete the Pause Game behavior and in its place add an Unpause Game behavior.

5. Save your project and preview it by clicking the Preview button. Test it out after first reaching Room A. Press the spacebar to make the inventory panel appear and press the spacebar again to make it go away. Then find the pass card and pick it up. Press the spacebar once more. Notice when you do that the pass card has disappeared from here. You want it to do the opposite in your inventory. You want the pass card to show up in your inventory only when it has been picked up and be absent before that.

6. Return to the Editor and go to the Inventory scene. Select the Pass Card instance. In the Backstage panel, go to the Pass Card (Instance) tab and click the lock to unlock this instance and edit its rules separately. The first rule is for when the Has Pass Card attribute is false, and the last one is for when the Has

Pass Card attribute is true. Go to the false one first. Delete the behaviors from its "do" area. In their place, add a Change Image behavior and leave the image to set it to at No Image. Go to the true condition, delete the behavior from its "do" area, and add another Change Image behavior here, setting the image to passCard.png.

7. This would be fine, but when there is no image selected for the actor, it will still show up as its default color. With the Pass Card actor still selected, go to the Actor tab of the Attributes panel and set its Color attribute to R 0, G 0, B 0, and A 0. Now it will be completely hidden.

8. While in the Inventory panel, select and use the same rules and behaviors on the screwdriver, opting for the Has Screwdriver game attribute instead of the Has Pass Card attribute and the screwdriver.png image instead of the passCard.png image.

9. Save your project and preview it again to test your changes. Now, when you first reach Room A and press the spacebar, you should not be able to see the pass card or the screwdriver present, but when you get to Room B and touch it to pick up the pass card and press spacebar, you will see the pass card has been added to your inventory, as shown in Figure 7.31.

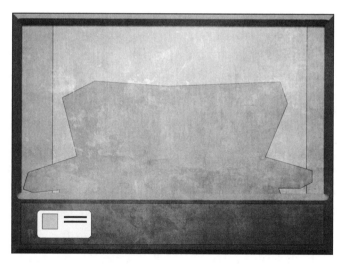

Figure 7.31
The pass card will appear in the player's inventory after picking it up.
Source: The GameSalad Creator, © 2013 GameSalad®, Inc.
© Michael Duggan.

Accomplishing the Quest

Once in the lab, the player will need to find the screwdriver and use it to repair the guidance system. This will work in the same manner as finding the pass card. If you wanted to get fancier with the search for the screwdriver, you could add an extra scene that is an up-close view of tools scattered across a work bench, and just like a hidden-object puzzle, give the player a limited time to find the screwdriver (and any other items as needed) hidden amid the mess. In the case of this lesson, however, having the screwdriver hanging on a wall next to some other tools is enough, albeit simple.

1. Select the Screwdriver actor from the Actors tab in the Library panel. Go to the Screwdriver (Prototype) tab in the Backstage panel and add a new rule. For the condition, type Attribute and select that option when it appears. Set the attribute of choice to if the Has Screwdriver attribute is false.

2. Add another rule and drag it to the "do" area of the first. Set this new rule's first condition to Touch > Pressed and the second to Touch > Inside. In the "do" section, choose Change Attribute; for the attribute, choose the Has Screwdriver game attribute and set it to true. This way, when the Screwdriver actor is touched, it will change the game attribute.

3. After the Change Attribute behavior, add a Destroy behavior so the screwdriver will disappear from the scene after being picked up. Add another rule below the first that checks to see if the attribute Has Screwdriver is true, and if so, set it to Destroy.

4. Select the CGS actor from the Actors tab in the Library panel. Go to the CGS (Prototype) tab in the Backstage panel and add a new rule. For the condition, add a Touch > Pressed condition and then a Touch > Inside condition. Add another rule, and drag it to the "do" area of the prototype actor's rule. For this new rule's condition, type Attribute and select that option when it appears. Set the attribute of choice to if the Has Screwdriver attribute is true. Click the Scenes tab in the Library panel and click the plus (+) button to add a scene beneath the others. Name this new scene Finish. Return to the CGS (Prototype) rules and behaviors. For the "do" area of the new rule, type Change Scene and choose that option when it appears. Choose the Finish scene as the target scene.

5. Go to the Finish scene. In the Actors tab in the Library panel, add a new actor and name it Victory. Set its default Color attribute to R 0, G 0, B 0, and A 0 so it has an invisible background color. With the Victory actor selected, go to the Backstage panel and the Victory (Prototype) tab. Add a Display Text behavior that says "All systems go! You did it." Set the font style to Trebuchet MS, 65 point, centered. For the font color, set it to R 255, G 240, B 0, and A 255, so it is bright yellow. Drag and drop an instance of the Victory actor into the Finish scene. Set its Position attributes to X 512 and Y 384. If you wanted to, you could

add a Play Again? button to this scene, but it is not required. If you did, you would set its rule and behavior to Reset Game on Touch.

6. Save your project and play it all the way through, until you see the conclusion message (see Figure 7.32). You are finished.

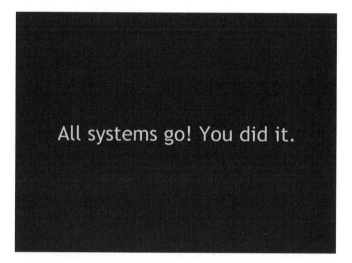

Figure 7.32
The big finish.
Source: The GameSalad Creator, © 2013 GameSalad®, Inc. All Rights Reserved.

That is it! You have a basic adventure game built and have learned tried and tested methods for building adventure games using GameSalad.

CHAPTER 8

TAKING YOUR GAME TO MARKET

Eventually, you will have either reached the end of your game project development and want to advertise the home-brewed game you made using the GameSalad Creator or you would have a genuine decent start but need more help or cash flow to continue development. When you get to that point, you may know some friends you can tell, but to really get your game out there so strangers can also play your game or invest in it, you will have to be savvy. Whatever your intentions are to get the world to notice you and your game, this chapter shows you how.

DEVELOPING A PROPOSAL

If you have a decent start of a game but feel you could do much better with a whole team of developers or a bigger budget, you should consider developing a game proposal and seeking out people to help you or investors to give you money.

A game proposal is similar to and often based on your game-design document. When working on a game proposal, keep in mind the difference between those materials intended for internal use and those you want non-developers to see. When writing game proposals, most designers do not include every detail.

The most important details non-developers needs to understand are as follows:

- You know what you are doing and have the skills to pull off the project you propose.

- The game you propose looks good. Notice I said "looks." You can talk a good game, but until you have a demo (especially a playable prototype) to show someone, they usually won't give you the time of day.

- Your proposed game has all the earmarks of a best-selling game (e.g., it sounds fun to play, appears to have an original premise, has some amazing audio and/or graphics, and more).

- You have set your design above all the rest by being fresh, innovative, and appealing. You have a clear identity and a great gimmick (more about which I will discuss in a moment).

If you go before a publisher or investor, try to secure a face-to-face meeting to deliver and review your proposal. This way, you can elaborate on specific points that you think are important. You can also answer clarifying questions more quickly. Just remember to go in prepared, collected, and dressed nicely. Your proposal can be on paper, but it is recommended you use visual media. You can use Microsoft PowerPoint to develop a slideshow presentation. You could set up a demo of the game right there or show them a pre-recorded demo of gameplay. Remember, you'll want the freedom to discuss and evolve your game description while also answering questions. In most cases, the publisher or investor's willingness to listen will be directly related to the energy you impart, so go in pumped and excited about your game. Also, if you're under the age of 18, most people will want to work with someone older as an intermediary (if they give you the time of day at all).

Be forewarned that snagging a publisher is not an easy row to hoe. In fact, it is a whole lot easier to self-publish and self-promote your games, which is a possible strategy in this cyber age of garage game development.

Crowd-funding is one method for gaining funds to complete your game design and requires little to no physical contact with publishers. Crowd-funding describes the collective effort of individuals who network and pool their money together via the Internet to support efforts you initiate. The following sites have more information and will help you get started if you are interested in crowd-funding:

- **Kickstarter:** www.kickstarter.com
- **RocketHub:** www.rockethub.com
- **Indiegogo:** www.indiegogo.com
- **GoFundMe:** www.gofundme.com

ADVERTISE YOURSELF

Some people find it difficult to promote themselves. If you place yourself in this category, believe me, you are not alone. Even the sensational singing legends Madonna and Lady Gaga have admitted being prone to self-doubt, and they have been recognized the world over as some of the best self-promoters. You may be plagued by insecure feelings and doubts, or you may be self-confident but feel selfish or that you have to be humble. When it comes to advertisement, don't be! If you want people to notice you and play your game, you cannot act as a fly on the wall. You have to be as crazy, outlandish, and noticeable as possible.

Now, I'm not advocating dressing like Marilyn Manson when you stroll down the streets of your hometown. And if you plan to visit with a publisher or conduct yourself in a business atmosphere, you'd best wear a dress or a tie. You are expected to dress the style of the environment you are entering; as the adage goes, "When in Rome, do as the Romans do." If you hang around a game-design company where everyone's wearing T-shirts and blue jeans, you can wear a T-shirt and blue jeans. But if you go into a boardroom to negotiate a contract with a potential investor, you had best put on a dress or tie (whatever's acceptable for your gender and ZIP code).

What I am telling you to do is to stop being vague, colorless, wishy-washy, or the amazing invisible man or woman. People will never notice you if you do not want to be noticed—and that is a downright shame because you deserve to be noticed. You might say, "It's my game that I want people to notice, not me," and there is some truth in that. But if you are an unnoticeable person used to evading comment and keeping to yourself, then there is a great possibility your game will never get the notice it deserves.

DEVELOP A CLEAR IDENTITY OR GIMMICK

Many game companies use gimmicks to help sell their games. A *gimmick* is a clear image that represents an idea and helps sell products. You have probably noticed gimmicks all around you. Some can be very transparent or clumsy, but most often, a gimmick is purely an understandable image of an idea that takes too long to explain.

Think about your game. Can you express your game in a single, clear sentence? Can you express it in a single image or avatar? If you can, this can become a gimmick to help you advertise your game.

Taking time to write down your game idea helps you sharpen and clarify your idea to yourself and to the team you'll be working with. If you started making your game before taking time to simplify your core concept, you should stop and take a moment to work it out now, before going any further.

After you've simplified your game idea, consider the following and find one thing that would serve as a possible gimmick:

- **Character:** Do you have a cute, sexy, strong, or mysterious character that is different and exciting enough to serve as an icon for your game?

- **Place:** Is the setting for your game adventurous, glorious, beautiful, or mysterious enough to serve as an icon for your game? Think of Alice in Wonderland, where Wonderland becomes an iconic place.

- **Prop:** Does your character wield an interesting, powerful, cool, or different sort of weapon or artifact that looks neat enough to serve as an icon for your game? Think of the dragonlance in the fantasy novels by Tracy Hickman and Margaret Weis or the dark crystal in the Jim Henson movie by the same name.

- **Enemy:** Do you have a scary, awesome, powerful, or mysterious enemy that is enthralling enough to serve as an icon for your game?

- **Element:** Is there some gameplay element so infusive that it's found everywhere in your game and looks different and exciting enough to serve as an icon for your game?

Let me give you just a few examples of gimmicks other games have used, in case you're still confused.

- In *Tomb Raider*, the gimmick is Laura Croft. In *Super Mario Bros.*, it is Mario. In *Donkey Kong Country*, it is Donkey Kong. In *Zelda*, it is the green-clad elf Link. All these games have the main character as a gimmick.

- In *Prince of Persia*, the gimmick is a combination of the main character (the prince) and the place (a romanticized ancient Persia).

- In the games *Diablo* and *Rayman: Raving Rabbids*, the gimmicks are the enemies.

You have to find just the right look for yourself and the right gimmick for your game, and you want people to notice you and play your game. Because you worked hard at creating a fun game, which people will like, you know you are not offering empty promises. You are only giving players excellent entertainment.

So how do you get the world to notice you and your game? How do you clue folks in that you have something for them to play? One of the best ways in this beautiful cyber age is through the use of the Internet.

Publishing Your Game on the Web

These days, the easiest way to self-publish is to build a website, put your art on it, and get people to come to your website to see it—something anybody can do for little or no cost.

No one doubts that the Internet has profoundly changed our society. These days, people from all over the world chat over the World Wide Web (WWW), instantaneously sharing information in ways humans never considered possible before the birth of the Web. In this day and age, "I found it online" has become a household refrain.

WWW and Internet Speak

The Internet is really a global network of computers that enables people from around the world to share information. Many people use the terms interchangeably, but the Internet and the World Wide Web, often referred to as simply the Web, are not one and the same.

The WWW is a subset of the Internet that supports webpages, or specially formatted documents created using languages such as Hypertext Markup Language (HTML). Hypertext allows you to click words in a document that are linked to related words, graphics, and other elements in the same or in another document.

Put another way, you might think of the Internet as the connection between various computers worldwide, and the WWW as the content that resides on those computers and is transmitted via these connections.

Just as terms like the Internet and the WWW run together after a while, so, too, do terms like webpages and websites. Take a look at the following distinctions:

- **Websites:** A website is a location out on the Web. It is kind of like a neighborhood full of homes. For instance, www.msn.com is a website.

- **Webpages:** A website consists of two or more webpages. A webpage is a single HTML document found on the Web, residing at a website. It is like one of the homes on a neighborhood block.

- **Home pages:** A home page is the first webpage you see when you enter a website, and it is often referred to as the index page.

- **Web browser:** A Web browser is a software program that is used to locate and display webpages. More than likely you've used Web browsers without knowing what they were before, such as Internet Explorer, Mozilla Firefox, Google

Chrome, and Safari (among others). All these browsers display graphics in addition to text. Additionally, they can display sound and video, although many require special plug-ins for these features to work correctly.

Finding a Web Host

It all seems simple. You click, and a new page appears on your screen. But where do these pages live while not being viewed? Where are webpages stored?

Websites and their pages are stored on special computers called servers. A server is a computer hooked up to the Internet 24/7 and might have one or more websites stored on it at any given time. The number of sites and pages that can reside on a single server depends on the server's memory capacity. When you enter a webpage address in the Address bar of your browser, the server responds by sending a copy of that page to your browser.

To publish your website, you don't need to set up your own personal server. You can borrow someone else's server to put your files on. This type of server is called a Web host. There are countless choices in finding Web hosts: some free and others at a cost. What follows is a list of free Web-host services:

- **110 MB:** 110mb.com
- **AtSpace:** www.atspace.com
- **Byet Internet Services:** www.byethost.com
- **Freehostia:** www.freehostia.com/hosting.html
- **Webs:** www.webs.com
- **Tripod:** www.tripod.lycos.com

When choosing free hosting, go with a reputable host. Some free hosting sites add bulky code to your page, which increases the loading time or speed at which your page displays. Others place advertisements on your page. Avoid these types of hosts if you can.

Companies with dedicated servers cost you more, but as in everything in life, you get what you pay for. The top Web hosts with dedicated servers you can pay for at the time of this writing are listed here:

- **BlueHost:** bluehost.com
- **Dot5Hosting:** www.dot5hosting.com
- **HostMonster:** www.hostmonster.com

- **HostPapa:** hostpapa.com
- **StartLogic:** www.startlogic.com

Building Your Site

Think of your website as a neighborhood. In that neighborhood, you will need to put stuff. Just as a city planner would, you need a clear concept of what kind of stuff you want to include in your site before you start building it. I will give you a brief primer for Web development. If you decide you really want to publish your games on the Web, however, there are whole books devoted to Web design you should read. A few I'd suggest from Cengage Learning include the following:

- *Web Design for Teens* by Maneesh Sethi
- *Principles of Web Design, 4th Edition* by Joel Sklar
- *Web Design BASICS* by Todd Stubbs and Karl Barksdale
- *PHP for Teens* by Maneesh Sethi

Prepping Your Text

Before you build your site or update it with new material, take time to write all your text beforehand. Your best bet is to use a word-processing program like Microsoft Word, because it enables you to check your spelling and it even makes suggestions relating to grammar and usage. In addition, writing things down beforehand helps ensure you're conveying the message you wish to convey without being distracted by the coding or technical aspects sure to crop up later.

Prepping Your Images

Images must be small enough for transmission over the Internet. When I say "small," I am referring, of course, to the size of the file, not the dimensions of the image itself.

Unlike images you prepare for print, which must have a resolution of 150 to 300 dots per inch (dpi), an image bound for the Web needs to have a resolution of 72 dpi. To achieve this file size, you will likely need to compress your images. This reduces redundancy in image data, often without a noticeable loss in image quality. Compressing your images not only makes it more convenient for upload, but it also benefits your visitors because it enables them to download your site more quickly. Use an art or photo-editing software application to compress your images. Note that some sites where you upload images, such as Facebook, auto-compress images as they are uploaded, so you do not have to do it before uploading.

There are three image types widely supported on the Web. The differences between these three image types are marginal.

- **JPEG:** JPEG (pronounced jay-peg), short for Joint Photographic Experts Group, is among the most common image-compression formats available.

- **GIF:** The Graphics Interchange Format (GIF) is an eight-bit-per-pixel bitmap format that supports alpha transparencies. You can pronounce GIF with a hard or soft "G" sound.

- **PNG:** Short for Portable Network Graphics, the PNG (pronounced ping) format is a bitmapped image system with 24-bit RGB colors and improvements over the GIF format. PNG is of great help for creating smaller-sized files with excellent quality.

Putting It Together

You could code all your webpages by hand, using HTML. HTML is a simple markup language that tells the browser how to display code on the page. It's so simple, in fact, anyone can learn it. There are numerous HTML tutorials online that can get you up to snuff in hand-coding in no time. To find them, search Google for "HTML tutorial."

Note, too, that you don't need special software to hand-code webpages in HTML. You can use a text editor such as Notepad (Win) or BBEdit (Mac) to type your code and then save your resulting file with the .html extension. When you open it later, it will launch in your default browser to preview.

Cascading style sheets (CSS) is a computer language used to describe the presentation of structured documents that declares how a document written in a markup language such as HTML should look. CSS is used to identify colors, fonts, layout, and other notable aspects of Web document staging. It is designed to facilitate the division of content and presentation of that content so that you can, in fact, swap out different looks without having to alter the content at all. CSS can thus be kept separate from the HTML coding.

Save all your Web files to a single folder, with index.html for your home page. Once you have your pages created, upload them to your hosting server by way of file transfer protocol (FTP) or another upload option. This is usually dependent on which host you go with. Whatever you do, don't lose your FTP, login, or password information on any of the sites or servers you decide to use. If you lose this information, you might have problems retrieving access to your site. Write them down in a notebook so that you don't lose them.

Using Dreamweaver   Adobe Dreamweaver, shown in Figure 8.1, is the premier web-site construction kit for professionals. It allows pros to work in either a WYSIWYG (what-you-see-is-what-you-get) or code environment, or both simultaneously. Dreamweaver comes with several built-in site templates. All you need to do is add your content and create your custom logo. In addition, there are many free templates available online. Note that Dreamweaver can be fairly complicated to work with. As such, you will probably need to read a book that focuses on teaching you its inner workings, such as Sherry Bishop's *Adobe Dreamweaver CS5 Revealed* (Cengage Learning). You can learn more about Dreamweaver and how to use it from Adobe's site at www.adobe.com/products/dreamweaver.

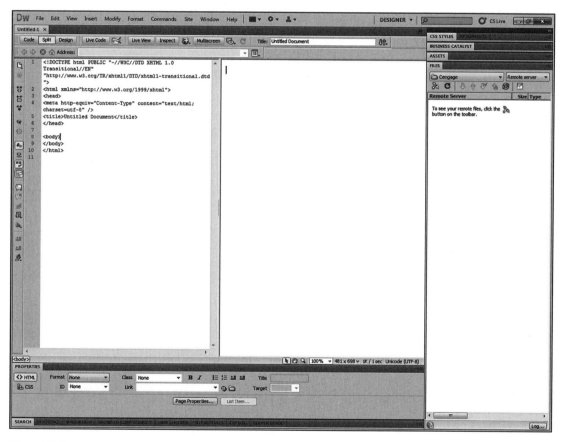

Figure 8.1
Adobe Dreamweaver CS5.

Source: Adobe Dreamweaver, © 2013 Adobe Systems®, Inc. All Rights Reserved.

Using Nvu   An alternative, especially if you don't have the budget for Dreamweaver, is Nvu (pronounced "N-view"), which is available online at www.nvu.com. Nvu is an open-source Web-authoring application for Windows, Mac, and Linux users. This free program provides a great WYSIWIG editing environment and built-in file transfer system to satisfy most designers' needs. If you've always wanted to get your feet wet building websites but don't have much in the way of disposable income, consider Nvu.

Using Free Online Web Builders   If you feel completely out of place trying to code your own website by yourself, or you would prefer whipping something together with very little effort and don't have to possess the most amazing or customized site, you can make use of one of several free online Web builders.

Some of these kits create websites for you on a trial basis, asking you to pay money for adequate hosting or maintenance, while others are free if you agree to use their hosting service. Be sure to read the fine print of any Web builder that says it is "free" because too many people have been disappointed before from using them.

- **DoodleKit:** www.doodlekit.com/home (see Figure 8.2)
- **Handzon Sitemaker:** www.handzon.com
- **Moonfruit:** www.moonfruit.com
- **Wix:** www.wix.com
- **Yola:** www.yola.com

Figure 8.2
The home page of DoodleKit's site.

Social Networks   Do you keep a blog or community profile, such as a Facebook, Google+, or MySpace page? These are other reputable ways to get your games noticed. You don't have to learn anything about HTML, and the blog or community service editors are nowhere near as complicated as Dreamweaver can appear. Some social networks will allow you to post HTML-ready messages, so you can embed your games that way, but if they don't, you can always add hyperlinks to your games.

What follows are instructions for making a Facebook page that advertises your game.

1. Log in to Facebook with your current Facebook account. If you do not have one, you can register for one.

2. Click the Like Pages link in the left navigation bar. On the Recommended Pages page that comes up, click the Create Page button near the top.

3. On the Create a Page page, click Brand or Product as your main topic (see Figure 8.3). In the options dialog box that appears, type the name of your game or the name you want to give your game company. From the drop-down category list, choose Games/Toys. Read the Facebook Pages Terms before selecting the checkbox that says you have read them.

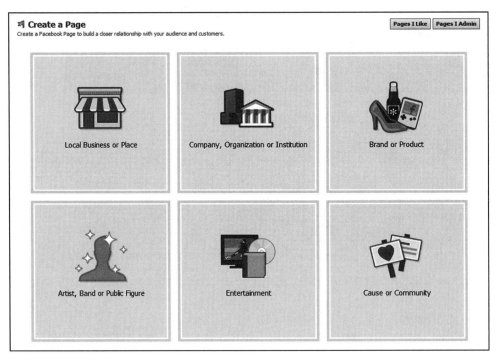

Figure 8.3
Pick Brand or Product.
Source: Facebook, © 2013 Facebook®. All Rights Reserved.

4. Add a square (1:1 ratio) avatar image for your game. Continue, and you will be directed through the steps to add a description, a cover image to go at the top of the Facebook page, and more.

5. When finished, you can send invitations to people you might have on your Friends list to "like" your page. From this point forward, you can use your Facebook page as a place to point people to when advertising your game.

Embedding or Linking to Your Game If you have an HTML-ready page where you can embed your game, nothing can be simpler. Log in to your account on the GameSalad website and go to http://publish.gamesalad.com/games. From there, select the game you made that you want to embed. As long as you have Allow Game Embed enabled in the Main Settings of this game, you will be able to grab the embed code. Copy and paste it into the HTML code of the webpage where you want to embed it.

Optionally, you could link to your game. This will be the preferred method if you are admin of a Facebook page or prefer to share links rather than embed the game. Provide a link to your game on the GameSalad Arcade servers to enable visitors to download your game.

Submitting Your Site to Search Engines

Now that you have some cyber real estate and you're confident in your overall design abilities, it's time to open the doors wide and let gamers in. For them to find you, your first step is to submit your site to search engines so that it can be indexed with them.

Pages are published to the WWW by their domain owners or contributors, and just as easily, they can be changed or taken off the site. Thus, a page may be there one week and gone the next. This makes the Web an ever-shifting environment. Humans can compile directories of Web links that point to subjects of interest, but if these same people don't check their links on a regular basis, they may quickly turn into dead ends. This is why we've developed other methods for searching the Web for the content we want: search engines.

A search engine is a Web program that searches the Web for specified keywords and phrases and returns a list of documents in which those keywords or phrases are found. Popular search engines include Google, Bing, Yahoo!, AOL, Alta Vista, Dogpile, and Ask.com. What follows is a list of search engines to which you should consider submitting your site:

- **Bing:** Visit www.bing.com/toolbox/submit-site-url to submit your URL.

- **Google:** Visit www.google.com/addurl.html and follow the onscreen instructions.

- **Open Directory Project:** A bunch of search engines use Dmoz.org for their search material, and you can submit to Dmoz.org, too. Go to www.dmoz.org/add.html and follow the onscreen instructions.

- **Yahoo!:** Visit http://search.yahoo.com/info/submit.html and follow the onscreen instructions.

Creating a QR Code

A QR code is a two-dimensional barcode that can be easily scanned using any modern mobile phone. After scanning, this code is then converted into a piece of text and/or a hyperlink. For instance, if you walk into a grocery store and notice a poster for an event that seems interesting, you can take out your mobile phone, scan the QR code, and instantly get more information about the event and/or a link to a website where you can book tickets. QR codes are typically small, square images and thus save a lot of space on the advert or product, making it a clever and ideal marketing strategy.

You can link to your game or the website you have advertising your game by using a QR code. QR codes are easy to make using Visualead's QR Code Generator online. Follow these steps:

1. Go to www.visualead.com/qurify2/en/ and type or copy and paste the URL of your game or website into the blank field. Then, click the Generate QR Code button.

2. A prompt will appear, asking you to choose a graphic for the background of your QR code. There are many to choose from (see Figure 8.4), and you can click the More button at the bottom of the list to show more. You could also select the blank white one to get the QR code by itself, without a background, or click the Browse Your Files and Folders button to upload your own background image.

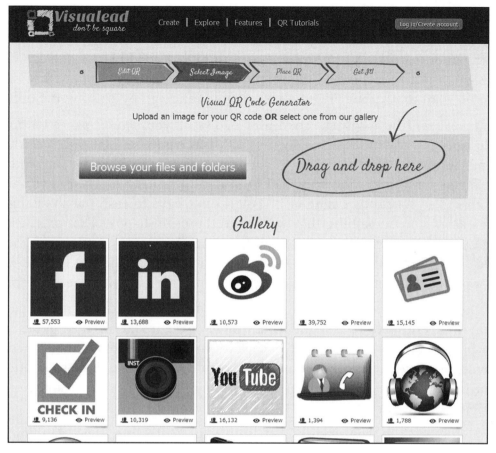

Figure 8.4
Pick a background graphic.

3. After you have chosen the image, the next prompt will show you where you can place your QR code on the background image. Click the Generate Silver button when you are satisfied with the placement of the code and wait for the code to be generated. When it is finished, click Next.

4. Register or log in with Facebook or Google to download your QR code for free. You can also keep track of all your generated QR codes, see how many visitors have scanned them, and re-download them as needed. Using an image editor, you can paste your QR code onto signs, flyers, posters, and more.

WHAT NEXT?

Be prepared for player feedback—good, bad, and ugly. Ignore the ugly, because sometimes there are just weak, insecure people who think it a good idea to attack amateur game designers just because they can. Never take it personally. I know that can be harder to do than to say, but preserve your dignity and ego by trusting me on this.

However, there will be feedback, good and bad, that you *should* pay attention to. Again, do not take any of it personally, but use it as signposts that indicate whether you are moving in the right direction. If someone tells you he likes the way you have brick platforms but thinks a disembodied head does not make much sense to him as a player character, jot down a note of it. You do not have to rush out to change the player character into something that will make the critic happy. That was just one critic, and you cannot please everybody all the time. As soon as you altered the disembodied head, someone else would probably complain that she liked it the way it was and wonder why you messed it up. Act prudently on the criticism you receive.

Some of the feedbacks you receive from others will be dire and necessitate edits to your game. For example, you might have thought you tested all your game levels, but perhaps you missed the fact that one platform physically blocked another, and now players are stuck and cannot continue. If you receive glitch information like that from your players, you are obligated to fix it as soon as possible and release a new version of your game.

While mulling over the feedback you get from your first game, start planning your next project. Now that you have at least one game finished, what is to stop you from making another? Just as they say, "Practice makes perfect," so too does frequent creativity. The next game you make will be even better, and the next one after that, and the next one after that, and so on. Eventually, you will have a stellar portfolio you will be proud to show off!

CHAPTER 9

CROSS-PLATFORM PUBLISHING

Using the GameSalad Creator, you have built two classic action games. One has been a shooter with quick motion, laser firing, and enhanced armor, in which the player is pitted against an alien ship and an enemy generator. The other game is a platformer, in which a disembodied head named Freaky merrily bounces around brick platforms in search of shiny red stars so he can exit without getting hurt by sharp spikes or luminous ghosts. This chapter shows you how to make games for platforms other than PC and Mac, and how to publish your completed games.

CREATING A MOBILE-READY GAME

So far, each of the games you built has been designed for play on a keyboard, requiring it to be a PC, Mac, or Web-based game. GameSalad Creator also offers you the ability to publish games for mobile devices. For PC users, this would be for the Android. Mobile devices do not have keyboards, at least not the type we are familiar with in game design, but they do often offer touchscreen input. The Android, iPad, and iPhone all offer touchscreen input, which you can put to your advantage when building a video game.

How, you might be asking yourself, do you make a touchscreen-ready video game? I will show you how you can take your existing platformer and turn it into a mobile game in simple, easy steps.

1. Open your basic platformer game project in GameSalad. Choose File > Save As and save it as a separate project called Platformer Touch. Saving a new version of the project, separate from the first, will enable you to continue

working on it, taking it in a completely new direction, without losing any of the work you put into the original.

2. Find the following images on the companion site for download, download them to your Images folder for your Platformer Touch game project, and import them within the GameSalad Creator: leftArrow.png, rightArrow.png, jumpButton.png, and pauseButton.png. As a reminder, you import them through your Library panel's Media tab.

3. Create four new actors: Left Button, Right Button, Jump Button, and Pause Button. Assign the leftArrow.png image to the Left Button actor, the rightArrow. png image to the Right Button actor, the jumpButton.png image to the Jump Button actor, and the pauseButton.png image to the Pause Button actor. See Figure 9.1.

Figure 9.1
The Left Button, Right Button, Jump Button, and Pause Button actors.
Source: The GameSalad Creator, © 2013 GameSalad®, Inc. All Rights Reserved.

4. Click the Game tab in the Attributes panel. Add four new Boolean attributes. Name them Left, Right, Up, and Pause. Set them to false (unchecked) by default. See Figure 9.2.

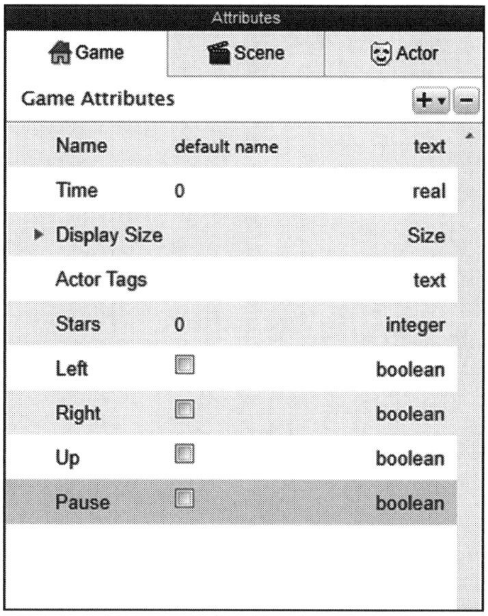

Figure 9.2
The Left, Right, Up, and Pause game attributes.
Source: The GameSalad Creator, © 2013 GameSalad®, Inc. All Rights Reserved.

5. Select the Left Button actor. Add a rule to it. You will add two similar conditions to this rule. For each, type Touch and select that option when it appears. For the first Touch condition, select Pressed from the drop-down list. For the second Touch condition, select Inside from the drop-down list. Make sure your conditions are set to All, so both have to be valid before any action takes place.

6. In the "do" section, type Change Attribute and select that option when it appears. For the attribute, select the Left game attribute you just made. Set it to be true. In the else section, drag and drop a duplicate of the Change Attribute you just made but setting the attribute to be false. Your Left Button actor's rule should look like Figure 9.3.

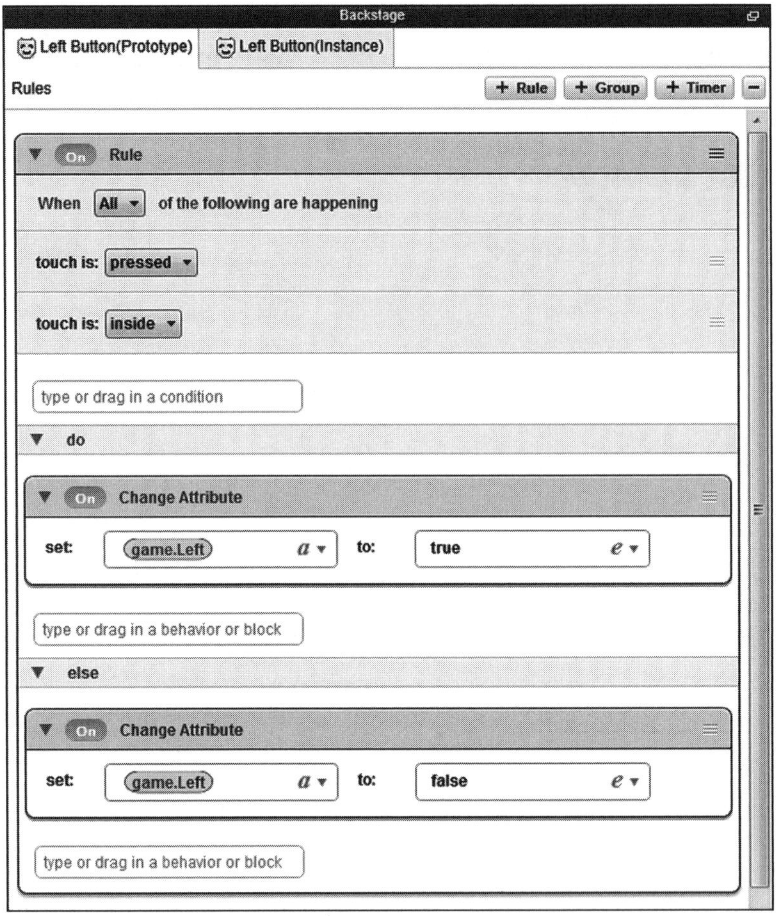

Figure 9.3
The Left Button actor's finished rule.

Source: The GameSalad Creator, © 2013 GameSalad®, Inc. All Rights Reserved.

7. Select the Player actor. Scroll down its list of rules until you find the one for Move Left. In the "conditions" area, add a new condition beneath the one that checks for the left arrow key being pressed. Type `Attribute` and select that option when it appears. Select the Left game attribute, and from the drop-down list, select True. Above the conditions, select Any from the drop-down list so that if either condition is true, the action commences.

8. Drag and drop an instance of the Left Button actor on the middle left of your stage in the Main scene. In its Position attributes, set Y to 404. Preview your game to test it. When you get to the Main scene, you should be able to click the left button to move Freaky left, the same as if you had pressed the left arrow key on your keyboard.

9. Repeat this procedure for the right movement. Add a rule to the Right Button actor that makes the Right game attribute true upon touch press inside and false if untouched. Then, in the Player actor's rules, go to the Move Right rule and add a condition that checks to see if the Right game attribute is true, and set your conditions to Any. Drag an instance of the Right Button actor to the middle right of your Main scene (with the Position Y attribute set to 404). Preview to make sure you did not miss a step. If you did, it is no problem to go back and check your work.

10. Add a Jump Button. For ease of use, the actor's instance should be placed on the right of the Main scene, beneath the Right Button actor, close to 270 Y. This way, the mobile user can tap it with their right thumb during play. Add a rule to the Right Button actor (the prototype, not the instance) that makes the Up game attribute true upon touch press inside and false if untouched. Then, in the Player actor's rules, go to the Jump rule and add a condition that checks to see if the Up game attribute is true, and set your conditions to Any.

11. The last step is to develop the Pause button. Drag and drop an instance of the Pause Button actor into the Main scene and center at the bottom of the stage (where X is 512 and Y is 50). Add a rule to the prototype of the Pause Button actor that makes the Pause game attribute true upon touch press inside and false if untouched. Then, in the Player actor's rules, go the Pause Game rule and add a condition that checks to see if the Pause game attribute is true, and set your conditions to Any.

12. You also have to go to the Pause scene and drag and drop the Pause Button actor here, too. Be sure to position it in the same place (512,50). With the instance selected, click the lock icon in the Backstage panel to modify the rules for this specific actor separate from its prototype. Delete the Change Attribute commands. In the "do" area, add an Unpause Game behavior. Now, when the button is pressed, the game will resume.

13. Your preview will show you if tapping the Jump button allows Freaky to hop around, but combining left or right movement with the jump action is near impossible with mouse control. You would have to preview on a mobile device to get the full effect. See Figure 9.4.

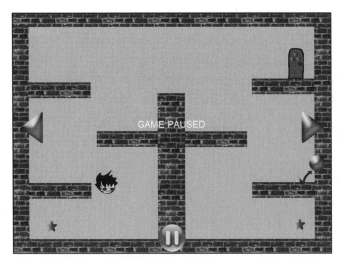

Figure 9.4
How the touchscreen interface should look.
Source: The GameSalad Creator, © 2013 GameSalad®, Inc. All Rights Reserved.

This is the start to a mobile-ready game. You would have to copy the buttons to every scene and keep their placement as static as possible so as not to confuse the player or make them hunt for where the buttons have moved. The important thing is that you can now see how onscreen buttons are used to direct action within a video game.

Publishing Your Game

Whether you are just putting the final additions on your latest game project and are ready to share your game with the rest of the world, or you are still hard at work on it and would like to *ad-hoc* test it on an Android device, you will first need to publish your handiwork from the GameSalad Creator. In addition to HTML5 publishing, which is available to all users, Professional users also have the option to publish for Android devices for both testing and distribution.

Mac users have the added capability of publishing to the Mac and to iOS devices (the iPhone, iPod Touch, and iPad). For more information about Apple publishing, you can go online to GameSalad's tutorials: *www.cookbook.gamesalad.com/tutorials*.

Publishing to the GameSalad Arcade

GameSalad offers a unique and fast way to publish your games directly online, through their website. They have a section of their site called GameSalad Arcade, where games you have made with GameSalad Creator can appear upon publishing.

Herein I will show you the systematic process for publishing your game project to the GameSalad Arcade:

1. Once you are ready to publish, whether your game is wrapped up or still a work in progress, the first step is to bring up the project file you have been hard at work on in the GameSalad Creator.

2. Click the Game tab in the Library panel of the GameSalad Creator. You will see an option to publish in the form of an Upload Game button, just above the Sign In/Sign Out button. Click the Upload Game button. A prompt will appear to confirm upload, after which you will be asked where you want to save a copy of the GameSalad project file on your local machine. Choose a file name and click Save.

3. If you are not already logged in to your GameSalad account at the time of upload, you will be asked to sign in, which is a requirement for publishing. (See Figure 9.5.) If you forget your password, do not panic. Just click the Forgot Password link, and a webpage will open to walk you through the password-reset process.

Figure 9.5
The GameSalad login.
Source: The GameSalad Creator, © 2013 GameSalad®, Inc. All Rights Reserved.

4. After your project has saved, it will begin uploading to the GameSalad servers. When the upload is complete, your default browser will bring up the second part of the publishing process, managed through the GameSalad website. A prompt will ask you to sign into the website, if you are not signed in already.

5. If this is your first time publishing with GameSalad Creator, click Create New (see Figure 9.6). Later, you can use the Update Existing button to swap out an

older, out-of-date version of the game project on the server with a more recent version that has all your improvements made to it rather than creating a new entry for each version of your game. Keep in mind that updating an existing game will overwrite the existing server file, so make sure to keep local backup copies of the various versions of your game.

Figure 9.6
Click the Create New button.
Source: The GameSalad Creator, © 2013 GameSalad®, Inc. All Rights Reserved.

6. The General Info tab contains several fields, which enable you to provide information about your game, including the game's title, description, instructions, tags, and so on. You can also upload screenshots (a must for picky gamers) and an icon. Providing these details and resources about your project will gradually fill up the progress bar in the upper-right corner of your window. After the bar reaches 78 percent (see Figure 9.7), you will be able to list your game on the GameSalad Arcade.

Figure 9.7
The progress bar must reach 78 percent before your game will be published in the Arcade.
Source: The GameSalad Creator, © 2013 GameSalad®, Inc. All Rights Reserved.

7. After you provide the requested information, click the HTML5 tab under Platforms on the left side of the page. The Publishing button on the right will appear intractable because you crossed the 78 percent threshold. Click it, and you will see a message that says, "Your app was queued for generation. It may take a couple of minutes—why not go brush up on your knowledge with the GameSalad Cookbook while you wait?"

8. In just a short while, your game will be playable worldwide on the GameSalad Arcade. If you want to take it a step further and embed your game in your own website or allow others to do so, you can enable the Allow Game Embed checkbox under Main Settings, as in Figure 9.8.

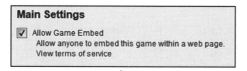

Figure 9.8
The Allow Game Embed option lets you or someone else embed your game in a website.
Source: The GameSalad Creator, © 2013 GameSalad®, Inc. All Rights Reserved.

When your game goes live, you will receive both a pop-up notification and an in-window notification that includes a link. In addition, the Play Game button should now appear clickable.

Downloading and Removing Your Game

There are two other options on the app page worth mentioning. The first is the Download button, located directly under the progress bar in the General Info tab. If you own or have access to multiple computers, you can use this feature to upload your project on one computer and then download a copy of the original project file on another. To access this page without having to go through the whole upload process again, log into your account on the GameSalad website and go to publish.gamesalad. com/games. From there, simply click the icon of the game you want to download and click the Download button.

The second option is the Remove button, located right beside the Download button. Clicking this will bring up a removal confirmation prompt. Clicking OK will remove your game from the Arcade, which will in turn break any links, embedded or otherwise, that point to your game. You will receive no further warnings or opportunities to change your mind after confirmation, so proceed carefully and be sure you have an up-to-date backup copy of your file on your machine before the Arcade removes your game for good.

Mobile Publishing

Professional users can take publishing even further by publishing signed and unsigned APKs that can be submitted to app distributors, allowing you to earn revenue off your game-making talent. Unlike HTML5 publishing, your Android-published game will not be made publicly available in the GameSalad Arcade, preserving exclusivity for you and your app distributors if you so choose.

Publishing Your Game for the Android

Unfortunately, the Pro version of GameSalad costs money, and publishing for Android is quite a bit more complicated than HTML5 publishing due to the configuration and setting requirements specific to that platform. If you are curious, though, here are the instructions for publishing to the Android.

1. Fill out the blank fields (Figure 9.9) under the Main Settings header using the formatting guidelines provided by the tool-tips that appear when you move your mouse over the question mark (?) book icons. After these fields are filled, you will see that the Generate APP button has become selectable. Clicking this button will queue the generation of an unsigned APK file, which will become available within moments.

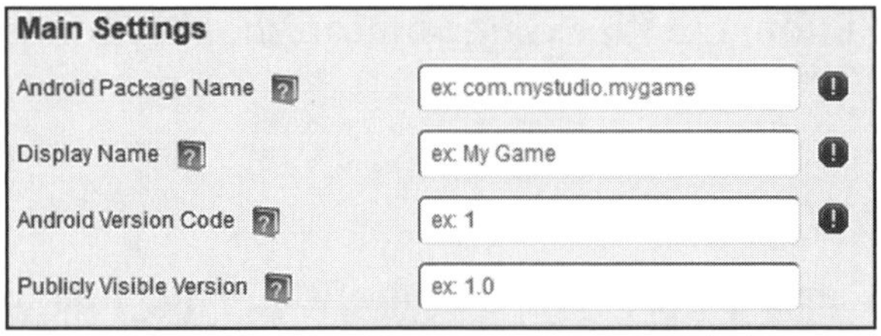

Main Settings

Android Package Name ⓘ	ex: com.mystudio.mygame
Display Name ⓘ	ex: My Game
Android Version Code ⓘ	ex: 1
Publicly Visible Version ⓘ	ex: 1.0

Figure 9.9
Enter the appropriate information in the blank fields.
Source: The GameSalad Creator, © 2013 GameSalad®, Inc. All Rights Reserved.

2. Once your unsigned APK is ready, you will receive both a pop-up notification and an in-window notification that includes a link to start the signing process. In addition, the Download and Sign App buttons will now be selectable.

3. In most cases, this is where you would click Sign App and begin the signing process. You will need a signed APK for most services. However, not all services require a signed APK, which saves your time if you do not have to sign it. For instance, Amazon requires you to submit to them an unsigned APK file because they prefer to sign the file on their end.

Signing the App

Before you even begin to go through the Sign App process, you need to know that you have to do certain things to set your local machine up before you can sign an APK file. The following instructions will walk you through this process. Of course, Android publishing is available only to Professional users, so you need to do this only if you are a Professional user and your distribution places require a signed APK file.

1. Download the Java software development kit (JDK). You can find the latest installer online at www.oracle.com/technetwork/java/javase/downloads/.

2. After downloading the installer, run it. You may see a user account control message saying, "Do you want to allow the following program from an unknown publisher to make changes to this computer?" If so, click Yes to proceed. You will have to click the Next button several times until you get to a Finish button, at which point you know you are finished installing JDK.

3. Download the Android SDK installer here: dl.google.com/android/installer_r18-windows.exe.

4. Run the Android SDK installer. Again, if you see the control message, click Yes to proceed. Click Next several times until you get to the Finish button, at which point you know you are through. Leave the checkbox for Start SDK Manager selected and click Finish.

5. When the Android SDK Manager loads, make sure the following folders are selected: Android SDK Tools, Android SDK Platform-tools, Latest Android API, and Google USB Driver. Click Install Packages. In the Choose Packages to Install dialog box, select the Accept All option button and click Install, as shown in Figure 9.10. Note that this install takes a while.

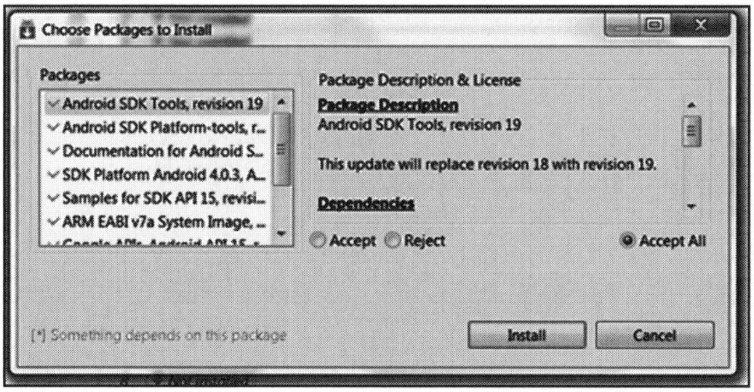

Figure 9.10
Select the proper folders and make sure Accept All is selected before you click Install.
Source: The GameSalad Creator, © 2013 GameSalad®, Inc. All Rights Reserved.

6. Once the update is finished, click OK and close the Manager Log. Finally, close the Android SDK Manager by clicking the × button in the top-right corner.

7. Navigate to the Android SDK folder on your computer and go to the Platform-tools folder. Right-click Platform-tools in the address bar and select Copy Address. This will copy the location of this folder.

8. Click the Windows icon in the lower left. Right-click Computer, click Properties, and click Advanced System Settings. Click Environment Variables. Under System Variables, click Path and then click Edit. Add a semi-colon to the end of the entry in the Variable Value field, and then paste the Platform-tools folder's address here. Do not click OK yet.

9. Navigate back to the Android-SDK folder on your computer. Go to the Tools folder. Right-click Tools in the address bar and click Copy Address. Then go back to the Edit System Variable dialog box, and add another semicolon to the end of the entry in the Variable Value field, and paste the Tools folder's address, as shown in Figure 9.11.

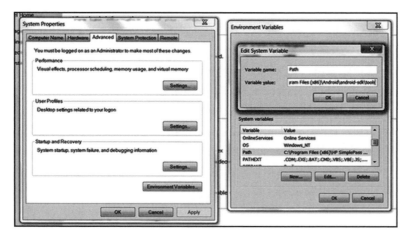

Figure 9.11
Enter the address after a semicolon at the end of the entry in the Variable Value field.
Source: The GameSalad Creator, © 2013 GameSalad®, Inc. All Rights Reserved.

10. Click OK when you are finished with the open dialog boxes. Now you can run the Android developer commands from any directory in the Command Prompt.

With your local machine set up to accept and run the Sign App process, return to GameSalad Creator to do so. Again, this is only if you are a Professional user who wishes to create a signed APK file.

1. Click the Sign App button. It will ask you to launch through the GameSalad Creator. Doing so will bring up the Android Package Signer, which is in four parts: Signing Tools Location, Keystore, Key, and Package to Sign.

2. For Signing Tools Location, use the browse icon beside each field to locate the appropriate EXE file. While the specific location of each of these may differ

from computer to computer, you will most likely find these in the following directories (after you've installed JDK and the Android SDK, that is):

- Keytool: C:\Program Files\Java\jdk1.6.0_30\bin\keytool.exe

- Jarsigner: C:\Program Files\Java\jdk1.6.0_30\bin\jarsigner.exe

- Zipalign: C:\Program Files (x86)\Android\android-sdk\tools\zipalign.exe

3. Click the New button to begin creating your first Keystore. Choose an easy to locate place to save your Keystore.

4. Fill out the remaining fields. Your Keystore and Key passwords can match, but they each must be at least six characters long. The final part, Package to Sign, has a field that should automatically be populated with the directory address of the file you are signing.

5. Click the Sign button, and pick someplace to save your signed APK file.

Testing on an Android Device

With that, you are ready to test your game on an Android device prior to submitting it to app distributors. Follow these steps:

1. On your Android phone/tablet, go to Settings and then Manage Applications (or simply Applications on some devices). Select the Unknown Sources checkbox to allow installation of your test builds. Then, navigate to Storage, which is typically found in Settings > SD Card > Phone Storage or Settings > Storage, and deselect the USB Storage checkbox. Turn on USB Debugging, which is typically found in Settings > Applications > Development.

2. Connect your Android device to your computer via USB cable. To verify the connection, run the following from the Command Prompt on your computer: `adb devices`. If your device is connected but not being detected, you might need to download the specific USB driver for your remote device. Refer to the manufacturer's website for assistance if that is the case.

3. When you are ready to test your game, you can install it directly to your device. You need to have generated a signed APK file for testing purposes. You will also need to know the path to the signed APK file, as it will be required. From the Command Prompt, type `adb devices` to make sure that your device is connected and being detected by your machine. Next, type `adb install` followed

by the path to your signed APK file. For example: `adb install desktop \mysignedfile.apk`. You will be prompted with a message indicating success or failure of the install.

Tip

A fast and easy way to send files, including APKs, to other devices than your source one is to use cloud sharing like Google Drive or Dropbox. I use both on a daily basis to ferry and fetch files between all the devices I operate regularly. You can create a 5 GB free Google Drive account by going to www.drive .google.com or a 2 GB free Dropbox account by going to www.dropbox.com/features.

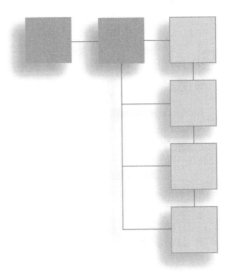

APPENDIX

RESOURCES

Herein you will find all the websites mentioned in this book and online resources you might find useful.

MAIN RESOURCES

- **GameSalad:** www.gamesalad.com
- **GameSalad Publisher:** http://publish.gamesalad.com/games
- **This book's companion site:** www.cengageptr.com/downloads

GAME DESIGN

- **GamaSutra:** www.gamasutra.com
- **GameDev:** www.gamedev.net
- **David Freeman Group on Creating Emotions in Games:** www.freemangames.com/idea/

IMAGE EDITOR

- **Face Generator:** http://lovelymoro.web.fc2.com/moromagalabo.html
- **GNU Image Manipulation Program (GIMP):** www.gimp.org
- **Lunapic Editor:** www151.lunapic.com/editor/
- **Photoshop Express Editor:** www.photoshop.com/tools/expresseditor

- **Picmonkey:** www.picmonkey.com
- **Sumopaint:** www.sumopaint.com/app/

GRAPHICS

- **Color Hex Color Codes:** www.color-hex.com
- **GameSalad Marketplace:** http://marketplace.gamesalad.com
- **Noctua Graphics:** www.noctua-graphics.de

FONTS

- **1001 Free Fonts:** www.1001freefonts.com
- **Dafont:** www.dafont.com

MUSIC/SOUND EFFECTS

- **DeusX.com:** www.deusx.com/studio.html
- **Flashkit.com:** www.flashkit.com
- **FlashSound.com:** www.flashsound.com
- **GameSalad Marketplace:** http://marketplace.gamesalad.com
- **Looperman:** www.looperman.com
- **Shockwave-Sound.com:** www.shockwave-sound.com
- **Sound-Ideas.com:** www.sound-ideas.com
- **Sound Rangers.com:** www.soundrangers.com
- **MusicBakery.com:** www.musicbakery.com

SOUND EDITORS

- **Audacity:** http://audacity.sourceforge.net/
- **Audio Expert:** www.audioexpert.com/
- **ClubCreate:** http://remixer.clubcreate.com/v2/musiclab/launch.html
- **Musicshake:** http://eng.musicshake.com/create/
- **Soundation:** http://soundation.com/

Free Web Hosts

- **110 MB Hosting:** 110mb.com
- **Atspace.com:** www.atspace.com
- **Byet Internet Services:** www.byethost.com
- **Freehostia:** www.freehostia.com/hosting.html
- **Webs:** www.webs.com
- **Tripod:** www.tripod.lycos.com

Paid Web Hosts

- **Bluehost:** bluehost.com
- **Dot5Hosting:** www.dot5hosting.com
- **HostMonster:** www.hostmonster.com
- **HostPapa:** hostpapa.com
- **StartLogic:** www.startlogic.com

Web Editors

- **Adobe Dreamweaver:** www.adobe.com/products/dreamweaver
- **NVU:** www.nvu.com

Web Builders

- **DoodleKit:** www.doodlekit.com/home
- **HandzOn:** www.handzon.com
- **Moonfruit:** www.moonfruit.com
- **Wix:** www.wix.com
- **Yola:** www.yola.com

Search Engine Submission

- **Bing:** www.bing.com/toolbox/submit-site-url
- **Google:** www.google.com/addurl.html

- **Open Directory Project:** www.dmoz.org/add.html
- **Yahoo!:** http://search.yahoo.com/info/submit.html

OTHERS

- **Java Development Kit (JDK):** www.oracle.com/technetwork/java/javase/downloads
- **Android SDK:** dl.google.com/android/installer_r18-windows.exe
- **Visualead (QR code generator):** www.visualead.com/qurify2/en/

GLOSSARY OF TERMS

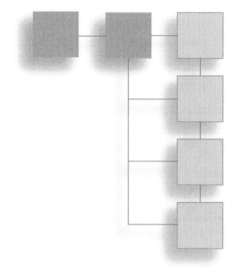

abs function   This provides the absolute value of a number. In other words, it will make a negative number into a positive number. For example, abs (−5.23)=5.23.

Accelerate behavior   Specifies the speed and direction of acceleration for an actor. Actors will continue to accelerate unless drag is applied or another movement behavior takes precedence.

Accelerate Toward behavior   Allows the user to specify the precise location toward which an actor will accelerate.

Accelerometer (attribute)   Determines the angle and rate of movement of the device. This can be useful for determining when a user rotates or tilts their device.

acos function   This is the trigonometric arccosine (inverse cosine) function. Values for x should range from −1 to 1, with results from 180 to 0, respectively. Any other input values will result in "nan."

actions   These are behaviors that are not meant to fire continuously, such as movement, changing image, color, or size, or accepting keyboard input. They are best used when governed by a rule.

actor   All the items (both visible and invisible) in your game are actors. They are governed by behaviors that control how they interact with other actors as well as with people playing your game.

Actor mode   This is the default mode for the Scene Editor. It enables actors to be placed, moved, rotated, and resized in the scene.

actor tag   Actor tags are used to categorize actors. They can be added and removed through the Editor.

Actors Library   A repository of the actors created in GameSalad Creator.

alpha color   Alpha controls the transparency of an actor. It can be set to any real number between 0 and 1, with 0 being completely transparent and 1 being completely opaque.

Animate behavior   Displays a series of images in rapid succession to create animation.

asin function   This is the trigonometric arcsine (inverse sine) function. Values for *x* should range from −1 to 1 with results from −90 to 90, respectively. Any other input values will result in "nan."

atan function   This is the trigonometric arctangent (inverse tangent) function. Results will range from −90 to 90.

attribute   Attributes contain numeric or text values that govern various aspects of the game, scene, and actors.

Behavior Library   A list of all available behaviors that can be assigned to actors.

behaviors   Behaviors are actions or states of being that apply to actors. They can change how actors move, look, sound, and act.

ceil function   The integer when you round up a value. For instance, ceil (0.3095)=1; ceil (9.2850)=10; and ceil (−3.5)=−3.

Change Attribute behavior   Allows user to set or change a game, scene, or actor attribute. For instance, users can create score-keeping systems, instructing the game to add points to (or remove points from) a specific actor or to remove health/life from a player or actor.

Change Image behavior   Changes an actor's image to a new image. This can be useful for showing damage or other changes to an actor without having to create multiple actors.

Change Scene behavior   Goes to a specific scene. This can be useful for moving to the next level, opening a credits scene, or showing a game menu.

Change Size behavior   Grows or shrinks an actor. (Use a negative number to shrink.) Insert a timer container to control how long the growth or shrink should take.

Change Velocity behavior   Specifies movement changes relative to another actor or to the scene.

Collide behavior   Use this behavior in conjunction with a tag to control which actor or groups of actors the primary actor will bounce against.

Collision Shape attribute   This option determines whether other objects will collide with this object as if it were round (or rounded) or square (or rectangular).

Constrain Attribute behavior   Continuously updates an attribute. For instance, you could use this to constrain the actor's location to that of the mouse. Essentially, this behavior ties two attributes together.

Control Camera behavior   Allows users to cause the camera to follow an actor, keeping it in view.

cos function   This is the trigonometric cosine function. cos (0)=1. For more information on sine and cosine, check out www.sosmath.com/trig/Trig2/trig2/trig2.html.

Density attribute   This setting dictates the heaviness of the actor. A higher value will make the object harder to move by less dense actors. A value of 0 will make an object immovable but still affect other actors in the scene. Density can be set to any real positive number.

Destroy behavior   Removes the actor from the scene. You can apply this behavior to objects that can be destroyed, like the blocks in *Breakout* or the bricks in *Super Mario Bros.* Best used with a rule (for instance, if a collision occurs with the ball in *Breakout*).

Display Text behavior   Allows users to change the color, size, font, and other elements of text displayed in-game. Change the actor's Color > Alpha attribute to 0 to make all parts of the actor invisible except for the text.

Editor   Used for editing all the details of your game.

exp function   The exponential function e^x, where e is approximately 2.71828182818. For more information, check out www.freemathhelp.com/exponential-functions.html.

Fixed Rotation attribute   Select this option to prevent the object from rotating when it collides with other actors in the scene. Leaving this box unchecked means the actor will rotate normally when it collides with other actors.

floor function   The integer when you round down a value. For instance, floor (1.5)=1, floor (9.2850)=9, and floor (−3.5)=−4.

Friction attribute   Increasing this setting will slow the object down more when it interacts with other objects. Set it to 0 for no friction (and hence no slowing).

function   Functions are various mathematical formulas available through the Expression Editor that enable you to have GameSalad Creator calculate sines, cosines, logs, and much more.

GameSalad Creator   The best software in the world for making games with no coding!

Gravity   Each scene can be set up with an X and Y Gravity attribute. These are real numbers that affect all the actors that are movable.

Group behavior   Creates a group container that holds a set of rules or behaviors.

In function   The natural logarithm of a value. The natural logarithm is the logarithm to the base e, where e is approximately 2.71828182818. For more information, check out www.betterexplained.com/articles/demystifying-the-natural-logarithm-ln/.

instance   An instance is a unique example of an actor, with altered behaviors, attributes, or abilities from the prototype actor.

Interpolate behavior   Allows you to cause an attribute (location, value) to go from A to B in a set amount of time. For instance, you could do a countdown from 100 to 1 or a preprogrammed movement of an actor from position X to position Y.

iOS   The operating system created by Apple, Inc. to run on the iPhone, iPad, and iPod Touch devices.

Keyboard Input behavior   Saves keyboard input text into a specified attribute.

Kiip   Kiip is a system to provide real-world rewards when players complete an achievement in your game. GameSalad Creator Pro-level account holders have the option to integrate Kiip rewards into their games and will receive a revenue share when players accept a real-world reward offer.

layers   Layers enable you to prevent actors from interacting with each other. This can enable you to create backgrounds, scores, and more without having the player's actors bump into them.

Load Attribute behavior   Loads the value stored by a custom key name from persistent storage. It can be used to allow gamers to change an attribute to specific input or events.

Log Debugging Statement behavior   Logs a statement in the debugging window. Statements can be attribute values for error-checking or text entry to flag an event when your game is running for testing purposes.

log10 function   The base 10 logarithm of a value. For instance, log10 (10)=1, log10 (100)=2. For more information, check out www.mathsisfun.com/algebra/logarithms.html.

logic   The combination of rules and behaviors that jointly define how a project operates.

magnitude function   Finds the length of a line segment drawn directly from the origin 0,0 to the given point. You can also include an offset to find the length between two points—for example, magnitude (x-x', y-y'). Say you have one actor at 100, 240 and another at 25, 30. To find the distance between them, use magnitude (25-100, 30-240).

max function   Returns the higher value of two numbers or variable units. This can be very useful for determining if a new score is higher than an existing score or for other similar comparisons. For example, max (12, 35)=35.

Max Speed attribute   This attribute controls the maximum speed an actor can reach through acceleration and gravity. Note that some behaviors, such as Change Velocity and Interpolate, override Max Speed.

Media Library   A repository of the assets that have been imported into GameSalad Creator.

min function   Returns the smaller value of two numbers or variable units. For example, min (12, 35)=12.

Movable attribute   Enables you to specify that an actor is or is not able to move when interacting with other actors. Select the checkbox to enable it to move.

Move behavior   Specifies an actor's movement in a particular direction relative to the actor or scene. Movement is perpetual unless stopped by some other rule or object.

Move To behavior   Specifies an actor's movement toward a particular X and Y coordinate. On arrival, it stops.

Note behavior   Enables users to write a note to themselves or other creators about a particular behavior, rule, actor, or group. This can be useful for explaining why something is done a particular way.

Open URL (Pro behavior)   Available only to individuals with a Pro-level membership. This option enables the developer to specify a specific URL to open when a certain action takes place, such as a button being clicked or pressed. The URL will open in the user's default browser.

Orientation attribute   This determines whether your game runs in up-and-down mode (portrait) or side-to-side mode (landscape) on iPhone, iTouch, and iPad.

Otherwise   An optional component of a rule. Behaviors placed under this heading trigger whenever the conditions of the rule are invalid.

padInt function   Displays an integer with the specified number of digits. For instance, padInt (32, 5) will display 00032. However, padInt (38025, 2) will display 38025. It will always display at least the minimum number of digits needed to retain the value of x.

padReal function   Displays a floating point with padding and precision. For instance, padReal (9.1234, 15, 6) will display 9.1234 with at least 15 total digits (including the decimal) and at most 6 digits to the right of the decimal (for example, 00000009.123400).

particles   Small objects that move out from the actor in a defined way. See "Particles behavior" for more information.

Particles behavior   Creates an explosion, rain, snow, sparkles, and more with particles. You can use a radial or fountain of particles. You can also set an image, color, lifetime, and other parameters.

Pause Game behavior   Pauses the scene by freezing all activity in it and opening another scene that you specify. Use this to open in-game menus or to simply pause the current action. Use the Unpause Game behavior to resume the scene.

Pause Music behavior   Pauses a currently playing music file on a particular event.

platform   The devices or locations where your game will be able to run. Current platforms include iOS, Mac Desktop, Android, and HTML5.

Play Music behavior   Triggers a music file to play. Can play once or loop.

Play Sound behavior   Triggers a sound file to play. Can play once or loop.

Playhaven   A creative ad network that provides an interstitial app referral immediately before gameplay. Pro accounts have the option to include the interstitial or not. Pro account holders also receive a revenue share for completed referrals in their games. PlayHaven is the first partner is GameSalad's game-referral system, included on all the games published under a Basic account.

pow function   Returns the value of x to the power of y. For example, pow (2, 3)= 2*2*2=8.

prec function   Displays a floating-point number with the specified number of decimal places. For instance, prec (1234.234, 2) will display 1234.23.

Preview   Enables you to see how your game will look and run instantly. Preview often to ensure that the rules and actions you are giving your actors are working properly.

Project Size indicator   The current memory needs of your project can be found in the bottom-right corner of the GameSalad Creator. The recommended maximum size for GameSalad Arcade games is 20 MB.

Prototype (Actor)   An actor that possesses all the overall governing behaviors but does not possess some of the specifics that an actor instance possesses (such as a spawning location).

publishing   Publishing uploads your game to GameSalad's servers, where it is turned into a binary that you can then submit directly to Apple, GameSalad Arcade, or the Android store.

random function   Returns a random integer equal to or between the first integer and the second. For instance, random (1, 5) could return any of the following values: 1, 2, 3, 4, or 5.

Replicate behavior   Creates copies of an actor based on an attribute or integer. Useful for displaying the number of lives a player has left, having an item duplicate itself, and much more.

Reset Game behavior   Resets the game and all scenes. This behavior is best used within a rule to specify when and/or how this happens.

Reset Scene behavior   Resets the current scene and all the actors in it. This behavior is best used within a rule to specify when and/or how this happens.

resolution independence   Allows your game to be displayed in low or high resolution, depending upon the capabilities of the device.

Restitution attribute   Makes your actor bouncy, with 0 having no bounciness and 2 being rubber-ball bouncy. Any real positive number from 0 to 2 can be used.

Rotate behavior   Causes consistent clockwise or counterclockwise rotation. It can also cause an item to rotate only when an event happens, such as a keyboard key being pressed or a collision with another actor occurring.

Rotate to Angle behavior   Causes rotation to an angle relative to another actor or to a scene.

Rotate to Position behavior   Causes rotation to a specific X and Y coordinate on the screen or relative to the actor.

rule   Creates a condition or set of conditions that, when met, cause actors to act in specific ways.

Rule behavior   Creates a condition or set of conditions to check for player input or an attribute change.

Save Attribute behavior   Saves a particular value into persistent storage with a custom name. It can also be used to enable users to save their games. See "Load Attribute behavior" for information on loading saved information.

scene attributes   Attributes that specifically affect a scene rather than an actor or the entire game. They include Name, Time, Size, Wrap X, Wrap Y, Gravity, Color, Camera, and Autorotate.

Scenes Library   A repository of the scenes created in GameSalad Creator.

Show iAd (Pro behavior)   Shows an ad whose text and destination are determined through Apple's iAd system.

sin function   The trigonometric sine function. This is similar to the cosine function but is offset by one quarter of a wave cycle. For more information, see www.sosmath.com/trig/Trig2/trig2/trig2.html. Note: If you use the sine function and start your incrementing variable at 0, your actor's movement does not start at the middle point between the minimum and maximum points of the wave.

Spawn Actor behavior   Creates a new actor instance in the scene. Useful for projectiles, dropping items, etc.

sqrt function   Provides the square root of a value. Input values less than 0 will result in "nan."

Stop Music behavior   Causes a music file to stop playing.

tableCellValue function   Returns the value of a cell of a selected table at a certain row and column. Tables are numbered starting at 1. You can also use the row or column name as an input for this function. For example, tableCellValue (game.Data, 1, 15) will return the value in table Data at row 1, column 15.

tableColCount function   Returns the number of columns in the selected table.

tableRowCount function   Returns the number of rows in the selected table.

tan function   The trigonometric tangent function. For more information, check out www.morethanmaths.com/learn/shape/trigonometry/.

Timer behavior   Enables you to perform behaviors or rules at specified intervals. These intervals are defined as after a certain number of seconds, every couple of seconds, or for a certain number of seconds.

Unpause Game behavior   This behavior removes the pause screen and resumes the game.

vectorToAngle function   Finds the angle relative to the origin 0,0, given an X and Y coordinate. For instance, vectorToAngle (100, 200)=63.435. You can also find the angle relative to an offset—for instance, vectorToAngle (x-x', y-y'). VectorToAngle (100–200, 150–250) will find the angle between the points 100, 150 and 200, 250, or –135 degrees.

INDEX